BEC Higher

Business BENCHMARK

Advanced

Student's Book

Guy Brook-Hart

CAMBRIDGE UNIVERSITY PRESS

CAMBRIDGE
UNIVERSITY PRESS

University Printing House, Cambridge CB2 8BS, United Kingdom

One Liberty Plaza, 20th Floor, New York, NY 10006, USA

477 Williamstown Road, Port Melbourne, VIC 3207, Australia

314–321, 3rd Floor, Plot 3, Splendor Forum, Jasola District Centre, New Delhi – 110025, India

103 Penang Road, #05-06/07, Visioncrest Commercial, Singapore 238467

Cambridge University Press is part of the University of Cambridge.

It furthers the University's mission by disseminating knowledge in the pursuit of education, learning and research at the highest international levels of excellence.

www.cambridge.org
Information on this title: www.cambridge.org/9780521672955

First published 2007

40 39 38 37 36 35 34 33 32 31 30 29 28 27 26

Printed in Italy by Rotolito S.p.A.

A catalogue record for this publication is available from the British Library

ISBN 978-0-521-67295-5 Student's Book BEC Higher Edition
ISBN 978-0-521-67294-8 Student's Book BULATS Edition Advanced with CD-ROM
ISBN 978-0-521-67297-9 Personal Study Book Advanced/Higher
ISBN 978-0-521-67296-2 Teacher's Resource Book Advanced/Higher
ISBN 978-0-521-67298-6 Audio Cassette BEC Higher Edition
ISBN 978-0-521-67299-3 Audio CD BEC Higher Edition
ISBN 978-0-521-67661-8 Audio Cassette BULATS Edition Advanced
ISBN 978-0-521-67662-5 Audio CD BULATS Edition Advanced

Introduction

Who this book is for

This book is intended to be an interesting and stimulating course for Advanced students of Business English (Common European Framework Level C1). It provides a general Business English course for students who have not yet worked in business and for people who are working and have experience of business environments.

It provides the practical reading, speaking, listening and writing skills necessary for people who need English for working in business. It also contains a wide range of essential business vocabulary and grammar.

For students who want to study for a Business English qualification, this book gives you a complete preparation for the Cambridge Business English Certificate (BEC) Higher exam, together with a complete BEC Higher practice exam.

What the book contains

The book contains the following elements:

- **24 units for classroom study.** These units are organised in groups of four around a theme: management, competitive advantage, etc. While each unit gives training and practice in a variety of skills, the first unit in each group mainly concentrates on reading skills, the second on listening, the third on writing and the fourth on speaking. Each unit contains essential vocabulary input for business students. Many of the activities in the units are similar to those found in the BEC Higher exam.
- **Grammar workshops.** For each group of four units, there is a two-page Grammar Workshop section. These explain and extend grammar work introduced in the units. In the units, you will from time to time see a cross-reference, e.g. > **page 20** (Future simple or future continuous?), which indicates where further explanation and exercises on a specific point can be found.
- **Exam skills and Exam practice section.** This section, which starts on page 121, gives you detailed guidance on how to approach each BEC Higher exam task, the skills required and what the exam task is testing. The Exam skills pages also contain exercises to build up your exam skills. The Exam practice pages contain all the questions/tasks from a BEC Higher exam.
- **Answer keys** to all the exercises and activities in the Student's Book. Sample answers to writing activities have not been included at this level because the range of possible answers is too great for this to be useful. However 'models' are provided for all writing tasks.
- **Transcripts** for all the listening activities in the book.

The book is accompanied by:

- **3 audio CDs/cassettes,** containing a variety of recorded material, including interviews with business people and BEC exam listening tasks.
- **Teacher's Resource Book**, containing guidance and suggestions on how to approach activities in the book and a large number of extra photocopiable activities and case studies to supplement the units in the Student's Book.
- **Personal Study Book**, containing activities and exercises based on the vocabulary, grammar and skills covered in each unit, and intended as reinforcement of material which you have studied in class. The Personal Study Book contains keys to all its exercises, so you will be able to check your answers yourself. It also contains a Word list of vocabulary from the Student's Book.
- **Website**, containing additional resources and information. Go to http://www.cambridge.org/businessbenchmark.

Map of the book

Speaking	Vocabulary	Language work
Describing company culture Why is it important to have a strong corporate culture?	Company culture Phrasal verbs *Board, bottom line, revenues*, etc.	Defining and non-defining relative clauses
Talking about good leaders Getting the most from staff Producing a more effective workforce	Leadership skills: *founder*, etc. Types of management	*As* or *like*?
The best way of communicating different things Must a manager be a good communicator?	Abbreviations	Future simple or future continuous?
The function of the chair Holding meetings	Evaluating meetings	Language functions for chairs
or future continuous?		
Discussing customer–supplier relationships Discussing the 80–20 rule, etc. The shortcomings of CRM, etc.; A CRM strategy	*Helpdesk*, etc.	
How does your company achieve a competitive advantage? Pricing	Elements that give a company an advantage; Submitting tenders; *Dedicated*, *resources*, etc. Phrasal verbs; Verb–noun collocations	Speaking hypothetically
	Linking words and phrases *Existing*, *identify*, etc.	Compound nouns The passive
The ice-cream market in your country Presenting information from charts Presenting from a text		Embedded questions
How does your company advertise? Cost-effective advertising How to advertise software	*Brand-building*, etc. Types of advertising *Households*, etc.	Adverbs
How you use the Internet to buy things How could your company use the methods of the car industry?; Using the Internet for advertising	*Straightforward*, etc.	*Although*, *however*, *despite*, etc.
The best medium for selling different products and services Structure of a report	Synonyms for *increase* and *decrease*	Present perfect simple or continuous?
How do you react to a cold-call?; Finding out about work problems; Role-play 1: Cold-calling; Advising on breaking into a new market; Role-play 2: Making a sales pitch	*Solicit*, *risk-averse*, etc.	Cleft sentences

Speaking	Vocabulary	Language work
How different elements help to make forecasts What makes forecasts inaccurate? How to prepare a sales forecast, etc. What type of forecaster do you think you are?	Phrasal verbs and expressions *Go bust, stock price*, etc. Vocabulary from profit-and-loss account and balance sheet	Conditional sentences
Should the arts be subsidised? How sponsorship can promote a company's image, etc. Role-play: Continental Bank and Tate Modern	Theatre vocabulary *Break down, running costs*, etc.	Infinitive and verb + *–ing*
How late payers affect a business Discussion: How should you deal with late payers? Presentation: How to deal with late payers, etc.	*Bank charges, bookkeeping,* etc. Formal expressions	Complex sentences
What you need to know before negotiating Negotiation, problems and advice Role-play: Negotiating an office lease	*Compromise, the bottom line*, etc.	Conditional sentences: alternatives to *if*
What makes people work harder Types of management–employee relationship; Trends in accidents and stress, etc.; Our attitudes towards stress	*Trends, pronounced*, etc.	Reference devices
Workers of the future; Working practices in the future Talk: teleworking, etc. Talking about your present job	Types of worker; Ways of working *Stuck in a rut, going rate*, etc.	
What factors affect productivity?; Describing charts: productivity at Magro Toys; Presentations on productivity; Raising productivity	*Assembly line, churn out*, etc.	Expressing causes and results
Company reorganisation; Would you be prepared to relocate?; Thinking about an offer Role-play: Negotiating an agreement	Phrasal verbs and expressions Phrases for negotiating	Variations on conditional sentences
Corporate responsibility CSR and corporate culture; Fair trade What is the connection between fair trade and CSR, etc.?	*Benefits, premise*, etc. Adverbial phrases	Articles
Expanding into foreign markets Describing the company you work for Wolseley's expansion strategy; Supervising subsidiaries The advantages of making acquisitions	*Acquisitions, year on year,* etc. *Surged, FTSE 100*, etc. Adjectives and adverbs of frequency	
The problems of expanding into a new market Replying to a letter		Complex sentences Tenses in future time clauses
Useful hints for making presentations Making a presentation; Business risks Discussion: Staff retention, market share	Discourse markers for short talks	Concession

Acknowledgements

Practice test material written by Elaine Boyd.

The author and publishers are grateful to the following for permission to reproduce copyright material. While every effort has been made, it has not always been possible to identify the sources of all the material used, or to trace the copyright holders. If any omissions are brought to our notice, we will be happy to include the appropriate acknowledgements on reprinting.

Text

pp.10, 11, 13, 16, 17, 25, 32, 33, 34, 52, 61, 65, 68, 69, 72, 86, 88, 92 and 101: *Cambridge Advanced Learner's Dictionary*, Cambridge University Press, 2005, www.dictionary.cambridge.org, for various of the definitions; p.12: *Corporate Board Member Magazine* for the text 'Who is responsible?' written by Rob Norton. Reprinted by permission, Corporate Board Member Magazine; p.15: Knowledge@Wharton for the text 'Leader of Virgin', pp.82–83: 'Giving employees what they want, pp.128–129: 'Call centers: How to reduce burnout, increase efficiency', p.127: 'How to avoid the biggest mistakes', p.130: 'Getting the best out of your staff', p.133: 'How soon will your product sell?', p.135: 'A dynamic approach to change', p.137: 'Dressing casually for work'. Reprinted with permission from Knowledge@Wharton http://knowledge.wharton.upenn.edu, the online research and business analysis journal of the Wharton School of the University of Pennsylvania; p.22: TeamWorx Innovations for the text 'Chairing a meeting' taken from http://www.meetingwizard.org/meetings/chair-a-meeting.cfm. Used by kind permission of TeamWorx Innovations; pp.28–29: *The Economist* for the text 'Giving people what they want' by Shoshana Zuboff, 8 May 2003, p.47: 'The effectiveness of advertising' by Paul Markille, 31 March 2005, pp.48–49: 'Target practice' 31 March 2005, p.51: 'Motoring online' 31 March 2005, p.87: 'Know future' 21 December 2000, p.101: 'CSR – worthy cause?' 20 January 2005, pp.114–115: 'Be prepared', 22 January 2004, p.115: 'Easy to lose', 22 January 2004, p.123: 'But can you teach it', 20 May 2004, p.126: 'Why do so many badly run companies survive?' 9 June 2005. © The Economist Newspaper Limited; p.31: Pars International Corporation for the text 'Masters of the Customer Connection' written by Mindy Blodgett, excerpted from *CIO Magazine*, 15 August 2005, p.31: 'Customer relationship management' written by Michael Johnson, excerpted from Darwinmag.com, September 2001, p.65: 'Forecasting disaster' written by Scott Kirsner, excerpted from Darwinmag.com, July 2001. Copyright © CXO Media Inc. All rights reserved; p.33: 'How the JJ Group prepares tenders' by Phoebe Hart, taken from the Business Link website, http://www.businesslink.gov.uk. © Crown Copyright; p.42: Decision News Media for the text 'Nestlé in Thailand' published on www.dairyreporter.com, 11 June 2004; p.42: for the text 'The Philippine market' by Rosalie B Bernardino. *Food and Agri Business Monitor*, June 2001. Used by permission of The University of Asia and the Pacific. Pasig City, Philippines; p.43: 'Nestlé expands ice-cream lines in China' published on www.foodnavigator.com, 23 February 2002. Used by permission of Decision News Media (UK) Limited; p.60: Inc.com for the text 'Cracking the big company market' by Evelyn Roth. *Inc.Magazine*, November 2002. Used by permission of Inc.com; p.73: Clearlybusiness.com for the text 'The impact of late payments on small businesses' taken from the website www.clearlybusiness.com. Used by permission of Clearlybusiness.com; p.77: AllLaw.com for the text 'Negotiating your office lease' by Celeste Marchland. Used by permission of AllLaw.com; p.103: *The Guardian* for the text 'The effort of ethics' by Oliver Balch 10 March 2005, p.116: 'Nestlé launch of fair-trade coffee divides company's critics' by John Vidal, 7 October 2005, p.135: 'Workshops miss their target' by Nick Pandya, 13 August 2005. Copyright Guardian Newspapers Limited 2005; pp.104–105: Wolseley PLC for the text 'Wolseley's strategy' taken from the website www.wolseley.com. Used by kind permission of Wolseley PLC; p.106: *The Sunday Times* for the text 'How Wolseley's boss plumbed to new heights', by Andrew Davidson. © The Sunday Times, London 9 January 2005; p.136: Guy Clapperton for the text 'Langloffan cheese' *The Guardian* 30 October 2003. Used by kind permission of Guy Clapperton.

Logos

p.12: © Nucor Corporation; p.14: © Virgin Enterprises Limited; p.16: © Disney Enterprises, Inc.; p.32: © Gifford Engineering Consultancy; p.33: © JJ Group; p.48: © Mediacom UK; p.102: Fairtrade logo. The use of the Fairtrade mark is by kind permission of the Fairtrade Foundation. The FAIRTRADE Mark, an independent consumer label, is a certification mark and internationally registered as a trademark by Fairtrade Labelling Organisations International (FLO) of which the Fairtrade Foundation (UK) is a member; p.104: © Wolseley PLC.

Photos

Cover photo: Corbis

Advertising Archives for p.46 (item b); Alamy for pp.10 (bl) (Imagestate), 36 (t) (Digital Archive Japan), 50 (t) (Christoph Papsch), 54 (t) (Mark Baigent), 68 (t) (Chuck Place), 71 (Arcblue), 78–79 (Maciej Wojkowiak), 86 (t) (3C Stock); Alvey & Towers for pp.18 (mr), 50 (r), 90 (r); Courtesy of Arbitron for p.48 (b); Art Directors & TRIP for pp.46 (item e), 54 (br), 64 (extreme r); Rachel Babington for p.16, by kind permission; Camera Press for p.86 (br); Corbis for pp.36 (b) (Tim McGuire), 50 (exreme r) (Joson), 60–61 (Jim Craigmyle), 64 (m) (Ricj Gomez), 72 (Jim Craigmyle), 74 (Helen King), 76 (r) (Chuck Savage), 89 (r) (Tim Pannell), 89 (extreme l) (Scott Areman), 93 (Louie Psihoyos), 100 (Jose Luis Pelaez, Inc.); Courtesy of Domino's Pizza for p.30 (b); Education Photos for p.30 (t); Eye Ubiquitous for pp.24 (b), 115; Chris Fairclough Worldwide Images for pp.94–95 (br); Courtesy of The Fairtrade Foundation for p.102 (t); Fair Trade Media for p.102–103 (b) (Christof Krackhardt); Getty Images for pp.10 (t) (Zubin Shroff), 14 (Anderson Ross), 18 (t) (Reza Estakhrian), 22 (t) (Ryan McVay), (b) (Justin Pumfrey), 28 (t) (DCA Productions), 29 (Sean Justice), 32 (Altrendo Images), 40 (t) (Ingram Publishing), 46 (t) (Mitchell Funk), 50 (m) (Kent Matthews), 58 (t) (Thomas Northcut), 64 (t) (Camelot), 76 (t) (Peter Cade), 82 (t) (Stewart Cohen), 89 (m) (Ryan McVay), 90 (t) (David Buffington), 94 (t) (Chabruken), 104 (t) (Pankaj & Insy Shah/Gulfimages), 108 (t) (DCA Productions), 112 (t) (Stewart Cohen), 114 (Fredrik Skold); Imagestate for pp.34 (t), 40 (b); Gifford Engineering Consultancy for pp.32 (b), 34 (b) and 75, by kind permission; Haymarket Publishing for pp.46 (item a) and 52 for the screenshot of Alfa Romeo Spider. Taken from the website www.whatcar.co.uk, by kind permission; International Photobank for pp.110–111; Lebrecht Art & Music Library for p.69(Tristram Kenton); MediaCom UK for p.48 (t) and p.53, by kind permission; Ian Middleton Photography/Photographersdirect.com for p.46 (item c); OnAsia.com for pp. 42–43; Nucor Corporation for p.12, by kind permission; Photolibrary.com for pp.92 (m, l & r), 112 (l); Punchstock for pp.10 (br & mr), 18 (br) (PhotoAlto), 18 (bl), 54 (ml) (Digital Vision), 28 (b), 64 (l) (Comstock), 36 (mr) (Fancy), 40 (r) (Creatas), 50 (extreme l), 55, 59, 83, 86 (bl), (Bananastock), 50 (l), 54 (mr) (Uppercut), 58 (br), 89 (extreme r) (Corbis), 64 (r) (Photodisc), 88 (Goodshoot), 108 (b) (Glowimages), 112 (r) (Imagesource); Rex Features for pp. 54 (bl), 64 (extreme l), 68 (br); Courtesy of Dr D. Sirota for p.82 (m); Superstock for pp. 24 (t), 51, 58 (bl), 89 (l), 94 (bl); TIPS Images for pp.39, 46 (item d); Topfoto for p.68 (bl); Virgin Enterprises Limited for p.15 (Richard Branson) by kind permission; Wolseley PLC for pp.104, 105 and 106, by kind permission.

Illustrations

pp.11, 21, 23 and 95 ©Rupert Beasley; pp.41, 55, 56, 85, 90, 144 and 145 Hart McLeod; p.53 *The Economist* for Chart 'Advertisers and their target audiences', 31 March 2005, p.84 Charts 'Fatal accidents at work in the UK' and 'Work-related stress in the UK', 26 August 2004. © The Economist Newspaper Limited; p.64 CartoonStock; p.72 © 2002 by Randy Glasbergen. www.glasbergen.com; p.96 Tim Oliver.

Every effort has been made to trace the copyright holders and we apologise in advance for any unintentional omissions. We would be pleased to insert the appropriate acknowledgement in any subsequent edition of this publication.

Photo research: Kevin Brown
Design and Layout: Hart McLeod
Project management: Jane Coates
Edited by: Catriona Watson-Brown
Production controller: Gemma Wilkins

Thanks

The author would like to thank the editorial team for their help, advice, guidance, enthusiasm, feedback and ideas throughout the project, especially Charlotte Adams (Senior Commissioning Editor), Sally Searby (Publishing Manager), Jane Coates (Series Editor), Catriona Watson-Brown (Freelance Editor), Gemma Wilkins (Production Controller) and Michelle Simpson (Assistant Permissions Clearance Controller). Special thanks also to Susie Fairfax-Davies for using her compendious list of contacts to search out and interview business people for the book, and thanks to the following people for kindly giving up time and agreeing to be interviewed: Rachel Babington (Disney Channel), William Brook-Hart (Gifford Engineering Consultancy), Neil Ivey (MediaCom), Philip Franks and Richard Coates (Wolseley PLC).

The author would also like to thank his Business English students at the British Council, Valencia, from 2004 to 2006, who kindly and good-humouredly worked through and trialled the materials, pointed out faults, suggested improvements and, by applying their business expertise, provided essential input.

The author would like to give his warmest thanks and love to his wife, Paz, for her help, enthusiasm and encouragement throughout the project. He dedicates the book to his son, Esteban, and his daughter, Elena, with much love.

The publishers would like to thank Elaine Boyd for her invaluable feedback when reviewing the course material.

Recordings by Anne Rosenfeld at Studio AVP (studio engineer: Dave Morritt).

UNIT 1

Corporate culture

Getting started

1 Work in small groups. Match the sentence beginnings (1–7) with their endings (a–g).

1 My company/organisation has a **vision**;
2 We have an **entrepreneurial** culture;
3 People in my company are highly competitive;
4 My company is pretty bureaucratic;
5 My company has a supportive culture;
6 My company has a controlling culture;
7 My company is quite informal;

a for example, it doesn't have a **dress code**.
b I know where it's going; I share its **goals**.
c the boss is **autocratic**, and we do as we're told without question.
d there are lots of regulations and 'correct procedures'. We're encouraged to **do things by the book**.
e we battle each other for promotion and for **bonuses**.
f when we need them, we're sent on training courses. Every employee has a **mentor**.
g we're encouraged to look for new business and take risks.

2 Look at the words and phrases in bold above and match them to the following definitions.

1 a person who gives another person help and advice over a period of time and often also coaches them in their job *mentor*
2 a set of rules for what you can wear
3 aims
4 demands total obedience from staff
5 extra amounts of money given to you as a reward
6 follow the rules exactly
7 view of how the company will be in the future
8 involving risk-taking

Aspects of corporate culture

Talking point

Discuss these questions in small groups.

1 Which of the things mentioned in Exercise 1 on page 10 are typical of your company's/organisation's culture?
2 Which would you like to be part of your company's culture? (If you don't work for a company or organisation, talk about one you would like to work for.)

Listening

You will hear four students on an MBA course discussing their companies' cultures.

1 Before you listen, match these words or phrases (1–10) with their definitions (a–j).

1 cut-throat	a informal meetings
2 back-up	b Internet company
3 get-togethers	c making more efficient
4 sink or swim	d paperwork
5 red tape	e responsible to the government
6 publicly accountable	f standard by which you can judge the success of something
7 streamlining	g fierce; not involving consideration or care about any harm caused to others
8 dotcom	h struggle of individuals in a competitive environment
9 yardstick	i succeed or fail without help from anyone else
10 rat race	j support

02 **2 Look at the list of aspects of company culture in *Getting started*. Listen to the four speakers, and for each one, decide which aspect of their company's culture he/she mentions. Write one number by each speaker. You will not use all the numbers.**

Candela: .... Sonia: ....
Henry: .... Omar: ....

Task tip

The speakers talk about the subject without using the exact words in the list. You must listen for clues in what they say to decide which is the correct answer.

Vocabulary

02 **Complete each of the phrasal verbs below with one or two words (the definitions are given in brackets). When you have finished, check your answers by listening to the conversation again.**

1 starting *out* (*beginning*)
2 talk things .... (*discuss thoroughly*)
3 come .... ideas and solutions (*produce ideas and solutions*)
4 stick .... (*follow, obey*)
5 .... up (*arrive*)
6 .... ahead (*making progress*)
7 it boils .... to (*the essential thing is*)

Speaking

Work in pairs or groups of three. Describe the culture of the company where you work, or a company you are familiar with, using the following procedure.

- Before you speak, plan what you are going to say and select words and phrases from the vocabulary you have studied so far in this unit.
- Speak for about a minute.
- When you are listening to your partner's talk, think of a question to ask at the end of it.

Useful language

I think there are three main aspects to my company's culture: first, there's …
Another feature is …
Finally, I should say that …
So, it's a good place to work, especially because … / I'd prefer it to be more …

Creating a corporate culture

Reading

1 Read this passage fairly quickly and find out:

1 who is responsible for influencing the culture within a company.
2 how company culture affects a company's performance.
3 what weakness many companies have with regard to corporate culture.

2 When you have finished, discuss your answers with a partner.

3 Choose the correct sentence (A–G) from page 13 for each gap in the text (1–6). There is one sentence you will not need.

Company background

Nucor Corporation is the largest steel producer in the United States. It is also the nation's largest recycler.

It's Our Nature.

WHO IS RESPONSIBLE FOR CORPORATE CULTURE?

F. Kenneth Iverson

How should a director think about the "corporate culture" of the company on whose board he or she serves? Consult a management text on organizational culture and you'll find a chapter or more of definition which boils down to something like "a pattern of shared basic assumptions." Peter C. Browning, dean of the business school at Queens University, North Carolina says: "Every organization has a culture which manifests itself in everything from entrepreneurship to risk-taking all the way down to the dress code. **1** ..G.. " In some cases, it can do both. Recall how IBM's insular, conservative culture first helped the company soar to success—and then nearly destroyed it before a new CEO, Louis Gerstner, arrived in 1993 and saved the company.

Browning considers corporate culture an important part of a board's responsibilities. And he's not alone. In a recent survey, an overwhelming majority of directors say that culture has a powerful effect on their company's ethics, risk-taking, and bottom-line performance. **2** ...... Furthermore, 79% say they believe a board can alter a company's culture.

Even so, many directors are less comfortable dealing with issues of corporate culture than they are with more easily quantified concepts like profitability or market share. Says Edward Lawler, a professor at the University of Southern California: "**3** ...... An understanding of corporate culture is one of the main things missing on boards, but they really need it if they're going to monitor what's going on inside the corporation."

So what should directors be doing to evaluate corporate culture, and what actions can they take to influence it?

Peter Browning's favorite example is Nucor, the steel company. Nucor's culture, which he describes as "extraordinarily powerful, effective, and unique," can be traced back to the values and vision of its legendary founder, F. Kenneth Iverson. The Nucor story—of an egalitarian, collaborative, high-performing business that's been consistently profitable in a notoriously tough industry—has been recounted in dozens of newspaper and magazine articles and books: **4** ...... Although the company earns $6.3 billion in revenues and has 9,900 employees, it has fewer than 60 people in management. There are no company cars or corporate jets. The company offers four-year scholarships to children of employees to help them pursue higher education or vocational training after high school. When business is slow, Nucor reduces hours but doesn't make workers redundant. There's a highly effective incentive program. **5** ...... Ditto for the shareholders: Nucor's total return to investors last year was 37.9%, better than almost two-thirds of the other companies in the Fortune 500.

To ensure that Nucor's collaborative, trusting culture continued, Browning recounts how he "went out and visited innumerable factories. I walked around, talked with people on different shifts." Then he made sure the other non-executive directors did the same. **6** ...... "It was important for the board to get to know the culture so that we could support the next generation of management as they move forward, while preserving the values that really distinguish this company," Browning says.

From *Corporate Board Member*

A The result is that employees have come to trust management and share its vision.
B And having a supportive culture can produce surprising gains in terms of productivity.
C CEO, Daniel R. DiMicco, answers his own phone and email and shares an assistant with CFO, Terry Lisenby.
D Most boards are poorly equipped to deal with their organization's corporate culture, because their staffing is not right.
E The entire board now goes once every year to a mill or plant and spends two days observing operations and talking to workers and managers.
F When asked to rate its importance for these issues on a scale where 1 equals "greatly affects" and 10 means "no effect", the respondents ranked corporate culture at 2.
G It can be a very powerful influence for good, or it can get companies in lots of trouble.

Task tip

Look at the clues in the sentences, e.g. in **A**, what has caused the result that is mentioned? In **F**, what does *these issues* refer to?

Vocabulary

Match these words and phrases from the text (1–7) with their definitions (a–g).

1 board	a dismiss employees, so they no longer have a job
2 bottom-line performance	b group of people appointed to manage a company
3 revenues	c money earned from sales
4 make workers redundant	d people who own shares in a company
5 shareholders	e set periods of time when people work, e.g. 6 a.m. to 2 p.m.
6 return	f the amount of profit on an investment
7 shifts	g whether the company makes a profit or a loss

UNIT 1

Grammar workshop

Defining and non-defining relative clauses

1 Read these five extracts from the text. Find and underline the five relative pronouns.

1 How should a director think about the "corporate culture" of the company on <u>whose</u> board he or she serves?
2 Consult a management text on organizational culture and you'll find a chapter or more of definition which boils down to something like "a pattern of shared basic assumptions."
3 Every organization has a culture which manifests itself in everything from entrepreneurship to risk-taking all the way down to the dress code.
4 An understanding of corporate culture is one of the main things missing on boards, but they really need it if they're going to monitor what's going on inside the corporation.
5 Nucor's culture, which he describes as "extraordinarily powerful, effective, and unique," can be traced back to the values and vision of its legendary founder, F. Kenneth Iverson.

2 Decide which relative pronouns above could be replaced with *that*.

page 26 (Defining and non-defining relative clauses)

Talking point

Discuss these questions in small groups.

- Why is it important for a company to have a strong corporate culture?
- What sort of culture would work best for you?
- What aspects of corporate culture do you think can have a negative effect on performance?
- What things can managers do to change the corporate culture of the company where they work?

Task tip

- Before you start discussing, take a little time to think about what you want to say.
- You can talk in general, but try to give examples from your knowledge and personal experience, too.
- Make sure that everyone in your group has a chance to express their opinions.

UNIT 2

Leaders and managers

Getting started

1 Read each of these things people said about their business leaders or managers (1–8) and match them with one of the qualities or skills listed in the box (a–h).

1 'Amongst other things, she has this tremendous ability to see how things could be in the future, and how the organisation should develop.'

2 'He's just great at producing new, unusual ideas, things other people would never have thought of.'

3 'I really like the fact that he gives us all plenty of responsibility. We all feel so empowered.'

4 'I'd say one of his strong points is his ability to get down to the nitty-gritty; nothing is so minor that it escapes his attention.'

5 'One thing I have to say about him is that he has excellent people skills; he can handle even the most awkward member of staff.'

6 'One thing she's particularly good at is problem-solving. You know, in our line of work we seem to go from crisis to crisis, but she seems to be able to get everything running smoothly again.'

7 'She has a totally practical approach. I mean, she doesn't just sit in her office theorising. She rolls up her sleeves and gets down to work with the rest of us.'

8 'She's just excellent at getting her ideas across. To give you just one example ...'

a A hands-on approach
b Ability to delegate
c Attention to detail
d Good communication skills
e Good interpersonal skills
f Originality
g Trouble-shooting skills
h Vision

2 Discuss the following questions in small groups.

1 Which of the above skills or qualities do you think are necessary for business leaders, which for managers and which for both? (Write 'L' for leader, 'M' for manager or 'B' for both by each of them.)
2 Add three other skills or qualities to the list and say whether they are more necessary for leaders, their managers, or both.

Great leaders and great managers

Reading

Company background
Started in 1971, the Virgin Group operates in a wide range of markets, from music to finance and travel.

1 Before reading, discuss in small groups what you know about Richard Branson and Virgin.

2 Skim the web page very quickly (in two or three minutes) to find out what qualities Branson has which make him a good leader.

RICHARD BRANSON

leader of Virgin

Richard Branson – the founder and owner of the Virgin Group, an empire of 350 companies that includes Virgin Atlantic airlines as well as ventures in other industries like telecommunications, trains, cosmetics and credit cards – says his goal is to turn Virgin into 'the most respected brand in the world'. Branson's skill as a brand builder is one of the reasons underlying his longevity as a business leader.

It is difficult to separate the success of the Virgin brand from the flamboyant man behind that brand. He travels the world weekly, reinforcing his good-natured, visible, jet-setting, billionaire reputation – a reputation like the reputation of the companies he owns. 'Generally speaking, I think being a high-profile person has its advantages,' he says. 'Advertising costs enormous amounts of money these days. I just announced in India that I was setting up a domestic airline, and we ended up getting on the front pages of the newspaper. The costs of that in advertising terms would have been considerable.'

What is the most important quality of a good leader? 'Being someone who cares about people is important,' he says. 'You can't be a good leader unless you generally like people. That is how you bring out the best in them.'

How does a man who owns 350 companies get it all done? Branson places enormous value on time-management skills. As chairman of a large group of firms, Branson says he spends about a third of his time on trouble-shooting, another third on new projects, both charitable and business, and the last third on promoting and talking about the businesses he has set up. 'As much as you need a strong personality to build a business from scratch, you must also understand the art of delegation,' says Branson. 'I have to be good at helping people run the individual businesses, and I have to be willing to step back. The company must be set up so it can continue without me.'

In order for this process to work, employees must be happy. Branson says his philosophy of 'look for the best and you'll get the best' helped him build an empire recognised for its young, fun culture. 'For the people who work for you or with you, you must lavish praise on them at all times,' Branson says. 'It's much more fun looking for the best in people. People don't need to be told where they've slipped up or made a mess of something. They'll sort it out themselves.' Branson feels strongly that if an employee is not excelling in one area of the company, he or she should be given the opportunity to do well in a different Virgin Group job. Firing is seldom an option.

Motivational strategies extend to innovative ideas. The key to encouraging innovation within the Virgin ranks, suggests Branson, is to listen to any and all ideas and to offer feedback. Employees often leave companies, he reasons, because they are frustrated by the fact that their ideas fall on deaf ears. Interaction between employees and managers is fundamental.

Branson has developed a level of trust with his top managers by setting the direction and then stepping back to let them navigate. 'I come up with the original idea, spend the first three months immersed in the business so I know the ins and outs, and then give chief executives a stake in the company and ask them to run it as if it's their own,' explains Branson. 'I intervene as little as possible. Give them that, and they will give everything back.'

From http://www.knowledge@wharton

3 Read the text again and check that you have understood the main points by choosing the best answer, A, B, C or D, to these questions.

1 What is Branson's business aim?
   A To diversify Virgin's activities
   B To make Virgin a global company
   C To survive longer than other business leaders
   D To enhance Virgin's brand image

2 What, according to Branson, is the business advantage of being well known?
   A It is easier to establish new ventures.
   B It saves money on publicity.
   C He is offered special advertising rates.
   D It makes his brands easily recognisable.

3 What, for Branson, is the key to managing his workload?
   A Being continuously involved at all levels of the enterprise
   B Concentrating on problem-solving
   C Making his companies independent of him
   D Continually expanding his empire

4 How, according to Branson, can you ensure optimum performance from staff?
   A By having an enjoyable corporate culture
   B By pointing out your employees' mistakes
   C By dismissing incompetent workers
   D By telling people that they are performing well

5 Why, says Branson, do many businesses lose good employees?
   A Managers do not listen to employees' suggestions.
   B Managers do not know how to communicate with staff.
   C Managers do not encourage innovation.
   D Managers do not delegate.

6 How does Branson optimise performance from his CEOs?
   A By giving them specialist training
   B By giving them a financial interest in the company
   C By giving them a three-month trial period
   D By offering them innovative ideas

Vocabulary 1

Find words or phrases in the text which mean the following.

1 someone who establishes an organisation (para. 1) *founder*
2 a new activity, usually in business, which involves risk or uncertainty (para. 1)
3 which are real but not immediately obvious (para. 1)
4 very confident behaviour (para. 2)
5 from the beginning (para. 4)
6 say a lot of nice things about (para. 5)
7 made a mistake (para. 5)
8 dismissing (para. 5)
9 completely involved (para. 7)
10 the detailed or complicated facts (para. 7)
11 share or financial involvement in a business (para. 7)

Talking point

Discuss these questions in groups of three.

- How much of Branson's leadership style do you think is a question of personality, and how much is a question of technique?
- Which things do you most admire about Branson's leadership style?
- Would you like to work for him?

Listening

03 **Listen to Rachel Babington, Head of PR at Disney Channel UK, talking about leaders and managers. Complete the notes at the top of the next column, using up to three words in each gap.**

Company background

Disney Channel is a cable TV network run by The Walt Disney Company and started in 1983.

© Disney Enterprises, Inc.

Task tip

Before you listen, read through the notes and predict:
- what type of information you will need in each gap
- what type of words (nouns/adjectives, etc.) you will need.

Good leaders ...
- have 1 .... , i.e. to make the business progress
- inspire staff.

Managers deal with the 2 .... of leaders' ideas.

Good leaders also ...
- avoid being too 3 ....
- are not too involved when working with 4 ....
- give people the 5 .... their professional lives.

Grammar workshop

As or *like*?

Study the examples from the text about Richard Branson (a–d) and say which one includes *as* or *like* in a sense that ...

1 means 'he is that thing' (e.g. a brand builder)
2 means 'for example' or 'such as'
3 means 'similar to'
4 is included in an expression which means 'and also'
5 can be used with adjectives or adverbs as a form of comparison

a ... an empire of 350 companies that includes Virgin Atlantic airlines **as** well **as** ventures in other industries **like** telecommunications, trains, cosmetics and credit cards ...
b Branson's skill **as** a brand builder is one of the reasons underlying his longevity **as** a business leader.
c ... reinforcing his good-natured, visible, jet-setting, billionaire reputation – a reputation **like** the reputation of the companies he owns.
d **As** much **as** you need a strong personality to build a business from scratch, you must also understand the art of delegation.

page 27 (Some meanings of *as* and *like*)

UNIT 2

Vocabulary 2

Match these management expressions (1–7) with their definitions (a–g).

1 time management
2 quality management
3 line management
4 middle management
5 brand management
6 crisis management
7 risk management

a direct management of staff
b how a company tries to control its brands and brand image
c level between senior management and junior management
d managing systems in a company so that each department works effectively and produces products of the required standard
e process of dealing with difficult situations
f process of assessing and measuring possible dangers and evolving strategies to deal with them
g the skill of administering your time so as to work effectively

Managing staff

Talking point 1

Discuss these questions in small groups.

- What things can managers do to get the most from their staff?
- What typical mistakes do managers make when managing staff?

Listening

You will hear Rachel Babington talking about empowerment.

1 **Before you listen, work with a partner and predict what she might say to complete the notes below.**

04 **2** **Listen and complete the notes on what she says, using up to three words for each space.**

Talking point 2

Work in groups of three or four.

Your local Chamber of Commerce has asked you to investigate ways of motivating staff in local companies in order to produce a happier, more effective and more productive workforce. Study these ways managers can motivate staff:

- performance pay and bonuses
- annual performance reviews/appraisal
- competitions for new ideas
- empowerment
- working in teams
- regular training

1 What are the advantages and disadvantages of each?
2 Add two or three more to the list.
3 Which would you recommend companies in your area to adopt and which would you ignore?

Empowerment

Workers empowered by:

- deciding their job's **1** ....
- being given **2** .... of their job.

Changes in management style

In last ten years, management has only changed at a **3** ....

Managing people

People need:

- **4** .... in the future to work towards
- reasonable work pressures
- a **5** .... to help them progress.

UNIT 3

Internal communications

Getting started

1 Discuss these questions in small groups.

1 Which of the methods in the box do you use most often for communicating with colleagues?
2 Does your choice depend on …
- who you are communicating with?
- the purpose of the communication?
- something else?

email
one-to-one interview
memo
meeting
handwritten note
notice on the notice board
suggestion box
article in the in-house magazine
informal chat
phone call

2 What methods from Exercise 1 would you use to communicate each of the following inside a company?

1 Informing office staff of a visit by senior managers (you are the office manager).
2 Reminding staff about the annual meeting to discuss the sales budget and sales targets next Wednesday morning.
3 Asking for staff suggestions on ways in which production could be streamlined.
4 Informing a manager that his present job is being transferred to another office in another city (you are the human resources director).
5 Communicating the need for better timekeeping to unpunctual staff (you are the team leader).
6 Informing staff about changes in the way they will work (you are the managing director).
7 Asking your assistant to address envelopes and send letters (he's out at the moment and when he comes back, you'll be in a meeting).

Internal messages

Reading

1 Read the four internal messages (a memo, an email, a note and a notice) on page 19. Decide which of these statements (1–8) refers to which message (A–D).

1 Could you deal with this urgently? [C]
2 Employees can arrange how they want to put this change into effect. [ ]
3 I realise my colleagues are making a considerable effort. [ ]
4 I've got a technical problem. [ ]
5 It's important to keep costs within the agreed limits. [ ]
6 This is where you can find further information. [ ]
7 We want to be able to check the types of problems our clients are having. [ ]
8 Working practices will undergo some reorganisation. [ ]

A memo

Memo

To: New Product Development Team
From: Max Fauré
Subject: Timekeeping

Dear all,

I've noticed in the last few weeks that a number of team members have been arriving late for work and, as a result, arriving late for our daily team meetings. This unfortunately means that:

- the meetings themselves start late and as a consequence, we don't have time for all the items on the agenda
- valuable time is wasted while latecomers are updated on discussions and decisions.

I'm very aware of the hard work and long hours you are all putting in on this project, so, rather than speaking to the individuals concerned, I would ask you all to please make an extra effort with timekeeping. This will help to ensure that the project finishes on time and within budget.

Many thanks,

Max

B email

Delete | Reply | Reply All | Forward | New | Mailboxes | Get Mail | Junk

To: Jennifer Lang
From: Mohammed Aziz
Subject: Our phone conversation

Hi Jenny,

Good to talk to you on the phone this morning, and thanks for your useful ideas. Here's a summary of what we decided. Let me know if you disagree or understood something different from the points below:

- Customer-service staff to work half an hour more Mon–Thurs and have Fri p.m. free in lieu.
- Members of existing staff to organise rota amongst themselves so that there is one member of staff on duty on customer service desk on Fri p.m.
- I will advertise and recruit one more part-time post to provide extra cover at peak times.
- Staff to keep a computerised record, from now on, of all customer queries and complaints and the action they have taken.

BW

Mohammed

C note

Carl,

Sorry – no time to speak to you – directors' meeting starting in 3 mins. Can't get my printer to work – pls cd you print out the envelopes for these letters on yr printer and post the letters asap? Thanks,

Janice

D notice

IMPORTANT
Visit from Haneul Corporation

As you will already know, we are engaged in important negotiations for a contract to supply Haneul Corporation. As a result of this, a group of senior managers from the Haneul Corporation will be visiting our offices on Wed 29 and Thur 30 April. The visit will include meetings with the board of directors and the marketing department. We shall also be showing them round the offices and the production facilities during the course of the two days, so they will be meeting staff on an informal basis. I'm sure you will all make them feel very welcome.

The provisional programme for their visit, which you can find on the Intranet under Forthcoming Events, will include coffee and a chat on Thursday morning from 10.00 to 11.00. Please let my PA, Melanie Ehlers, know if you would like to attend.

Many thanks

Manfred Schüller
CEO

2 **Work in pairs. Read these statements (1–7) about the style and match them to the messages (A–D). Some statements refer to more than one message.**

1 None of these messages is written in a very formal style, but this is the most formal. ....D....
2 Some of the sentences in these messages are not complete sentences. ....
3 There are some abbreviations in these messages. ....
4 These messages use bullet points. ....
5 This is the only message which does not have a subject heading. ....
6 This message contains informal punctuation. ....
7 This type of message does not need to be addressed to anyone. ....

Writing

1 Work in pairs. Choose one of these tasks (1–4). Decide what would be the most appropriate format for your message (memo, email, note or notice) and write your reply together.

1 Reply to the memo. Apologise for your poor time-keeping and explain the reasons for it (e.g. heavy traffic). Suggest team meetings be held later.
2 You are Jenny: reply to the email – there are two points you think are not *exactly* what was agreed. Point these out to Mohammed.
3 You are Carl: reply to the note – you printed out the envelopes, but haven't posted the letters. Give a reason. Also, the technician has fixed her printer. Say what was wrong.
4 Reply to the notice. You want to go to the coffee and chat (give a reason). Ask if this is possible.

2 Exchange your message with another pair of students. Discuss how the messages could be improved.

Useful language

Thanks for your email, etc.
Just a brief note to say / let you know ...
There are a couple of things I'm not sure about: ...
Do call me if you'd like to discuss this further.
Apologies for ... This has been due to / this is because ...

Vocabulary

1 Work in pairs. Decide what these abbreviations from the messages mean.

1 BW	4 cd	7 PA
2 mins	5 yr	8 CEO
3 pls	6 asap	

2 Complete the phrases (1–9) used in written messages with the words from the box.

advance answer details further good hearing input know note ~~reference~~

1 With *reference* to your memo concerning training courses in negotiating skills, ...
2 .... to our discussions this morning, it occurs to me that ...
3 .... talking to you on the phone this morning and thanks for your very useful .... to this project.
4 As you probably ...., Don Grant will be retiring at the end of this month and ...
5 Just a brief .... to say ...
6 Thanks for this information. In .... to your queries ...
7 Many thanks in .... for your co-operation.
8 Further .... can be obtained from ...
9 I look forward to .... from you.

Grammar workshop

Future simple or future continuous?

1 Read the four messages again and underline the examples of the future simple (*will do*) and future continuous (*will/shall be doing*).

2 Complete these rules for using the future simple and future continuous (1–4) with one of the phrases (a–d).

1 The future continuous is often used ...
2 The future simple is often used ...
3 The future simple is also used ...
4 Stative verbs (e.g. *know*) are not normally used ...

a in continuous tenses.
b to express a decision, promise or offer.
c to express the writer's opinion about a future event.
d to talk about future plans and arrangements.

3 Say which of the verbs you underlined in the messages are examples of each rule.

page 27 (Future simple or future continuous?)

Advice for communicating with colleagues

Listening

You will hear four people at a training workshop giving advice on how to communicate effectively with colleagues.

05 **1 Listen and decide which piece of advice (A–H) each speaker gives.**

A Avoid interrupting their work
B Always be polite
C Keep to the point
D Be grammatically correct
E Avoid over-formal language
F Don't send too many emails
G Have an email routine
H Send a clear message

Larry: .... Magdi: ....
Marina: .... Thérèse: ....

2 Work in pairs. Which advice do you agree with? Is there any advice you disagree with?

UNIT 3

Vocabulary

05 **Listen to the recording again and read the transcript printed at the back of the book at the same time. Find words or phrases which mean the following.**

1 do something in a way that is too extreme
2 stop working, usually at the end of the day
3 walking into a room quickly, without being invited
4 question
5 polite behaviour
6 having to work too much

Writing

1 **You all work in the same company. Work in pairs and choose one of these tasks (A–C).**

Task A

Write a memo to your department:
- informing them about a change in working procedures which is going to be implemented
- explaining the reasons for the change
- inviting suggestions for further changes.

Task B

Write an email to your manager (who is on an extended business trip):
- informing him/her that you wish to apply for a post in another department of the company
- explaining the reason(s) why you are applying
- asking him/her to recommend you for the post.

Task C

Write a notice to all staff:
- telling them about a big contract the company has landed
- explaining why it's so important
- thanking them for the part they played
- informing them that there will be a celebration in the office.

2 **Pass your memo, email or notice to another pair of students and do one of the tasks below. (Before writing, decide whether you should use a memo, email, note or notice to reply.)**

Task A Reply to the **memo**
- saying that you think the change(s) are unnecessary, and explaining why
- suggesting an alternative procedure.

Task B Reply to the **email**
- explaining why he/she is not ready for the post
- suggesting you discuss the matter together when you return from your business trip.

Task C Reply to the **notice**
- expressing congratulations about the contract
- saying you will attend the celebration

Pass your reply back to your colleagues.

Talking point

It is often said that a good manager must be a good communicator. Work in small groups and discuss these questions.

- How true do you think this is?
- How can managers learn to communicate better?
- What can managers do to improve communications within their organisations?

Useful language

Well, I think there's a real need (in companies) for ...
Another requirement of managers is ...
One weakness which many managers have is ...
Where many organisations fail is ... , and so managers should ...
Managers have to make sure that / ensure that ...
Another thing we should take into consideration is ...

UNIT 4

Chairing meetings

Getting started

Discuss these questions in small groups.

- What is the function of the chair (or chairperson) at a meeting?
- What personal qualities should a good chair have?
- What things should a chair do to make sure a meeting achieves its aims?
- Does every meeting need a chair?

Advice for chairs

Reading

You will read some advice for people chairing meetings. The advice comes under four headings: *impartiality*, *assertiveness*, *staying on course* and *summarising*.

1 **Before you read, discuss in small groups: what advice would you give about these four aspects of being a chair?**

2 **Read this advice for chairing meetings (ignore the gaps for the moment). Was the advice the same as yours or different?**

Chairing a meeting means ensuring that a meeting **1** ...B.... its aims. The meeting should have been **2** .... for a specific purpose, and all discussion at the meeting must be conducted to this end. These are some of the skills required:

Impartiality

A chairman should ensure that all participants have an opportunity to express their point of view.

Assertiveness

Ensuring that everyone gets a(n) **3** .... will almost certainly involve stopping someone from dominating the **4** .... The more **5** .... the issue, the more likely you are to require firmness, although phrases such as 'I think we should hear from Ms. Smith on this' or 'Can we have some comments from the engineering department on this?' should be sufficient in most cases. Once you provide this opening, however, you need to ensure that there are no interruptions while the next speaker has their **6** ....

Staying on course

A chair must **7** .... the importance of each item on the agenda, and **8** .... time to each topic as required. If one issue begins to dominate, the chair must take control. You might **9** .... a further meeting to discuss the issue at a later date, or that the main parties concerned could continue the discussion at the end of the meeting.

Summarising

Summarising can be used at the end of a meeting to ensure that everyone has a clear **10** .... of what took place or what action is now required. It is a skill which is **11** .... for a chair and which requires active **12** .... You have to state concisely what was said and end with a clear statement about what is expected to happen next and what each participant has agreed to do.

From http://www.meetingwizard.org

3 **Read the text again and choose the best alternative, A, B, C or D, for each gap. This will help you to study a number of useful collocations connected with meetings.**

	A	B	C	D
1	**A** meets	**B** achieves (circled)	**C** arrives	**D** manages
2	**A** summoned	**B** required	**C** called	**D** gathered
3	**A** listening	**B** attention	**C** notice	**D** hearing
4	**A** procedure	**B** proceedings	**C** dealings	**D** undertakings
5	**A** contentious	**B** argumentative	**C** disagreeable	**D** quarrelsome
6	**A** speak	**B** say	**C** state	**D** opinion
7	**A** assess	**B** advise	**C** weigh	**D** appraise
8	**A** share	**B** set	**C** budget	**D** allot
9	**A** suggest	**B** advise	**C** indicate	**D** move
10	**A** insight	**B** preview	**C** hindsight	**D** overview
11	**A** valueless	**B** invaluable	**C** valued	**D** priceless
12	**A** hearing	**B** audition	**C** attention	**D** listening

4 **Compare your answers with a partner and discuss the following.**

- Which do you think is the best advice? Is there anything you disagree with?
- What training could you give someone to become a good chair?

UNIT 4

Key phrases for chairs

Listening

You will hear five different extracts from business meetings where people are discussing problems.

06–10 **1** **Listen and for each meeting (1–5), decide which problem (A–H) is being discussed.**

Meeting 1: .... Meeting 2: ....
Meeting 3: .... Meeting 4: ....
Meeting 5: ....

A How to deal with a late payer
B How to improve timekeeping
C Whether a product is suitable
D Who would be the best person for the job
E Which would be the best hotel to use
F How to treat a potential customer
G When to hold an event
H Why a deadline can't be met

2 **Complete these sentences (1–14), used by the chairs of the meetings, with the words from the box.**

about	break	copy	~~get~~	have	look
minutes	other	purpose	sum	summary	
to	views	what			

1 OK, let's ..*get*.. started.
2 Has everyone got a .... of the agenda?
3 Would anyone like to take .... , or shall we just keep a list of action points?
4 Thank you all for coming. The .... of this meeting's to …
5 Jane, could you give us your .... on this?
6 So, if I could just .... up, what you think is that …
7 Thanks very much for that. Now can we hear what other people .... to say?
8 Look that's all very interesting, but can we keep .... the issue in hand?
9 So, in a nutshell, ... you think is that …
10 Well, we don't have to decide on this today. Let's think .... it a bit more and come back to it next week.
11 Now, let's take a five-minute .... and then start on point number 6.
12 So we need more information on this issue. Sandra, can you .... into it for the next meeting?
13 So, in .... , we've agreed about where we're going to stay …
14 Well, thanks all of you for your time. I think this has been very profitable, and we'll meet again to talk about the .... points on Wednesday 4th at the same time. See you all then.

06–10 **3** **Listen to the conversations again to check your answers.**

4 **Classify each of the sentences from Exercise 2 by writing a number in the table below.**

Starting and managing a meeting	Asking for other opinions	Keeping the meeting focused	Summarising
1			

Holding meetings

Speaking

4 UNIT

Work in groups of four or five and take turns to chair the meetings below. Each meeting should take about five or six minutes.

The chair should:
- start and administer the meeting
- get everyone's opinions and give everyone a chance to speak
- keep the meeting focused
- make sure the meeting finishes on time
- summarise discussion points or decisions when necessary.

The other attendees should:
- study the agenda of the meeting beforehand
- quickly prepare a few ideas or opinions.

Meeting 1

You work for a large company. Your meeting is to consider the regional sales conference to be held next autumn. You have the following points on the agenda:
- conference location (somewhere attractive and enjoyable)
- length of conference
- suggestions for entertainment of delegates during conference.

Meeting 2

You work for a medium-sized company. Each of you is from a different department. The chair is the training manager. The meeting is to discuss training needs for next year. The points on the agenda are:
- training needs for managers
- training needs for other staff
- training budget (the company has a turnover of $7m and gross profits of $2m p.a.).

Meeting 3

Your company is thinking of moving its head office. You are meeting to discuss this. Points on the agenda are:
- where the new head office should be located (city centre / near the airport, etc.)
- design of the offices (open plan, individual offices, etc.)
- facilities for staff which should be provided.

Meeting 4

You are all senior sales personnel. Your company is expanding rapidly, and you are going to take on new sales staff. Your meeting has the following agenda:
- whether to recruit experienced sales people or train up relatively inexperienced sales people
- the most suitable incentives for new sales staff.

Meeting 5

You work for the sales department. An important customer is visiting the company next week. Your meeting is to decide:
- where she should stay
- how to entertain her
- who she should meet when she visits the company.

Vocabulary

1 **Study these common words and expressions used in connection with meetings (1–8) and match the words in bold with their explanations (a–h).**

1 Which meeting was the most **productive**?
2 Were any of the meetings **totally unproductive**?
3 Which chair was most successful in making people **stick to the point**?
4 Was anyone guilty of **wandering off the point**?
5 Did anyone **miss the point**?
6 Did any of the chairs let the meeting **run over time**?
7 Did all the participants get a chance to **make their point**?
8 Did all the meetings have satisfactory **outcomes**?

a a complete waste of time
b digressing
c misunderstand what someone was trying to say
d results
e express their opinion
f take longer than scheduled
g talk about the matter in hand
h useful

2 **Work with a partner. Discuss the meetings you have just held by asking the questions above.**

Summarising action points

Reading

Checking writing for mistakes is an important business skill. Read this memo from a chair to participants in a meeting. In most lines, there is one word which should not be there. Write the extra word in the space on the right. If you think a line is correct, write *correct* in the space.

Task tip

Although you have to find extra words in lines, the mistakes are at sentence level, so you should read the text *sentence by sentence*, rather than line by line.

MEMO

To: Departmental Heads
From: Human Resources Director
Subject: Meeting to discuss new recruitment procedures

Dear colleagues,

Many thanks for attending ~~to~~ the highly productive meeting held yesterday — 1 ...to...
and apologies also for letting it run somewhat over time. I hope this did not — 2 ....
cause any of you too much more inconvenience. As promised at the end of — 3 ....
the meeting, here is the list of action points and decisions which we were — 4 ....
agreed on during the meeting:

1 The HR Director will look into the suitability of doing psychometric tests — 5 ....
for all of applicants to management positions within the organisation and — 6 ....
report you back at the next meeting in a month's time. — 7 ....
2 In future time, when interviews for posts in the company are held, a — 8 ....
trained interviewer from the HR department will chair the interview — 9 ....
panel and the head of the department concerned will also be at present. — 10 ....
3 The HR Department will design a standard application form intending to — 11 ....
be used by candidates for all posts at all levels in the company. — 12 ....
4 The HR Director will propose in writing down to the Board of Directors — 13 ....
that there should be made a change in company policy to the effect that — 14 ....
all vacancies should, if possible, be filled up internally and that external — 15 ....
applications should only be sought for if no suitable internal candidate — 16 ....
can be found.

Many thanks for your contributions on these subjects.

Amalia Fayed
Human Resources Director

Writing

Write a memo to your colleagues summarising the action points and decisions taken during the meeting you chaired. Use the corrected memo as a model if you wish.

Grammar workshop 1

Defining and non-defining relative clauses

- **Defining relative clauses** are used to define what we are talking about. They give **essential** information:
  The contract ***which we want to negotiate*** *will run for six years.*
  The relative clause (in bold) tells you which contract is being talked about.
- **Non-defining relative clauses** give extra, **non-essential** information:
  My contract, which I negotiated last week, runs for six years.
  You already know which contract – it's *my* contract – and *which I negotiated last week* does not tell you which contract is being talked about.

Both defining and non-defining relative clauses use the following relative pronouns: *who, whom*, which, whose, where, when, why*. There are differences in grammar:

Defining relative clauses
- have no commas
- can replace *who* or *which* with *that*
- can omit *who, which* or *that* when they are the object of the clause:
  The contract we want to negotiate will run for six years.
  (*We* is the subject and *the contract* [*which*] the object of the clause.)

Non-defining relative clauses
- use commas (or pauses in spoken English)
- do not use *that*
- cannot omit the relative pronoun

* *whom* is used instead of *who* when preceded by a preposition in formal written English, e.g. *The person to whom you are referring is unfortunately no longer employed in this company.*

1 Write a relative pronoun in each space, or '–' if a relative pronoun is not necessary.

1 My company has introduced a strict dress code, *which* we will all have to adhere to.
2 The company .... culture I admire most is Microsoft.
3 The new product launch, ... we had all worked so hard for, was a disappointment.
4 He had forgotten about the budget-planning meeting, ... incidentally is being held in the boardroom, until I reminded him.
5 The report .... he wrote was well received by the board of directors.
6 Mr Samuels, ... you met last year, is taking over as chief accountant.
7 The sales manager .... left the company last month is now working for one of our main competitors!
8 Our former sales manager, ... left the company last month, is now working for one of our main competitors!
9 He turned the company around at a time .... things were going badly for us.
10 The woman .... we really want for the job is asking for rather a lot of money.

2 Join these sentences from an email about a report using a relative clause.

1 Thank you for circulating the report. You wrote it.
Thank you for circulating the report (which/that) you wrote.
2 The head of the department would like to discuss it with you. I work there.
3 She would like several of the marketing people to be present at the meeting. You obtained their input.
4 Could you suggest a time? It would be convenient for us to meet then.
5 Please pass my congratulations to Andy Drake. He did the graphics.
6 The report contained a number of statistics. I thought they were surprising.
7 I had an interesting conversation with Maria Kalitza. You included her comments in the conclusion.

Some meanings of *as* and *like*

As

You use *as*:

a to say someone or something is that thing, or has that function:
He works ***as*** *an accountant.*
She uses email ***as*** *a way of keeping in touch with her friends.*
Can I give you some advice ***as*** *a friend?*

b before a subject + verb:
Things happened exactly ***as*** *I had predicted.*

c to mean 'because':
As *Brian's away today, I'm going to chair this meeting.*

d as a preposition after certain verbs, for example *describe as, consider as, regard as*:
I know it lost money, but it was ***regarded as*** *a good investment at the time.*

e with adjectives and adverbs to make comparisons:
It's not ***as*** *profitable* ***as*** *our other businesses.*

f to mean 'for example' in the phrase *such as*:
Several producers, ***such as*** *Repsol, have increased their prices.*

g with the *same … as*:
You work exactly the ***same*** *hours* ***as*** *me.*

Like

You use *like:*

h to mean 'similar to':
Our company is ***like*** *one big happy family! We just love working together!*

i to mean 'for example':
Several companies, ***like*** *Shell and Repsol, have achieved record profits this financial year.*

Write *as* or *like* in each gap and write the correct meaning (a–i) from the box above after each sentence.

1 ...As... someone who's new to this department, she'll need a bit of guidance. ....a....
2 .... you already know, we're going to close these offices and move to Prague. ....
3 He was recruited into the company .... a trouble-shooter. ....
4 I, ... you, think that it's time to change. ....
5 I can't see any difference. It looks just the same .... the previous model. ....
6 It's just .... I thought – they've sent the wrong instructions! ....
7 Our company, ... Virgin, is a privately owned business. ....
8 Several departments, such .... budgeting and accounts, are going to be amalgamated. ....
9 There are several aspects of our culture, ... not wearing ties or having flexible working hours, which are quite informal. ....
10 They closed the factory, ... it was no longer profitable. ....
11 This factory is often described .... a showcase for good working practices in the region. ....

Future simple or future continuous?

You use the future simple:

- in written English
The meeting ***will be held*** *in the boardroom at 10 a.m.*
- to make predictions based on our opinions
*He's highly ambitious. One day he'****ll be*** *head of this company.*
- to express a decision made at the moment of speaking
*Oh, that's the phone! – Don't worry, I'****ll answer*** *it.*
- to make an invitation, a promise, or an offer
Will *you* ***have*** *lunch with me?*
*I'****ll send*** *you the report by Monday at the latest.*
*I'****ll ask*** *him if you're too busy.*

You use the future continuous (*will* + *be* + *–ing*):

- to talk about a future event that is going on at a specific time
*No, you can't use the boardroom tomorrow – they'****ll be using*** *it for a board meeting all morning.*
- to talk about a future activity which is the result of a previous arrangement
We ***will be showing*** *some Japanese clients round the factory on Thursday afternoon.*

Stative verbs (e.g. *appear, believe, contain, own, remember, seem, suppose*) are not normally used in the continuous.

Choose the best form of the verb in each of these sentences.

1 To all staff: Javier Muñoz *will be giving* / ~~*will give*~~ a presentation on The Future of Solar Power in the meeting room tomorrow at 12. I hope you can all attend.
2 She's not determined enough. I honestly don't think *she'll make / she'll be making* it to senior management.
3 In five years' time, our factory in Mainz *will produce / will be producing* 50,000 units a year.
4 Don't worry about the design problem for now. I've talked to my colleagues, and *we'll discuss / we'll be discussing* it at a management meeting next week.

UNIT 5

Customer relationships

Getting started

1 Discuss the following in small groups.

Look at these aspects of customer relations and categorise them according to whether they are:

a something companies look for in the relationship
b something customers look for in the relationship
c both

- after-sales service
- loyalty
- information about future needs
- information about product updates
- cost savings
- personalised treatment

2 Brainstorm a list of activities companies can do to build customer relationships, e.g. publishing a company newsletter.

3 Talk about the company you work for, or a company you know about. What methods does the company have for building customer relationships? Which do you think are more successful?

Problems with customer relations

Reading

1 Work in small groups. Make a list of things that can go wrong in companies' relationships with their customers.

Companies don't answer customers' queries efficiently.

2 Skim the article from *The Economist*. Which problems on your list are mentioned in it? Does it mention any problems which aren't on your list?

Giving people what they want

Companies are still failing to put their customers first

by **SHOSHANA ZUBOFF**

YOU know the feeling all too well. Some widget in your home computer breaks down. Result: it no longer talks to your printer. You telephone the PC maker's helpdesk, only to be told to 'press nine for immediate assistance' and 'your call is important to us'. After 15 minutes of nasty music, a voice tells you to call a different number: that particular widget is their responsibility, not ours. Eventually, a new widget is said to have been shipped to you. Two weeks and many phone calls later, it has not arrived. You throw the PC away and start again.

Life is full of experiences such as these, curiously different from the silvery promises of television advertisements and the salesman behind the counter. A chasm now separates

individuals and firms, and that gap is the next big business opportunity. People long for support to help them through life's complexities and those moments when the promise of reliability turns sour.

Everyone has stories of how firms fail to give consumers the service they have promised. Managers talk of taking care of customer relationships; the reality is the frantic woman dashing from one airline's gate to another, trying to get onto a flight home and finding one cancellation after another and unpleasant, unhelpful staff. When firms cut costs, they often do so in ways that upset consumers: they put pressure on frontline staff who handle complaints, cutting the time each call-centre operative is allowed to spend on a pacifying call; or they use customers' data to pretend to an intimacy and understanding of their needs that does not really exist; and when they raise prices, it is sometimes in ways that turn a good deal into a lousy one when something goes wrong.

Promises, promises

The difficulty begins with companies promising customers support that they cannot deliver. Electronic networks mean that firms now know more about their customers than ever before, so they believe that they can treat customers as individuals. Meanwhile, customers' expectations have risen: they want choice, reliability and to be looked after as individuals. This is, after all, what the advertising promises.

Every manufacturer these days wants to offer service as a distinguishing characteristic; and every service business wants to build relationships with its customers, because it knows that retaining existing customers costs far less than recruiting new ones. But providing services turns out to be expensive and complex. Outsourcing services, whether a bank outsources its credit-card business or a hotel its reservations, is harder to manage than outsourcing the manufacture of chips or tyres. Besides, the prices of many goods have been falling; but the cost of services, including the helpdesk, continue to rise. And the more reliable goods become, the fewer customers need help – and the more redundant (and expensive) the helpdesk seems to be.

But does the solution really lie in new corporate structures and new businesses, designed to support customers in trouble with their airline or computer company? That depends on whether consumers are willing to pay for support. If they are not – which many firms fear – support will remain a cost with no matching benefit, at constant risk of being squeezed.

From *The Economist*

3 To check your understanding of the main points, read the article again and choose the best answer, A, B, C or D, for each question.

1 What is the purpose of the story in the first paragraph?
A to criticise the speed at which companies respond
B to complain about unsatisfactory customer care
C to show the shortcomings of new technology
D to highlight the unreliability of some computer manufacturers

2 What does the writer say is the result of the difference between promises and reality in the second paragraph?
A Customers no longer trust the companies they buy from.
B Consumers now have low expectations of customer service.
C There is an opening for businesses to exploit.
D Companies and customers are unable to cope with difficulties when they arise.

3 What effect do budget cutbacks have on the way companies service their customers?
A Less personal attention is given to customers with problems.
B Products become more expensive than before.
C Companies misuse private information about their customers.
D Products become more unreliable than before.

4 What is the effect of new technology on customer relationships mentioned in paragraph 4?
A Customers expect more from companies than is reasonable.
B Companies use advertising to mislead their customers.
C Companies treat each customer differently.
D Companies think they can offer a better service than is in fact possible.

5 What incentive is there for companies to provide a customer helpdesk?
A Customer helpdesks permit companies to provide better services than their competitors.
B Customers increasingly require after-sales service when they buy a product.
C Customers are prepared to pay extra for after-sales service.
D Keeping the customers they already have happy is more cost-effective than finding new customers.

6 In paragraph 6, what does the writer imply would be the benefit to customers of closing the helpdesk?
A A source of irritation with the company would be removed.
B The company's products would be less costly.
C Companies would find alternative methods of dealing with customer problems.
D Companies would make their products more reliable.

5 UNIT

Vocabulary

Complete the following sentences with a word or phrase from the article about giving people what they want.

1 If you have difficulty installing your new software, you should ring the manufacturer's *helpdesk* . (para. 1)
2 Your new computer was .... to you this morning, so it should arrive in the next couple of days. (para. 1)
3 Our company's products have an unrivalled reputation for .... However, if they do break down, we promise to replace them immediately. (para. 2)
4 One of the duties of our customer-service staff is to .... customers' complaints. (para. 3)
5 Our marketing budget is directed at .... existing clients more than at recruiting new ones. (para. 5)
6 We can reduce our exposure to risk by .... many of our services to other companies. (para. 5)
7 New computerised data-collection systems have made more traditional systems .... (para. 5)

Talking point

Discuss these questions in small groups.

1 What are the implications for businesses of these statements?

a The truth is that not all customers are equally valuable to your company. The well-known 80–20 rule of business says that 20% of your customers will account for 80% of your sales – or even more in some industries.

b One study indicates that it's five to ten times more expensive to gain a new customer than it is to retain an existing one. Other studies show that increasing customer retention by just 1% can produce an 8% increase in profitability.

c Domino's Pizza tells its franchisees that the lifetime value of the average customer is more than $1,000. So when that customer says he doesn't like his $10 pizza and wants a new one free, the lifetime-value formula is simple: make him another pizza.

2 It is often said that 'the customer is always right'. Is this true? Why? / Why not?

Customer Relationship Management (CRM)

Listening

You will hear an interview with Boris Shulov, a lecturer from a business school, about Customer Relationship Management.

1 Before you listen, read the notes and decide what sort of information you need to complete them.

11 **2 Listen and complete the notes by writing up to three words in each gap.**

Customer Relationship Management (CRM)

CRM is: integration of marketing, sales and after-sales service within an organisation.

Purpose: to maximise 1 .... of customer relationships.

CRM applications allow companies to be different from 2 ....

Central to CRM are 3 ....

Key areas include:

- Marketing automation: best customers targeted so 4 .... employed more rationally.
- Sales automation: provides support during the 5 ....
- Customer service: resolves customer issues and thereby builds customer 6 ....

CRM systems delivered over 7 .... are the norm, permitting efficient communication between users.

Talking point

Discuss these questions in small groups.

1 From the article on pages 28–29 and what you have just listened to, what do you imagine are the shortcomings of CRM systems?
2 When do you think computer databases are better at predicting customers' comments and needs, and when is this done better by sales people on the ground?
3 What information do you think it is acceptable for companies to keep on their databases and what information is not acceptable?

Reading

1 **Skim the extracts below fairly quickly and note down all the ideas for how CRM can be used by companies.**

2 **Work in pairs and compare what you have noted down.**

A

Customer relationship management (CRM) is a business strategy that helps a company integrate itself and forge a tight connection with the customer. The promise is that by using technology and human resources strategically, businesses can transform themselves into the proverbial friendly general store – to provide the same levels of customer service that were typical decades ago.

But the goal goes beyond simply satisfying customers. While providing customer service, clever companies are also gathering data on their customers' buying habits and needs, then storing and analysing that data and using it to improve products or services as well as management policies, with the ultimate aim of turning consumers into customers for life.

From *CIO Magazine*

B

Managing customer relationships is only part of an overall business system that links internal quality (both with respect to people and internal processes) to customer experiences, satisfaction, loyalty, retention and profitability. This is not an easy undertaking. It simply can't be the 'project of the month'. To be customer-oriented, organisations must excel at understanding their customers and providing them with improved goods and services.

From *Darwin Magazine*

C

Unfortunately for telecoms companies, how they handle even the most general customer queries remains the cause of the most dissatisfaction. Consumers' greatest angst is one of astounding simplicity – that customer care representatives do not have all the required information to hand. According to our research, 87% of operators said bill inquiries were amongst the top three most common queries they received. The implication is that companies need to urgently reassess their customer-care and billing systems to address this significant shortfall in delivering up-to-date information to the customer.

The customer is more interested in service than the technology that delivers it. By reversing the current dissatisfaction in the telecoms industry, companies can really begin to address their profit margins and secure their future.

From *Communications Week International*

D

Most senior executives say their companies should be customer-focused. Yet when budgets are tight, some of the first expenditures to be cut are for marketing and IT, both of which are supposed to help companies better understand and serve customers.

While investors implicitly value product-development and R&D expenditures, considering them assets that are potentially useful over a long period of time, they undervalue marketing and customer-acquisition costs.

From *Optimize*

E

Our view of customer-based strategies suggests that companies should organise around customers rather than products. A bank should not have one manager for checking and savings accounts, another for investments and a third for credit cards. Such an organisational structure makes it difficult to comprehend the total value of a customer and therefore can't capture important opportunities such as cross-selling. Businesses should have customer managers, not product managers.

From *Optimize*

3 **Read these statements (1–8). Which of the five extracts (A–E) does each statement refer to?**

1 By changing management organisation, companies can sell a wider range of products to the same customers. ...*E*...
2 CRM combines customer care with consumer research.
3 It is a mistake to reduce spending on customer relationships when money is short.
4 CRM should be seen as a long-term activity.
5 Technology can be used to create a similar relationship with customers to one that existed in the past.
6 The ultimate purpose of consumer research is to create a long-term relationship with the customer.
7 Consumers give priority to quality over processes.
8 Companies concentrate too much on product innovation and not enough on attracting new customers.

Talking point

Work in groups of three or four to do the following task.

Your company has decided it needs a Customer Relationship Management strategy. You have been asked to decide how to implement this strategy. Discuss and decide together:

- how Customer Relationship Management can make a company more competitive
- how companies can reorganise themselves to improve their customer relations.

UNIT 6

Competitive advantage

Getting started

1 Work in groups. Combine the words and phrases on the left (1–7) with the words on the right (a–g) to form elements which give companies an advantage over the competition.

2 Explain how each of the things in Exercise 1 can give a company an advantage over the competition. Which do you think is the most effective?

1 a proven track	a identity
2 being one step ahead of the	b management
3 clear brand	c money
4 competitive	d prices
5 customer relationship	e record
6 good value for	f research
7 market	g competition

Submitting tenders

Listening

Public organisations which require private companies to carry out work for them usually organise a competition to find which company will do the best work at the best price.

1 You will hear a consultant engineer, William Brook-Hart, talking about what gives his company, Gifford Engineering Consultancy, a competitive advantage. Before you listen, match the words and phrases (1–8) with their definitions (a–h)

1 a tender	a amount of money paid for a particular piece of work
2 procurement	b computer program, used especially in business, which allows you to do financial calculations and plans
3 to assess	c detailed description of how something should be done, made, etc.
4 to itemise	d a formal written offer to do a job for an agreed price
5 specifications	e the obtaining of supplies or services
6 fee	f to compete against other firms by offering to do a job or contract for a certain amount of money
7 spreadsheet	g to judge or decide the value of something
8 to bid	h to list things separately

2 Read the notes below and decide what sort of information you need in each space.

12 3 Listen and complete the notes by writing up to three words in each gap.

Prospective clients interested in finding 1 .... at cheapest price.
Cheapest contract not always the best 2 ....
Gifford demonstrate excellence through:
- excellence of their 3 ....
- track record obtained from 4 ....

Company background

Gifford

Gifford Engineering Consultancy is an engineering and design consultancy employing 600 people, based near Southampton, UK.

UNIT 6

Speaking

1 Work alone for two or three minutes. Prepare to give a short talk (of about one minute) on the following topic.

How does the company you work for (or a company you know well) achieve a competitive advantage?

2 Work in groups of three and take turns to give your talk.

3 Discuss which is more important to clients and customers: price or quality?

Task tip

- Make brief notes with about three main points.
- Think of examples or reasons to support your points.
- Look at your partners more than at your notes when you are speaking.

Reading

1 Read this account of how the JJ Group prepares tenders and briefly, in your own words, answer these questions.

1 How does the JJ Group avoid submitting tenders for the wrong contracts?
2 How do they find out about contracts?
3 Who works on preparing the tenders?
4 How do they co-ordinate their work?
5 How do they set their price?

2 Complete the text by writing one word in each gap.

Task tip

- Gap-filling exercises help you to focus on grammatical details.
- If you can't think of the word, decide what type of word you need – preposition, pronoun, modal verb, etc.
- The context is important, so read the sentences before and after the gap.

3 Find these words (1–8) in the text and then match them with their definitions (a–h).

1	dedicated	a	good understanding of someone and ability to communicate well with them
2	resources	b	particular way of considering something
3	tracking	c	beginning
4	outset	d	choose to work on a particular job
5	allocate	e	designed for just one purpose
6	rapport	f	measure the quality of something by comparing it with something else of an accepted standard
7	benchmark	g	money and people
8	perspective	h	recording the progress or development of something

Company background

The JJ Group is a full service agency based in Oxford, UK.

How the JJ Group prepares tenders

Two years ago, we **1** ..set.. up a dedicated team to co-ordinate tenders **2** .... part of our growth strategy. We began by reviewing recent contracts, analysing revenue versus costs. We also identified which market sectors and company types we wanted to target. It's important to be specific **3** .... you don't waste resources chasing tenders that don't fit overall business objectives.

There are lots of ways to find out about contracts. As well as **4** .... members of relevant professional bodies, we monitor the trade press, attend networking events and use an online tool for tracking public-sector contracts. **5** .... the outset of a tender, we pick a team to work on it, balancing skills required against existing workloads. We always allocate the people who will actually work on the business **6** .... we win it, and we include **7** .... CVs in the tender document.

We hold meetings at key stages and map critical paths so everyone knows **8** .... they have to produce and when. Our golden rule is to focus **9** .... what the client is asking for. If we have queries, we contact the client, **10** .... also helps to build a rapport before the tender document is submitted.

Most tender briefs come with a budget to work to. We regularly benchmark ourselves against similar-sized agencies so we know our pricing is competitive. Tender documents will be read by several people within an organisation, **11** .... with a different perspective. We structure ours so that they're easy to read and the client can quickly reference the part they're interested in.

From http://www.businesslink.gov.uk

UNIT 6

Winning contracts

Listening

You will hear William Brook-Hart talking about how Gifford Engineering Consultancy wins contracts and sets prices.

1 Before you listen, discuss the following in pairs.

How can innovative designs (such as the ones shown below) give an engineering company or an architectural practice an edge over the competition?

> **Task tip**
> - Take about a minute to read the questions before you listen.
> - Concentrate on the **questions** rather than the options while you are **reading**.
> - Concentrate on the **options** while you are **listening**.

Gateshead Millennium Bridge

West Bay Harbour, Dorset

13 **2 Listen and, for each question, choose A, B or C.**

1 How were Gifford given the contract for the Gateshead Millennium Bridge?
   A They had a well-recognised brand.
   B They had worked on previous projects for Gateshead.
   C They competed successfully against other firms.

2 In what way has the bridge project benefited Gifford?
   A They have been able to reduce their promotional budget.
   B They have improved their reputation worldwide.
   C They have gained valuable experience in bridge construction.

3 How do Gifford find out about large new public projects?
   A They read about them in a periodical.
   B They are approached by potential clients.
   C They have personal contacts inside public organisations.

4 How are prices set on a 'top-down' basis?
   A by charging a fixed designer's fee
   B by estimating the amount of work involved for the designer
   C by charging a proportion of the total value of the project

5 How are prices set on a 'bottom-up' basis?
   A by estimating how much the client would be prepared to pay
   B by adding up the cost of all the work involved
   C by charging less than your competitors

6 How do companies meet the costs of unsuccessful bids?
   A The costs are paid by income from successful contracts.
   B The costs are shared with other consultants.
   C The costs are not recovered.

Vocabulary 1

There are many phrasal verbs connected with business, although they are generally used in more informal contexts.

1 Match these phrasal verbs (1–8) from the two listening exercises in this unit with their definitions (a–h).

1 bid for	a add up to
2 come out with	b approach the problem
3 come to	c calculate
4 go about	d offer to do some work for a particular price
5 go for	e prepare/organise
6 put together	f produce
7 team up with	g try to get
8 work out	h work together with

2 Complete these sentences using the phrasal verbs from Exercise 1 in the correct form. The sentences are all taken from the listening exercises.

1 If you ..go for.. the lowest price, you may not get the best value for money.
2 And Gifford .... a leading architectural practice, Wilkinson Eyre and Associates, and jointly we .... a completely new concept for a bridge.
3 How do you or Gifford's .... getting new contracts?
4 So you'd .... all the time on a spreadsheet from the bottom up and see what it ....
5 How many of the contracts that you .... do you expect to win?
6 .... a proposal or bid must be expensive and time consuming.

UNIT 6

Grammar workshop

Speaking hypothetically

1 Study this extract from the interview and answer the questions below.

Interviewer How many of the contracts that you bid for do you expect to win?

William We'd expect to win about one in three, one in four of straight competitive bids where we're competing against maybe six other similar consultants. And we would hope to achieve that rate.

1 Which verbs are in the conditional?
2 Why does William use the conditional in this context?
3 Which other tenses are used by William and the interviewer?
4 Is William talking about past, present or future time?

2 Complete the dialogue below by putting the verbs in brackets into the conditional where possible. Where it is not possible, use a present tense.

Interviewer How does your company react when you **1** ..don't land.. (*not land*) a contract?

Interviewee Well, it **2** .... (*not happen*) too much to us actually, but we **3** .... (*have*) a very good marketing director, who, if necessary, **4** .... (*approach*) the potential client in a very diplomatic way, and he **5** .... (*ask*) the client what it **6** .... (*be*) that we are doing wrong. We **7** .... (*hope*) that this **8** .... (*give*) us a clue so that, the next time, we **9** .... (*manage*) to get the contract ourselves. Our company **10** .... (*rely*) on building rapport with our target customers, so we **11** .... (*do*) a lot to maintain good relations with them.

page 44 (Speaking hypothetically)

Vocabulary 2

Collocations are words which are often used together, e.g. *raise prices*.

Complete these sentences using the verbs in the box in the correct form. They all contain collocations which have occurred in this unit.

~~assess~~	compete	cover	devote	establish
go	itemise	submit		

1 How do you go about ..assessing.. the value of a contract before .... your tender?
2 We .... a lot of time to building relationships with important private clients.
3 With our costs, it's sometimes difficult to .... on price.
4 If you don't .... costs, you will almost certainly .... out of business eventually.
5 We .... all the work we have to do on a contract; we find this is the best way to .... a fair price.

Talking point

Work in pairs. Imagine you are the sales and marketing directors for your company (or a company you know well).

1 Discuss how you would go about establishing a price for your products or services.
2 Which other members of your organisation would you need to involve in your decision?

Task tip

Before you start, look back at the vocabulary and grammar you have studied during this unit to see if you can use any of it during your discussion.

UNIT 7

A proposal

Getting started

Discuss these questions in small groups.

1. Why might a company decide to extend or diversify its product range?
2. When should a company decide *not* to extend its product range?

Think about:

- extensions of the same basic product
- competitors' activities
- diversification and market changes
- the company's skills base
- brand identity
- marketing and product development costs
- company expansion versus specialisation

Extending the product range

Listening

You will hear a conversation between Devika Chowdry, CEO of a dotcom company, and Naseem Bakhtiar, the company's marketing manager.

14 **1 Listen and complete the notes Naseem took during the conversation.**

Proposal

To be read by **1** ....

Subject of proposal: extending our **2** ....

Main reason for new activity: demand from **3** ....

Also include in proposal:

- reasons for adding to product range
- **4** .... , e.g. stock-control tools, online ordering applications, etc.
- **5** .... , i.e. staff, etc.
- **6** ....

Deadline: **7** .... (Weds 17th)

2 Discuss these questions with a partner.

1. What information should the proposal include?
2. Who is going to read it?
3. Should it be in a formal or an informal style?

Reading

1 **Read Naseem's proposal below. Has he covered all the points in Devika's instructions? (Ignore the gaps at this stage.)**

Proposal for adding to our product range

Purpose

The aim of this proposal is to suggest new products we could add to our existing product range and to **1** .....C..... ways in which the products could be developed.

Our current product range

At the moment, our company produces accounting software for small retail outlets, the purpose of which is to take managers of small businesses **2** .... the process of producing legally acceptable accounts step-by-step while at the same time producing VAT returns and, where necessary, the payroll.

The need for new products

While we know from the feedback that we are achieving high levels of customer **3** .... with our existing products, we have to recognise that we operate in a dynamic and swiftly changing market. Furthermore, more extensive market research among our clients has uncovered a **4** .... for compatible software to perform stock-control and ordering functions.

Resources

Our programming department **5** .... employs six systems engineers and produces regular updates for existing products, while **6** .... them to suit individual clients. Although two engineers could be assigned to the development of the new programs, it would probably be necessary to recruit two further engineers for the new project team. This, in turn, would give rise to higher overheads and other costs, particularly for salaries and equipment. I envisage that the **7** .... project will take 18 months, but at the end of that period will generate profits which will justify the **8** ....

Other costs

Apart from the recruitment requirements mentioned above, the only extra cost I have identified in connection with this project is a requirement for extra office **9** .... to accommodate the project team. Since the new products are being developed in response to demand from our existing clients, I do not foresee extra marketing costs at this stage.

Recommendation

I therefore recommend that we **10** .... with this project as soon as is convenient.

2 **In order to focus on the vocabulary of the proposal, read it again and choose the best alternative, A, B, C or D, for each gap.**

1	**A** discover	**B** search	**C** identify	**D** underline
2	**A** over	**B** into	**C** across	**D** through
3	**A** happiness	**B** interest	**C** satisfaction	**D** pleasure
4	**A** demand	**B** request	**C** necessity	**D** interest
5	**A** presently	**B** actually	**C** meanwhile	**D** currently
6	**A** matching	**B** tailoring	**C** fitting	**D** meeting
7	**A** first	**B** initial	**C** entry	**D** introductory
8	**A** input	**B** down payment	**C** output	**D** outlay
9	**A** room	**B** sections	**C** space	**D** capacity
10	**A** carry	**B** engage	**C** provide	**D** proceed

3 **Study Naseem's proposal and discuss these questions with a partner.**

1 What do you notice about the layout of the proposal?
2 Does the proposal have an introduction and a conclusion?
3 Which is more important in the proposal: the current situation or discussion of future activity?
4 Is the style formal or informal? Find examples to illustrate your answer.

Vocabulary

1 **Match these linking words and phrases from the proposal (1–9) with their meanings (a–g).**

1 at the same time (line 9)	a also
2 while (line 13)	b although
3 furthermore (line 16)	c as a result (of)
4 in turn (line 27)	d because
5 apart from (line 33)	e for this reason
6 in connection with (line 34)	f in addition to
7 since (line 36)	g related to
8 in response to (line 37)	
9 therefore (line 40)	

UNIT 7

2 Complete these sentences using words or phrases from Exercise 1. You will need to use one phrase twice.

1 .....*Since*..... our profits have fallen in recent months, it is unlikely that we shall be able to reinvest so much in new marketing initiatives.
2 .... we have met our targets in all of the last five years, this year we look likely to fall short by half a million euros.
3 Interest rates have risen, and this .... has led to an increase in the price of components.
4 The purpose of this proposal is to suggest a restructuring of our marketing department and .... to propose new marketing strategies.
5 There have recently been a number of errors in our stock-control system. .... we should seriously consider implementing a computerised system. This .... will reduce staff costs.
6 We're introducing a flexible working system .... requests from a number of staff.
7 Our sales force is looking rather depleted just now: two senior sales managers retired earlier this year and, ... this, several other sales staff have transferred to our overseas offices.
8 Unfortunately there have been a number of complaints .... our latest advertising campaign.
9 We need to launch new products. .... , these products need to be tailored to suit the needs of individual customers.

3 Find words or phrases from the proposal which mean the following.

1 present/current
2 find
3 shops
4 tax declarations
5 money paid to employees
6 improvements
7 create
8 expect

Grammar workshop

1 Compound nouns

1 Write compound nouns to express these ideas. Then check your answers by reading the proposal on page 37 again.

1 range of products .*product range*.
2 software used for accounting
3 small outlets for retailing
4 products which already exist
5 the satisfaction which clients feel
6 research which is carried out on the market
7 requirements for recruitment
8 costs incurred by marketing

Compound nouns are very common in business English, e.g. *product range, software solutions, business start-ups*.

In this case, a noun or a verb is used as an adjective to describe the noun which follows, e.g. *managing director* (the director who manages), *Internet service provider* (a company which provides service for the Internet).

The compound element, e.g. *product, managing*, etc. usually follows the rules for adjectives:

- It goes before the noun.
- It is normally not plural (exceptions to this are items 1 and 8 in Exercise 2 below).

2 Write compound nouns to express these ideas.

1 manager responsible for the services provided to customers (*three words*)
2 box where suggestions can be placed (*two words*)
3 pay you receive during your holidays (*two words*)
4 management of resources (*two words*)
5 satisfaction a person feels from doing a job (*two words*)
6 process of selecting candidates (*three words*)
7 response from clients (*two words*)
8 procedure for dealing with complaints (*two words*)

page 45 (Compound nouns)

2 The passive

In formal business writing, such as proposals and reports, the passive is commonly used because it is:

- more impersonal (and therefore more formal)
- often not important or necessary to say who is doing or who did something.

The passive is formed by the verb *to be* + past participle:

The product ***was launched*** *in January of last year.*
This product ***could be sold*** *at twice its present price.*

Remember: the passive is used more often in formal writing, but it is not used all the time.

Rewrite the phrases in *italics* in these sentences using a passive form. (Be careful: you may have to make a number of other changes.)

1 The market research, which *we carried out* in Liverpool between May and September, revealed that *we could raise the price* by 50% with only a 5% loss of market share.
2 *They have interviewed 27 candidates* for the job, but *they don't consider any of them* to be suitable.
3 *We received your order* the day before yesterday, and *we have just dispatched the goods*, so *the shippers should deliver them* within the next 24 hours.
4 *We will not supply you with any more goods* until *you have paid the outstanding invoice.*

Writing a proposal

Reading

Complete this email by writing one word in each gap.

Delete | Reply | Reply All | Forward | Compose | Mailboxes | Get Mail | Junk

From: Natalie Bowes
Date: 19th May
To: Francesca Jiménez
Subject: Finding new markets

Dear Francesca

Further **1** ...*to*... our discussion last week, I think it would be a good idea to **2** .... our ideas about investigating new markets for our products a stage further, especially as we've **3** .... expressions of interest from distributors in other parts of the country.

I'd be grateful, therefore, **4** .... you could write a proposal for this activity **5** .... we could then put to other managers for their reactions.

6 .... your proposal please include:

- reasons for researching new markets
- the types of market we might break into
- how the research should be **7** ....
- the resources which will be needed for carrying **8** .... the research.
- your recommendations.

I look forward to having your ideas as **9** .... as convenient.
Many thanks in **10** ....

Natalie

Writing

1 **Write the proposal outlined in Natalie's email above. Before you start, work with a partner and do the following.**

- Underline the points in the email that you must deal with in your proposal.
- Decide what details you must invent in order to write the proposal, e.g. the type of company you work for, what new markets you should research, etc.
- Decide what sections and section headings your proposal should have, and write a plan.
- Discuss what ideas you can express in each section and include these in your plan.

2 **Compare your ideas with the rest of the class.**

3 **Work alone and write your proposal, following your plan. You can use the proposal on page 37 as a model.**

4 **When you have finished writing, spend some time checking what you have written to improve it and to correct mistakes.**

UNIT 8

Presenting at meetings

Getting started

Discuss these questions in small groups.

- Who do you think eats more ice-cream in your country: children or adults?
- Which are the dominant brands? Are they local, national or multinational brands?
- Which factors are more likely to give an ice-cream company a competitive advantage in your country: price, advertising, quality, variety, tradition, fashion or something else?

The Chinese ice-cream market

Listening

You will hear an extract from an Export Department meeting at Helsingor Foods, a Danish ice-cream producer. Catalina (Cati) is giving a presentation to her manager, Nils, and to Paul and Tanya, European sales managers based in London.

1 **Before you listen, discuss in small groups: What do you imagine are the opportunities and dangers for a company trying to break into the ice-cream market in a different country?**

15 **2** **Listen and complete these notes with up to three words in each gap.**

- Total **1** .... last year: 23 billion yuan (€2.3bn) and **2** .... of 10% p.a.
- Five companies have 57% of **3** .... (30% foreign companies, 27% national companies).
- Average **4** .... of ice-cream: 1 litre per capita (compared with 23 litres in USA)
- Largest national producer, Yili, says it plans to:
  - increase **5** ....
  - reduce **6** ....
  - tailor products to **7** ....
- To capture market share, all companies have been involved in a **8** ....
- Main products cost 1-2 yuan (10-20 cents)

3 **Complete these charts by labelling the gaps (1–5) with information from the notes in Exercise 2.**

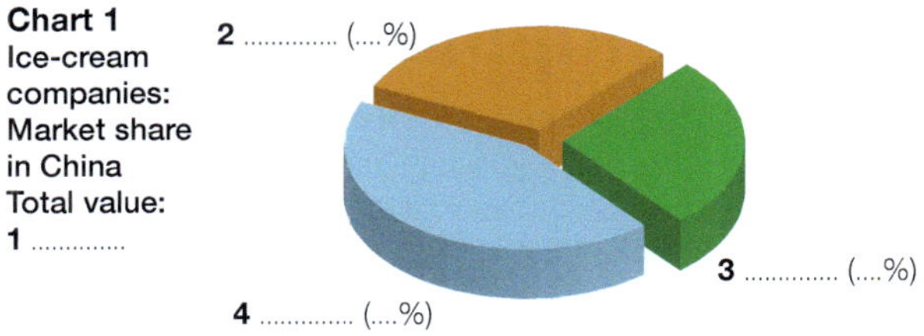

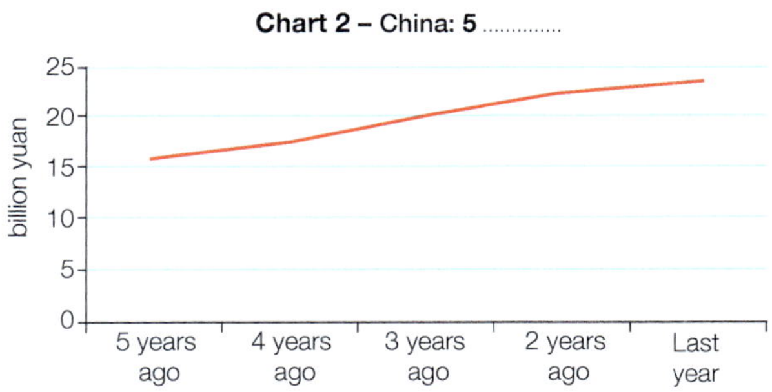

4 **Decide whether these statements about Catalina's presentation are true or false and say why. (You can look at the transcript for track 15 at the back of the book.)**

1 She starts her presentation with a brief introduction.
2 She speaks in a quite formal style.
3 She uses formal vocabulary.
4 At the end of her talk, she offers conclusions.
5 She structures her talk, so we know where she has reached in her presentation.
6 She makes clear which part of Paul's question she's answering.

Grammar workshop

Embedded questions

Rewrite these questions beginning with the words given.

1 What are the total sales for the Chinese market?
I'd just like to know ...*what the total sales for the Chinese market are.*...
2 How are Chinese companies reacting to this competition from abroad and also, how are these competitors going about increasing their market share?
Can you tell me .... ?
3 What sort of price do you think we could sell our products at?
I wonder ....
4 How would we position them?
How do you think .... ?

➲ **page 45** (Embedded questions)

More on the Chinese market

Speaking

You are going to present information at a meeting about the Chinese ice-cream market.

1 **Work in pairs and together study either File A or File B. Discuss together how you can present the information. If necessary, look at Catalina's presentation again and decide what features of her presentation you can use.**

2 **Change partners and work with someone who studied the other file. Take turns to present your information to each other.**

3 **While you are listening to your partner, take notes and think of a question to ask at the end.**

Useful language

Structuring your talk

I'm going to make three main points. The first one is …
The market has been growing for two reasons: firstly, …
There are three factors to be taken into account. The first one is …
Now, moving on to point number two, …
The second thing I'd like to point out is …
Finally, …
And my third and final point is …

File A

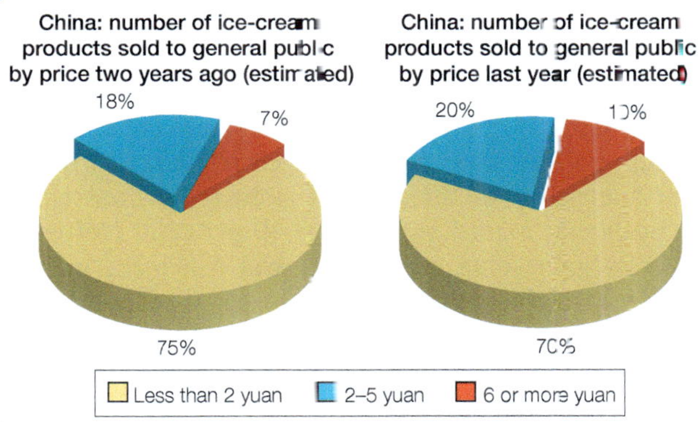

File B

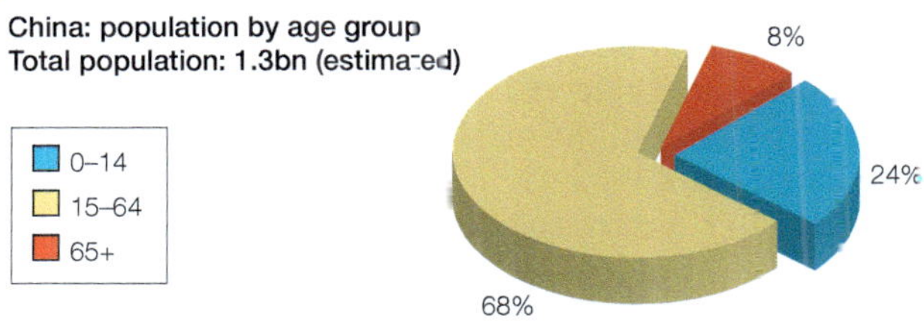

Income per capita: €1,000 p.a.
Economic growth rate (estimated): 8% p.a.

Trends in the ice-cream market

Reading and speaking

Work in groups of three. You have been carrying out further investigations into the ice-cream market. Each student should:

- read **one** of the three texts, A, B or C and take notes on the essential information in order to present the information at a meeting later
- present the information to your group using your notes as a guide
- listen to your partners' presentations and, while listening, take notes and prepare to ask a question at the end of the presentation.

A

Nestlé in Thailand

Swiss food giant Nestlé has said that its Thai division is about to introduce another major drive in its aim to consolidate the still fragmented ice-cream market in Thailand.

NESTLÉ ICE CREAM has said that it intends to invest a total of €23.4m in an attempt to further expand its business. The company said that approximately 75 per cent of budget had been allocated towards marketing activities which will feature new products and advertising. The company says it is also planning on doubling production capacity from 30–35 million litres a year to 60–70 million litres over the course of the next few years.

Currently Nestlé Thailand has a 36-per-cent share of Thailand's ice-cream market, which is estimated to be worth a total of €113m, but the latest programme aims to push that market share up to 40 per cent. Nestlé is keen to gain some ground on rival ice-cream maker Unilever which currently has a 40-to-45-per-cent leading share of the market.

Last year, the company successfully increased its share of the market by launching a range of take-home ice-cream products for the market, which helped to boost its market share from around 30 per cent. Nestlé launched seven varieties of ice-cream, including traditional flavours made with coconuts, peanuts and condensed milk.

Meanwhile, Unilever is also looking to maintain its leading position in the market by announcing this week the launch of a Wall's brand low-fat version of its ice-cream in an effort to capitalise on growing niche markets.

From *Dairy Reporter*

B

The Philippine market

The Philippine market is dominated by three companies, namely: Selecta-Wall's, Nestlé Philippines and Universal Robina. Selecta and Nestlé each claim market shares of 46%. There are also imported brands in the market, such as Dairy Queen, Häagen-Dazs and Baskin-Robbins.

Ice-cream consists mainly of milk. Since the country imports 99% of its milk, the ice-cream industry is vulnerable to foreign exchange fluctuations. Another concern is the presence of adequate storage and handling facilities, since ice-cream easily melts. The product's shelf life usually ranges from two weeks to one year, depending on the conditions of its storage.

Consumption is largely influenced by quality, such as flavor, body and texture, appearance or color of the product, and packaging. Increasing competition in the market has also led manufacturers to develop and launch new production techniques, flavors, and products.

Overall, there is still a large market for ice-cream. In the Philippines, where ice-cream is considered as a traditional dessert, there is definitely room for increasing the low per-capita consumption. The key is in providing quality products at competitive prices.

From *Asia Week*

c

Nestlé expands ice-cream lines in China

SUPPLIERS OF ingredients to the developing ice-cream market in China will welcome news that Nestlé, the world's number-one food maker, will deepen penetration and sharpen competitiveness in this burgeoning market through new launches.
Ken Donaldson, head of Nestlé's ice-cream business unit in China, announced the firm will launch 29 new ice-cream products onto the market, targeted at consumers of all ages. Nestlé hopes to attract new consumers with 'low-priced products as well as take-home items, which are specially designed for kids, teens and adults'.

Foreign giants Wall's, Nestlé and Meadow Gold have 30 per cent of the Chinese ice-cream market, while the two domestic brands, Yili and Mengniu, hold 27 per cent.

Growing affluence in China is transforming the landscape for food: industry sales took off in the mid 1990s, rising from under 100 billion yuan (€9.2bn) in 1991 to well over 400 billion yuan (€37bn) just ten years later. Driving the market is the increased spending power and changing eating habits of China's 1.3 billion people.

There has been an increase in per-capita income levels, and the consequent increase in disposable incomes has brought about a shift in favour of branded and packaged food. Changing lifestyles and growing urbanisation in larger cities have also contributed, bringing a wider acceptance of newer products and driving sales for foods like ready meals, pasta and frozen food.

From http://www.foodnavigator.com

Helsingor Foods: meetings

Speaking

1 Work together in groups of four or five. Study this information about Helsingor Foods.

HELSINGOR FOODS

DATA REPORT

Headquarters: Copenhagen
Established: 1977
Manufactures: High-quality ice-creams and desserts
Annual turnover: €950m
Main markets: Europe, South Africa, Australia and New Zealand
Ambition: To become a global brand
Positioning of brands in existing markets: Helsingor Foods signals the quality of its products by price and by selling in delicatessens and upmarket restaurants. However, brand quality and ingredients can vary according to the market.
Budget available for new ventures: €100m over 5 years.

2 Decide the best way for Helsingor Foods to break into the Chinese market. You should consider the following points:

- what price you should set
- whether to market the product nationally or in one or two selected cities
- whether you need a local joint-venture partner for marketing, storage and distribution
- how you will advertise.

Note down a brief suggested plan of action from what you have decided.

3 Now change groups and present your ideas and your suggested plan of action to your new group. One person in the group should act as chairperson.

Decide which is the best plan.

Writing

Write a proposal (about 250 words) for how to break into the Chinese market. Use the proposal on page 37 (Unit 7) as a model.

Grammar workshop 2

Speaking hypothetically

- To speak hypothetically about the present or future, you use the second conditional. This is formed by *if/unless* + past simple tense + *would/could/might* + infinitive.
  *If a customer **didn't pay**, we **would stop** giving them discounts.*
  Note that in this type of sentence, either *was* or *were* can be used as the singular past tense of *be*; however *were* (a subjunctive form) is more formal.
  *If the company **were/was** to go bankrupt, it would have huge implications.*
- To speak hypothetically about the past, you use the third conditional. This is formed by *if/unless* + past perfect tense + *would have / could have / might have* + past participle.
  ***If** we **hadn't landed** the new contract, we **might have had** to make some staff redundant.*
- Often the conditional clause (starting with *if/unless*) is understood and therefore omitted.
  *How **would you deal** with a customer who didn't pay? – **I'd be** very careful to give him every chance to pay* (We understand the conditional clause: *If this situation arose.*).
  *What **would you have done** in that situation? – I **might have offered** to lower the price.*
- If one part of the sentence speaks about the present/future and the other part about the past, you can 'mix' second and third conditionals.
  *If I **hadn't done** that MBA course last year, I **wouldn't be working** here now.*
  *I **wouldn't have replied** to that email if it **wasn't** part of company policy to reply to all correspondence.*

1 Write the verbs in brackets in the correct forms in the following sentences.

1 Do you advertise your products on television? –No, if we advertised (*advertise*) on TV, I think we .... (*find*) our costs too high.
2 We've always maintained good relations with our customers. If we .... (*not manage*) to do so, I think we .... (*go*) out of business long ago.
3 I'm not sure about CRM. I mean, if we .... (*have*) a complete database with all our customers' details, ... we .... (*be*) able to use it efficiently?
4 It's a pity that, with all his expertise, Don left the company. If he .... (*stay*), he .... (*know*) how to deal with the present situation.
5 I've never had such a terrible boss. If he .... (*be*) more polite when he speaks to me, I .... (*mind*) so much, but if I .... (*realise*) he was so rude when he came, I .... (*leave*) the company months ago.
6 If we .... (*put*) in a lower bid, we .... (*land*) the contract, but as it is, we've lost it.
7 Many business courses put too much emphasis on the technical aspects of business. If they .... (*teach*) more people skills, many managers .... (*be*) better at their jobs.
8 Fortunately we didn't buy that new machine which was recommended to us. If we .... (*order*) it, we could never have paid for it.
9 If we .... (*not win*) that contract we tendered for last month, we .... (*probably be*) out of a job now.
10 Fermal, as a company, is well known for paying their invoices on time. If they .... (*not have*) such a good reputation, we .... (*not sell*) them all that machinery last year.

2 Put the verbs in brackets in the following conversation into the correct tense to express hypothetical ideas.

Q How would you go about deciding whether to adopt some new piece of technology?

A Well, that very much depends. I think we **1** .... (*first have*) to look at whether it was likely to produce real cost savings. The question of productivity **2** .... (*also need*) to be taken into account. I mean, sometimes we have adopted new technologies in the past which haven't proven very satisfactory. For instance, if we **3** .... (*budget*) correctly for the real costs in staff training, in many cases we **4** .... (*not buy*) into new equipment so quickly. So, nowadays when considering these things, we **5** .... (*look*) at training costs, and we **6** .... (*even assess*) the level of staff dissatisfaction that implementing changes **7** .... (*cause*). In our business, we make it very clear that staff contentment comes first and leads to contented customers, so we **8** .... (*not want*) to do anything to upset our staff unnecessarily.

Compound nouns

- Compound nouns are formed by putting the noun or verb you want to use as an adjective before the noun you want to describe:
  shareholder meeting = a meeting of shareholders, i.e. describing the type of meeting
  meeting room = a room used for meetings, i.e. describing the type of room
- The first noun or verb is usually singular:
  cost savings, six-month contract
- To make a compound noun plural, add *-s* to the final element:
  retail outlets, customer complaints
- To make a compound noun using a verb use the verb + *-ing*:
  working party, negotiating skills
  but if there is a corresponding noun, use the noun: *application form, selection board* not ~~*applying form*~~, ~~*selecting board*~~
- Sometimes compound nouns can have three elements or more:
  basement meeting room, customer helpdesk
- Some compound nouns are written as separate words: *office worker*
  Some use a hyphen: *risk-taking*
  Some are written as one word: *businessman, database*
  A good dictionary will tell you how a compound noun is usually written.
- When compound nouns are formed with three elements, sometimes a hyphen is needed to show which nouns are being used adjectivally. A *working lunch arrangement* is a lunch arrangement that works; a *working-lunch arrangement* is an arrangement to have working lunches.
- The first part of a small number of compound nouns is plural, e.g. *complaints procedure, suggestions box*.

What do you call the following things?

1 a procedure for doing the accounting
2 a company which manufactures cars
3 a session used for negotiating
4 a firm which is a rival
5 the director in charge of finance
6 a list of prices
7 a survey made when researching a market
8 forms you must complete when applying for a job
9 a service for delivering things by motorcycle
10 an error made when typing

Embedded questions

- You put a short introductory phrase before a question to make it less direct and so more polite. When you do this, you do not invert subject and verb as you would in a normal question (auxiliary verb + subject + main verb):
  How long ***have they been operating*** *in China?* →
  Can you tell me how long ***they have been operating*** *in China?*
- If the introductory phrase itself is not a question, do not use a question mark:
  I'd like to know what their market share is.
  I wonder how much they spent on advertising and promotion.
- If the question expects the answer *yes* or *no*, use *if* or *whether* between the short phrase and the main part of the question:
  Could you tell me if you have been expecting me to call?

1 Rewrite these questions, beginning with the phrases given.

1 When will the new factory site become operational?
I wonder …
2 How long is the construction work expected to take?
Do you have any idea …
3 Why couldn't the goods have been delivered on time?
Could you please tell me …
4 Do we have to send the invoice with the goods?
Several people have asked me …
5 What time did you finally finish writing the report?
Tell me …
6 When must we have the work completed by?
I'd be grateful if you could tell me …
7 Did they bring the samples with them?
I'd like to know …
8 Could you answer a few questions for me?
I'd appreciate it …

2 Prepare to ask your partner a few questions about his/her job/studies. Introduce the questions with a short phrase from either the grammar explanation or Exercise 1 above.

UNIT 9

Advertising and customers

Getting started

1 Complete these reasons for advertising using the words in the box.

awareness	boost	building	customer	launch	market

- As a brand-**1** .... activity
- To increase **2** .... of the brand
- To **3** .... a new product onto the market
- To **4** .... sales and to increase **5** .... share
- To maintain **6** .... loyalty

2 Work in pairs or groups of three. Discuss these questions.

- Which do you think is the main reason for each of the advertisements a–e?
- Can you think of other advertisements which are examples of each of the reasons for advertising above?
- Can you think of other reasons for advertising?
- How effective do you think advertising is compared with other promotional activities?

The effectiveness of advertising

Vocabulary

1 Complete questions 1–5 using the words in the box. Then match each type of publicity (1–5) with the photos (a–e).

~~banner~~	classified	endorsement	point-of-sale	street

1 Do you pay attention to banner ads when you're using the Internet? a
2 Have you ever put a .... ad in the newspaper? ......
3 What sort of things are advertised on .... hoardings in your country? ......
4 When you visit shops, do .... displays ever persuade you to buy things? ......
5 Would you ever buy something as a result of a product .... from a famous person? ......

2 Work with a partner and discuss your answers to the questions.

Reading

1 Discuss this question in small groups. Give reasons for your answers.

Do you think consumer advertising is becoming more or less effective?

2 Read this text (ignoring the gaps). Does the writer believe that advertising is becoming more or less effective? Why?

The effectiveness of advertising

People still enjoy ads that are creative and entertaining. But it 1 ...A.... an awkward question: does it actually sell any more chocolates or cars? Although TV viewers tend to be able to 2 .... a particularly good commercial, many cannot remember the product it 3 .... And for the most 4 ...., they try to avoid the rising barrage of ads. Getting their attention is becoming increasingly difficult, because 5 .... are splintering as people use different kinds of media, such as cable television and the Internet. The choice of products and services available is multiplying, but at the same time, consumers have become more sceptical about 6 .... made for products. In today's 7 ...., consumers have the power to 8 .... and choose as never before.

This new consumer power is changing the way the world shops. The ability to get information about whatever you want, whenever you want has given shoppers 9 .... strength. In markets with highly transparent prices, they are kings. The 10 .... for business are enormous. For instance, the huge increase in choice makes certain brands more 11 ...., not less. And as old business divisions crumble, a strong brand in one sector can provide the 12 .... to enter another. Hence Apple has used its iPod to take away business for portable music players from Sony; Starbucks is 13 .... to become a big noise in the music business by installing CD-burners in its cafés; and Dell is moving from computers into consumer electronics.

'I am constantly amazed at the 14 .... level and sophistication of the average consumer,' says Mike George, Dell's chief marketing officer. If Dell changes prices on its website, its customers' buying 15 .... change literally within a minute.

From *The Economist*

3 Choose the best alternative, A, B, C or D, for each gap in the text.

	A	B	C	D
1	(A) raises	B arises	C arouses	D lifts
2	A remind	B memorise	C recall	D retain
3	A included	B featured	C revealed	D offered
4	A part	B time	C ways	D place
5	A groups	B audiences	C samples	D viewers
6	A messages	B suggestions	C proposals	D claims
7	A shopping mall	B open market	C retail sector	D market place
8	A catch	B pick	C hold	D take
9	A record	B unique	C unprecedented	D abnormal
10	A meanings	B suggestions	C connotations	D implications
11	A valuable	B worthwhile	C worthy	D essential
12	A trust	B credibility	C belief	D fame
13	A targeting	B designing	C aiming	D directing
14	A belief	B confidence	C assurance	D esteem
15	A patterns	B systems	C activities	D customs

Talking point

Discuss these questions in small groups.

- How does the company you work for (or a company you know well) advertise? How effective is the advertising?
- How should businesses decide the size of their advertising budget?

Grammar workshop

Adverbs

Adverbs can be single words, e.g. *often, yesterday, quickly,* or phrases, e.g. *every few weeks, in fact, before we had time to react.*

Find items 1–8 in the text. (In some cases, you can use the same answer twice.)

1 two single-word adverbs which come between the subject and the verb
2 a single-word adverb which means *in fact*
3 three single-word adverbs which modify adjectives
4 an adverbial phrase which means *more than ever*
5 an adverbial phrase which means *for example*
6 a single-word adverb which means *always/repeatedly*
7 a single-word adverb which modifies an adverbial phrase
8 an adverbial phrase which says how quickly something happens

page 62 (Position of adverbs)

Listening

You will hear Neil Ivey, a director of MediaCom, talking about the effectiveness of advertising.

1 **Before you listen, read the notes on the right and decide what type of information you need for each gap.**

16 **2** **Listen and complete the notes with up to three words.**

Company background

MEDIACOM
People First » Better Results

MediaCom was founded in 1986 and operates in over 80 countries. It provides media solutions for some of the world's largest advertisers and has sales of over $13 billion.

- TV generally 1 .... way to reach audience (despite expense).
- But according to some, consumers decide to buy at 2 ....
- Decision about which medium determined by:
  - extent of 3 ....
  - when advertising will take place
  - the 4 .... of the target audience
- Monthly magazines more suitable for advertising a 5 .... or a perfume.
- For a washing-up liquid, TV more suitable.
- To achieve maximum audience, television adverts broadcast 6 ....

Talking point

Discuss these questions in small groups.

- Do you think television is still the most cost-effective advertising medium? Have you ever bought anything as a result of seeing a TV advertisement?
- When do you make the decision to buy a new product: when you see an advertisement, at the point of purchase or at some other time?

Measuring the effectiveness of advertising

Reading

1 **Discuss these questions in small groups.**

1 Why is it difficult to measure the effectiveness of advertising?
2 Why is it important to measure its effectiveness?
3 How can it be measured?

2 **Read the five extracts A–E to find answers to the questions in Exercise 1.**

A

The most ambitious effort to measure the effectiveness of advertising is Project Apollo, which is now recruiting 30,000 households in America to become the most closely studied consumers ever. Apollo, run jointly by Arbitron and VNU, will collect information on these families' lifestyles. To measure their exposure to electronic media, they will carry an Arbitron device called a 'portable people meter'. This device, the size of a pager, was initially developed to detect inaudible codes placed in radio and TV commercials, as well as other forms of electronic media ranging from the cinema to background music in places like supermarkets.

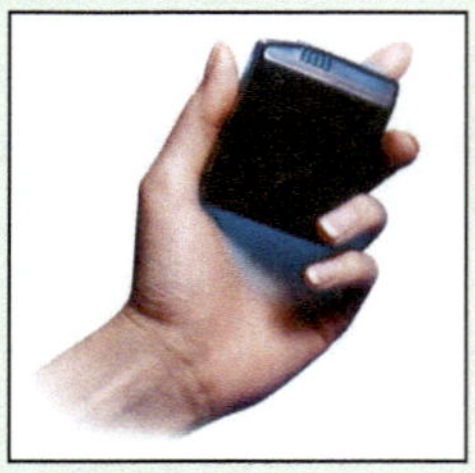

Portable people meter

B

A variety of methods will be used to find out how members of the households spend their day and what they buy. Nielsen's Homescan system, for instance, uses scanners to read the barcodes on all their purchases. Linda Dupree, in charge of new-product development at Arbitron, explains that although marketers gather lots of information, it has always been difficult to put it all together to establish a link between exposure to ads and buying behaviour. This is what Apollo is designed to achieve.

C

Mr Gossman, of *Revenue Science*, has his own ideas about the way advertisers will reach consumers in the future. His behavioural targeting software is already at work on many websites. For instance, it was used by the online edition of the *Wall Street Journal* to try to establish which readers were frequent flyers from their reading of travel-related stories and sections. Individuals using the websites remain anonymous, but they can be identified as users by 'cookies', electronic tracers that show which websites they have visited. When the frequent travellers returned to the *Wall Street Journal* site, they were presented with American Airline ads in whatever sections they read. 'The response to the ads increased significantly,' says Mr Gossman.

D

As most networked electronic media will probably be using Internet-based technology, the same user could be tracked even when he uses different devices, such as a mobile phone or an interactive TV set. This allows audiences with common interests to be grouped together, making them commercially attractive to advertisers, wherever they happen to be. Apart from delivering ads that are more likely to be relevant, the advertisers will also be able to limit the number of times an ad is shown to an individual in order to avoid irritating him.

E

'The consumer experience with advertising will improve,' predicts Arbitron's Mr Morris. The advertising industry must hope he is right. People are increasingly able to filter out ads. Whoever wishes to can pay to avoid them, use technology to block them or simply ignore them. The average American is now subjected to some 3,000 marketing messages every day and could not possibly take all of them in. Two-thirds of consumers feel 'constantly bombarded' with too much advertising and marketing, according to a survey by Yankelovich Partners, a firm of marketing consultants.

From *The Economist*

3 Read these statements (1–8) carefully. Which extract (A–E) does each statement refer to?

1 Advertisers will be able to target consumers who are using a variety of different media. ..A..
2 At present, most people feel excessively exposed to marketing. ......
3 Consumers will not be shown the same advertisements too often. ......
4 It will be possible to relate what marketing messages people hear with how they shop. ......
5 Nowadays, consumers have more ability to prevent advertising messages from reaching them. ......
6 This device will log what people listen to at different times of day. ......
7 This method boosted the effectiveness of the advertising. ......
8 This technology allows advertisers to target individuals without them being identified by name. ......

Task tip

If you think carefully about the meanings of the statements before you read the extracts, you will almost certainly have to spend less time reading the extracts.

Vocabulary

Find words or phrases in the extracts which mean the following.

1 groups of people, often families, who live together (extract A)
2 experience of (extract A)
3 unable to be heard (extract A)
4 devices for relaying information into a computer system (extract B)
5 patterns of black lines which can be read by and recorded on a computer (extract B)
6 devices which allow movements to be followed (extract C)
7 followed/monitored (extract D)
8 remove (perhaps using special equipment) (extract E)
9 forced to experience something unpleasant (extract E)
10 given so much information that it is difficult to deal with (extract E)

Talking point

Work in pairs or groups of three.

Your company sells software to other companies, not to the general public. It has decided it needs a new advertising campaign to promote its products. You have been asked to consider what form this should take.

Discuss and decide together:

- what forms of advertising you think will be most effective
- how you can measure the effectiveness of the advertising campaign.

Task tip

- Take a minute or so to gather your ideas before you start speaking.
- You may have to quickly invent a company and its activities with your partners before you start.

UNIT 10

Advertising and the Internet

Getting started

Discuss this question in small groups.

How/Why would you use the Internet when buying each of these products or services? You can choose from options in the box and use ideas of your own.

1 a car
2 a computer
3 a holiday
4 a course of study, e.g. for an MBA
5 a book
6 groceries
7 a house
8 a cinema ticket

a to check prices
b to find the nearest retailer/dealer
c to customise the purchase
d to compare different products
e to check availability
f to track delivery
g to make a reservation
h to make the final purchase

Internet sales

Listening

You will hear part of a radio programme in which five people talk about why they used the Internet to buy things.

17 **For each person, write down the product or service they were buying (from the list 1–8 above) and how they used the Internet (from the list a–h above).**

	Product/Service	Why used Internet
Bruce		
Tanya		
Paddy		
Petra		
Salim		

Task tip

You will hear each extract twice. When you listen the first time, try to complete as much as possible of both columns – don't do one column the first time you listen and the other the second time. The second time you listen, check your answers and fill in the gaps you haven't managed to complete yet.

Talking point

Discuss these questions in pairs.

Do you ever …
- click on banner ads?
- filter out online ads, e.g. in pop-up boxes?
- click on sponsored links when using a search engine?
- use online yellow pages or classified ads?

Reading

1 You will read an article about how customers and manufacturers are using the Internet to buy and sell cars. Skim it and decide which paragraph (a–g) explains:

1 how car buyers use the Internet to decide which car they want. ..C..
2 how much interest the Internet arouses amongst customers as opposed to other forms of advertising.
3 how people bought cars in the past.
4 how the Internet can be used for obtaining customer feedback.
5 how the Internet can be used for sales forecasting.
6 why buyers still need to speak to a salesperson before buying.
7 why car makers are spending increasing amounts on Internet advertising.

Task tip

When you do this type of reading activity, match the idea of each paragraph and the ideas expressed in the sentences. Check also that the sentence fits grammatically. Read the whole passage again when you have finished to make sure it reads logically.

Motoring online

a The Internet has transformed the car trade. Selling cars used to be a relatively straightforward business. **1** ..H.. They would then decide on a model, haggle over the price and the trade-in value of their own car, order and take delivery.

b With so many of its customers using the Internet to research their planned purchases, Ford is changing the way it is spending its marketing budget. Four years ago, most of its advertising dollars went on traditional media, such as television, print and outdoor hoardings. Non-traditional forms, such as the Internet, accounted for only around 2% of the total. Now the share is 20%. **2** ...... For instance, a click on a banner ad on a website can be traced through to the company's own website, the selection of a model, the response of a dealer and ultimately a sale.

c A website works like a living brochure. For example, Ford's F-150 pick-up truck, of which some 900,000 were sold last year, is shown in graphic detail. **3** ...... Users can check models and prices, browse through the inventory of local dealers or get a quote for the one they have designed for themselves using Ford's build-your-own option.

d So why bother with dealers at all? 'The dealership is even more important than it used to be,' says Mr Sullivan, a Ford director. '**4** ......' Besides demonstrating the product, dealers are also needed to manage the purchase and after-sales support. Moreover, they can play a big part in customising cars for buyers, fitting anything from different wheels to instruments and DVD systems, all of which could make a handy contribution to profits.

e Indeed, car makers would do well to study the way people compare vehicles online. Edmunds, an online car-buying service, has found that by tracking the behaviour of website users, it can predict with considerable confidence how many cars different manufacturers will be selling four weeks hence, and where. **5** ......

f The company also has a good idea of what people say about different cars. Its website receives 2,000–3,000 reviews a week from buyers of new cars who fill out an online appraisal form. They also suggest improvements to future models. **6** ...... Edmunds is now developing new products to commercialise this information.

g As the car makers have discovered, a website has become an essential part of doing business with consumers, and almost all their advertising now gives their website address. That makes a lot of sense. A typical television or print ad might get a few seconds of attention, but a website typically holds the browser's attention for two to five minutes. **7** ...... This makes it rather puzzling that many companies devote only around 2% of their advertising budget to it.

From *The Economist*

2 Choose the best sentence (A–H) for each gap in the text. There is one sentence you will not need.

A If there is anything wrong with a vehicle, complaints will soon pop up here.
B In Britain, the Internet is now the third most popular media form.
C It uses special software in order to screen out car enthusiasts who are just looking for information.
D Nowadays, dealers report, there are few people who visit their showrooms without a recommendation from a satisfied customer.
E One of the attractions of the Internet is that its effects can be measured.
F People want to touch the vehicle, to smell the inside, to kick the tyres and take it for a test drive.
G There was even a series of videos in which rival models were cut apart and their components compared, to support their claim that theirs is the toughest.
H Customers might see an advertisement in a newspaper, perhaps pick up a brochure, visit a couple of dealers.

Vocabulary

Match these words (1–8) from the text on page 51 with their definitions (a–h).

1 straightforward	a a method of buying a new product by giving your old one as part of the payment for it
2 haggle	b appear
3 trade-in	c argue/negotiate
4 browse	d easy to understand / simple
5 handy	e filter out / remove
6 appraisal form	f place where you can write your opinion of something
7 pop up	g look at information on the Internet
8 screen out	h useful

Talking point

Discuss these questions in small groups.

- How do the methods described in the article for buying and selling cars compare with how you would buy a car / have bought a car?
- What parts of the process do you think are a good idea?
- Which methods used by the car industry could be used by your company (or a company you know well) in its website?

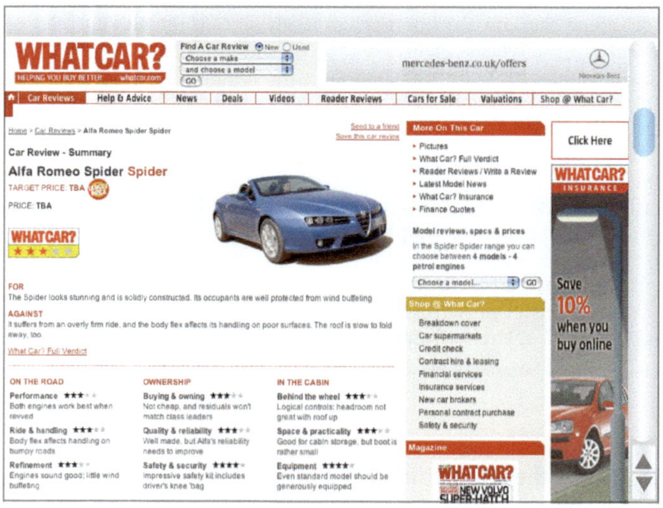

Grammar workshop

Although, however, despite, etc.

> ***Despite*** *a massive advertising campaign, brand awareness hardly rose.*
> ***Despite*** *mailing 30,000 households, the new product range didn't catch on.*
> *During the recession their sales fell.* ***However****, their market share remained unaffected.*
> ***In spite of*** *lowering the price, they were unable to sell the old factory site.*
> *Over-the-counter sales have fallen.* ***In contrast****, e-sales have rocketed.*
> *They managed to increase sales,* ***although*** *they had reduced their media advertising budget.*
> ***While*** *television advertising is able to reach mass audiences, the Internet is able to target more specialist audiences.*

1 Answer these questions.

Which word(s) or phrase(s) (*although, however, despite, in spite of, while, in contrast*):

1 join two sentences, each with a verb in a tense?
2 are followed by a noun phrase or an *-ing* form?
3 start a new sentence and refer to the sentence before?
4 joins two sentences and contrasts two similar but not necessarily related facts?
5 contrasts two similar but not necessarily related facts in two separate sentences?

2 Rewrite or join these sentences using the word(s) given in brackets. Remember, if you use *however* or *in contrast*, you will need to write two sentences.

1 Few people buy cars on the Internet. Many people research cars on the Internet. (*while*)
While few people buy cars on the Internet, many people research them there.
2 People study new cars on the Internet. However, they go to showrooms to buy them. (*although*)
3 Although it's difficult to measure advertising's effectiveness, few companies believe they can do without it. (*however*)
4 They employed a consultancy, but they couldn't improve their company's image. (*despite*)
5 While many dotcom companies have been struggling, eBay has been growing by 40% a year. (*in contrast*)
6 They had a large advertising budget but they kept their product prices low. (*in spite of*)

Advertisers and the Internet

Writing

1 Your manager has asked you to research how advertisers reach their target audiences. You have found the information in the chart on the right. Work in pairs. Study the chart and discuss what it shows.

2 Read the first half of a report based on the information in the chart. Write one word in each of the gaps.

> As the chart shows, there is a disparity **1** *between* the quantity US advertisers spend on advertising in **2** .... of the main media and US consumers' use of the media.
>
> While advertisers spend 38% of their budget on television advertising, US households nowadays spend only 32% of **3** .... time watching television. The difference between advertising spending and consumption of newspapers is **4** .... more accentuated, **5** .... advertising taking up 36% of the budget, although people **6** .... an average of just 9% of their time reading them.

3 Complete the report with information from the chart about magazines, radio and the Internet. Use the first half of the report as a model.

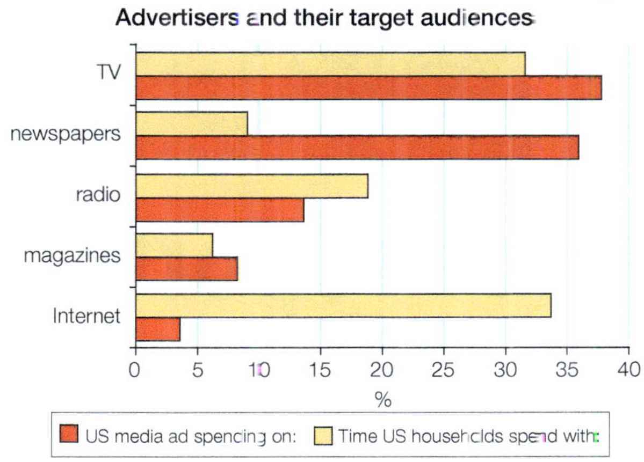

From *The Economist*

Listening

You will hear Neil Ivey, a director of MediaCom (see Unit 9), talking about advertising and the Internet.

18 **Listen to the interview and, for each question, choose the best answer, A, B or C.**

1 Why, according to Neil Ivey, is Internet advertising so successful at selling cars?
   A Customers feel more receptive towards car advertising while online.
   B Internet advertising provides useful information rather than publicity.
   C Advertisements on the Internet are more interesting than TV commercials.

2 What is 'direct-response advertising'?
   A Advertising where companies can respond immediately to questions from customers.
   B Advertising which allows sales people to get in touch directly with the customer.
   C Advertising where the customer can get in contact with the advertiser.

3 What method of advertising household products on the Internet does Neil outline?
   A People go directly to the advertiser's website when looking for a solution to a problem.
   B People looking for a solution on the Internet are told about the advertiser's website.
   C When you go to a search engine, you see banner ads for the product.

4 What are 'viral ads'?
   A Advertisements invented by people who are not advertisers to make fun of real advertisements.
   B Amusing advertisements which people send to their friends by email.
   C Advertisements which infect computers with destructive programmes.

5 How could a small e-commerce company compete with large corporations?
   A by offering something that cannot be bought elsewhere on the Internet
   B by having a more attractive website than large manufacturers
   C by undercutting big manufacturers

Talking point

Work in groups of three. Your manager has asked you to investigate ways in which your company could benefit from advertising on the Internet. Work together and discuss the following points.

- How the Internet can be used to promote products.
- What types of company and product benefit most from Internet advertising.
- How Internet advertising can be combined with other forms of promotional activity.

UNIT 11

Sales reports

Getting started

Discuss these questions in pairs.

1 Which of these sales activities do you think is most effective for selling the products or services in the box?

1 telephone sales
2 mail order
3 e-sales
4 sales events
5 visits from company reps
6 retail sales

a a time-share holiday home
b advertising space in magazines
c clothes for older people
d corporate catering services
e life insurance
f machine tools
g rare books
h theatre tickets
i web-design services

2 Which of these ways of selling does your company (or a company you know well) find most effective? Why?

3 Which method does your company (or a company you know well) use most often to source services or products? Why?

Evolving sales

Listening

You will hear Mehtar Tilak, a sales manager at a professional conference, talking about how sales activities in his software company, Software Solutions, have changed over the last ten years.

19 **Listen and complete the chart with some of the activities (1–6) listed in *Getting started*. (Note: The answers to the questions are not mentioned in the same order as they are presented in the chart, and there are two activities you will not need.)**

Task tip

Before listening, study the chart and what it shows. Familiarise yourself quickly with the statistics it expresses.

Software Solutions: sales by sales activity

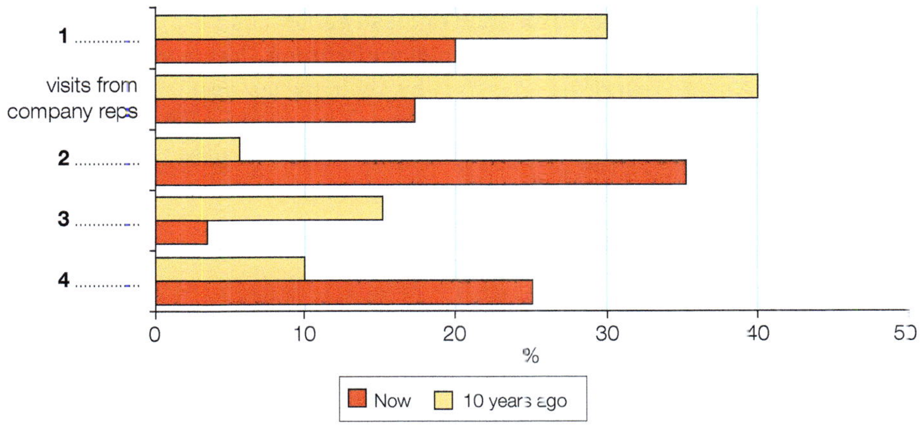

Vocabulary

19 1 **Listen again and say whether these verbs mean 'to increase' or 'to decrease'.**

1 decline 2 plummet 3 soar 4 rocket 5 recede 6 shrink

2 **Work with a partner. Brainstorm other words you can think of to express 'to increase' or 'to decrease'. When you have finished, compare your ideas with the rest of the class.**

Reading

1 **Mehtar Tilak wrote a brief report of the main points shown in the chart above. However, there is one wrong word in most lines. Correct the wrong word. If you think a line is correct, put a tick (✔) by the line.**

Breakdown of sales

In the last ten years, retail sales ~~had~~ fallen from 30% of total sales to just	1 *have*
20%, while at the same time, sales resulting of visits by company	2 ....
representatives have more that halved from 40% to 17%. Similarly, mail-	3 ....
order sales have dwindled from 15% ten years ago too just 3% this year.	4 ....
In the other hand, during the last few years, we have been concentrating	5 ....
more on e-sales. These have expanded spectacularly from 5% ten years ago	6 ....
to 35% now. Telephone sales had also taken off, increasing from 10% to 25% over the same period.	7 ....

2 **Find other verbs in the report that express 'to increase' or 'to decrease'.**

Grammar workshop

UNIT 11

Present perfect simple or continuous?

1 Study these two sentences from the corrected report and answer the questions below.

On the other hand, during the last few years, we have been concentrating more on e-sales. These have expanded spectacularly from 5% ten years ago to 35% now.

1 Which verb form (present perfect simple or present perfect continuous) do you use when you focus on the activity and length of time involved?
2 Which verb form do you use when you focus on the results or the quantity completed?

2 Choose the correct alternative for each of these sentences.

1 Dell, which was founded in 1984, *has been manufacturing / has manufactured* computers for more than 20 years.
2 Industrial output *has been rising / has risen* by 3% in the last year.
3 *She's worked / She's been working* in this department since she graduated, which is a really long time now.
4 Due to unfavourable exchange rates, several of our customers *have been going / have gone* bankrupt, and this is causing us real problems.

page 62 (Present perfect simple and continuous)

Writing

1 Work in pairs. Study the chart on the right and discuss what it shows.

2 Write a short report (120–140 words) covering all the information in the chart.

> **Task tip**
> - Use the short report on page 55 as a model.
> - Use some of the vocabulary and grammar you have just studied.

3 Exchange your report with another pair of students and discuss what things they did well and what they could improve. Then give them feedback.

Software Solutions: software sales by category

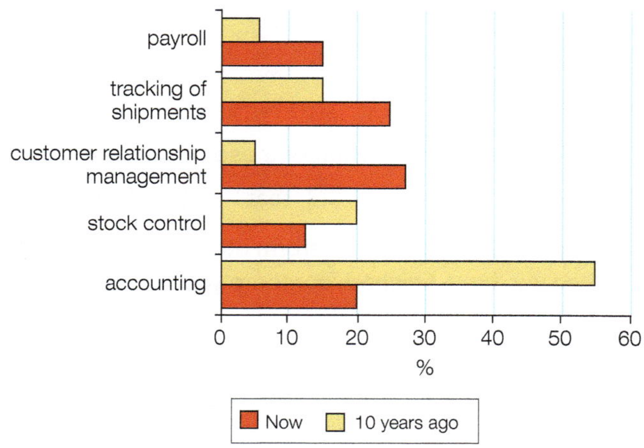

Report on a sales event

Reading

Recently, Software Solutions invited 145 of its clients to a sales event in Seville, Spain. Software Solutions' marketing director asked Mehtar Tilak to write a report on the Seville Sales Event.

1 Discuss these questions in pairs.

- What are the advantages of sales events for the company which holds them?
- How are they different from conferences or trade fairs?

2 Scan the report to find out a) if the event was successful or not, and b) what outcomes and reactions there have been to the event.

SOFTWARE SOLUTIONS

REPORT ON SEVILLE SALES EVENT

Introduction

The purpose of this report is to **1** ...B.... the success of the Seville Sales Event and to make recommendations for how future events of this nature are organised.

The Seville Event

One hundred and forty-five key clients from a range of European industries were invited to the España Hotel, Seville on 6th and 7th January at our company's **2** .... for a range of demonstrations of our new software packages. Also, talks were given by a number of expert guest speakers. During the event, the **3** .... were given the opportunity to network and share experiences with our software, and at the same time, we took the opportunity to obtain feedback on our products.

Sales

The event was highly successful. The initial investment of £550,000 **4** .... in immediate orders of £ .6m of software, and we have achieved a further £2.2m in sales in the **5** .... four weeks.

Feedback

Comments from clients have **6** .... a need for payroll and accounting software which allows companies to calculate their tax liabilities more easily over a number of EU countries. Several clients expressed a reluctance to invest in our CRM software, which was thought to be more **7** .... to the US market.

Conclusions and recommendations

Guests stated that they would be **8** .... for this event to be repeated in two years' time. It was also suggested that more informal presentations could be given by **9** .... clients speaking from their own knowledge and experience. Moreover, several clients requested that the next such event be held in a more central European venue, thereby **10** .... most clients' journey times.

3 Read the report again and for each gap, choose the best word, A, B, C or D.

1	**A** value	(**B**) evaluate	**C** appraise	**D** estimate
2	**A** expense	**B** cost	**C** outlay	**D** charge
3	**A** assistants	**B** attendants	**C** representatives	**D** delegates
4	**A** ended	**B** finalised	**C** resulted	**D** closed
5	**A** latest	**B** subsequent	**C** past	**D** coming
6	**A** revealed	**B** disclosed	**C** demonstrated	**D** uncovered
7	**A** matched	**B** adapted	**C** linked	**D** suited
8	**A** interested	**B** enthusiastic	**C** keen	**D** excited
9	**A** single	**B** individual	**C** sole	**D** only
10	**A** declining	**B** dropping	**C** reducing	**D** falling

Talking point

Discuss these questions in pairs.

1. What similarities can you see between this report and the proposal on page 37 in Unit 7?
2. How do you think a report is different from a proposal?
3. How would you describe the style of this report (formal/neutral/informal) and why did Mehtar choose this style?
4. This report is divided into sections with headings (*Introduction*, *The Seville Event*, etc.). Why are headings and sections useful? Can you think of other typical section headings for a report?

Writing

The company you work for has recently held a sales event to launch a new product. Your managing director has asked you to write a report on the effectiveness of the event, including the following points:

- who was invited to the event
- what guests' reactions were
- how successful the event was
- what recommendations you would make for future sales events of this kind.

1 Discuss these questions in small groups.

1. What would be a suitable new product to choose for this writing task?
2. What sorts of activities are held at new product launches? Brainstorm ideas.
3. What sections/section headings would be suitable for this report?
4. Who will read the report? What style would be suitable for this reader?

2 Work alone and write the report.

UNIT 12

The sales pitch

Getting started

Cold-calling is when you phone someone you have never spoken to before to sell them a product or service.

Discuss these questions in small groups.

1 How do you react when you receive a cold-call?
2 What are the problems of cold-calling for the salesperson?
3 When is it necessary to cold-call prospective customers?
4 What advice would you give to cold-callers?
5 Do you ever cold-call prospective customers?

Cold-calling

Listening

You will hear Rosa Levy, a salesperson from CSS Ltd, a security firm, cold-calling the human resources manager of Vogel Leblanc, a large property-management company.

1 Before you listen, discuss these questions with a partner.

1 What do property-management companies do?
2 Why might they need the services of a security firm?

20 **2 Listen to the conversation and complete Rosa's notes with up to three words in each gap.**

Vogel Leblanc
Contact: Richard Slade, HRM
Says employees are occasionally verbally or
1 ....
Incidents occur on phone, in office and when
2 ....
Present protection for lone workers through a
3 .... company
Normal procedure: call the worker and possibly
4 ....
Shortcomings of system:
• no cover when 5 .... is empty
• difficult to 6 .... worker in difficulties
Meeting: 4 p.m. Friday, at office 7 ....

3 Work in pairs. Say whether these statements are true or false.

1 Rosa states immediately what services she wants to sell.
2 She apologises for taking up Richard's time.
3 She spends time gathering information.
4 She asks for names of competitors.
5 She does not close a sale during the call.

20 **4 Check your answers by listening again and reading the transcript for track 20 at the back of the book.**

5 Match these phrases from the questions in the telephone conversation (1–5) with their function (a–e).

1 Do you mind … ?	a starting an opening question
2 First, can you … ?	b signalling that the questions are finishing
3 Would I be right in thinking …?	c checking an assumption
4 And one last question: tell me …?	d asking whether someone wants to do something
5 Would you be interested in … ?	e asking permission

Speaking

1 **Work in pairs. Try to recall the questions Rosa asked using the phrases in Exercise 5. When you have finished, check by looking at the transcript for track 20 again.**

2 **Take turns to ask each other questions using the phrases from Exercise 5 to find out about problems your partner has at work or when studying.**

Role-play 1

TopPlant Repairs Ltd is a company which specialises in repairing factory tools and machines. Technicians visit factories when required at any time of the day or night and either repair the equipment on site, or take it back to TopPlant Repairs' workshops and, when they have repaired it, they deliver and reinstall it.

1 **Work in pairs.**

Student A: You are the sales manager for CSS Ltd. Turn to page 118.

Student B: You are the operations manager for TopPlant Repairs Ltd. Turn to page 119.

Study your role cards carefully for a few minutes before you speak and decide what you are going to say. Use some of the phrases for questions you've just studied.

2 **Imagine you are going to cold-call someone in another company to sell one of your company's products or services (or a product/service of a company you know well).**

- Tell your partner which company and which person in the company you would cold-call.
- Ask your partner to role-play that person and then cold-call them.

Useful language

Dealing with cold-callers when you are busy

OK, I've only got a few minutes, so could you make it quick?

I'm sorry, it's not convenient at the moment. (Could you call my assistant / call back …?)

I'm afraid I'm rather busy at the moment. (Could you put all that in an email?)

Speaking to reluctant prospects

I'm sure you're very busy, so I'll be brief.

With your permission, I'd like to ask you a very few quick questions.

I won't take very much of your time.

If you've just got a minute, I'm sure you'll find what I have to say interesting.

Providing services to large companies

Speaking

1 **Work in groups of three. Read the problem in the speech bubble and answer the questions below.**

1 What service does this person want to provide for large companies?
2 What does he want suggestions for?
3 What advice would you give him?

2 **Compare your ideas for Question 3 with students from other groups.**

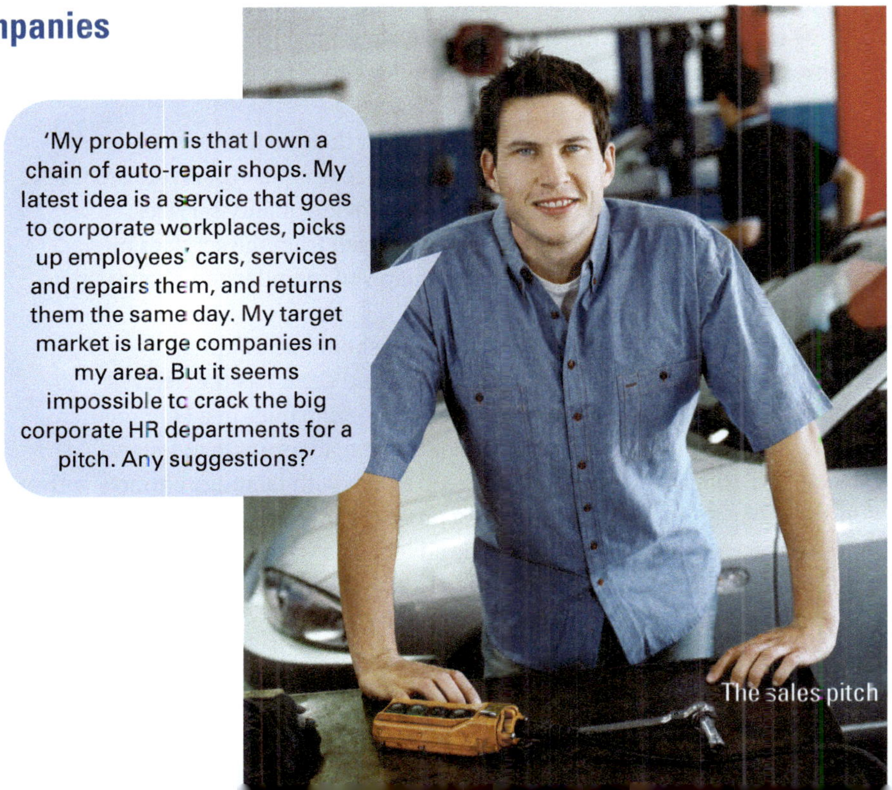

Reading

1 Scan the advice in this article and then discuss with your group whether it was similar or different to the advice you thought of.

Cracking the big company market

Networking is the best way to start, suggests Martin Babinec, founder and CEO of TriNet, a company that provides outsourced payroll, benefits, and HR services. "We've never had much success cold-calling a big company. Every one of our big-company opportunities has been brought to us by referrals," explains Babinec.

"One way we solicit referrals is by identifying the decision-makers in a big company and then determining if we know someone who knows them. We then educate the person that we know about the things we can offer that the big company couldn't find somewhere else.

"Make sure you can offer the company more than mere convenience to its employees. Large companies are often risk-averse, and unless they see a company benefit, they tend to focus on the things that could go wrong (for example, liability, upset employees complaining about poor screening of service providers, and so on).

"Find out which other local businesses provide employee services to the companies you're pursuing. What do those businesses offer that makes them unique? How is the large company benefiting? Can you track down the owners of those local businesses and gain insight into the relationship structure and the decision process that got them on board?

"One last note: In my experience, people at large, high-tech companies expect service providers to handle transactions over the Web. It's best to have that capability up and running before you contact your prospects."

Mary Naylor, founder and CEO of VIPdesk Inc., which provides concierge services to large corporations, questions whether you're aiming too high too soon. "Though it might seem efficient to sell to a large company because you believe there's more business in one location, you'll be trying to crack a bigger bureaucracy," she observes. "I recommend you first target mid-size companies, prove you have a track record with them, and then use that record to persuade a big company to work with you."

From *Inc Magazine*

2 Choose the best answer, A, B, C or D, to these questions.

1 According to Martin Babinec, how should you go about landing contracts with big companies?
   A by cold-calling the members of the board of directors
   B by using the Internet to contact their top managers
   C by telling someone outside the target company about your products and services
   D by explaining to the top managers why your products or services are unique

2 Why are large companies frequently unwilling to give contracts to external service providers?
   A They are reluctant to make life too easy for their staff.
   B They consider the problems which can arise from using service providers.
   C They believe that few service providers provide quality services.
   D They see no advantage for the company itself from the services offered.

3 How can certain local business owners help you to understand your target customers?
   A They can explain the type of service you should be offering.
   B They can explain how they managed to land contracts themselves.
   C They know what goods and services large companies need to procure.
   D They have a track record which makes them an example to follow.

4 According to Mary Naylor, what is the problem with landing contracts with large companies?
   A You may find the decision-making process slow and complicated.
   B Your company's efficiency may be adversely affected.
   C You may find big companies reluctant to work with a small company.
   D You may not have the capacity to provide the required services.

Vocabulary

Match these words and phrases from the text (1–8) with their definitions (a–h).

1 solicit	a when you are legally responsible for something
2 risk-averse	b operating
3 liability	c made them part of a group or team
4 screening	d have a strong dislike for taking risks
5 got them on board	e find a solution to a problem
6 up and running	f examining someone or something to discover if there is anything wrong with them
7 crack	g ask someone for money, information or help
8 track record	h all the achievements or failures that someone or something has had in the past

Making a sales pitch

Listening

You will hear Rosa from CSS Ltd giving her sales pitch at a meeting with Richard Slade of Vogel Leblanc.

21 **Listen and complete the notes Richard made during the meeting with up to three words in each gap.**

Service available every day for **1** .... hours
Security staff **2** .... for handling emergencies
To make an emergency signal, workers just **3** ....
When security company receives call, they:
- call the worker to **4** ....
- inform our office about **5** ....
- inform the police.

Equipment allows workers to be located to within **6** ....
Phone calls often mean that the attacker stops.
Security company:
- calls a **7** .... when office empty.
- monitors police every **8** .... mins.

Costs include:
- charge for **9** .... (sophisticated mobiles)
- payments: **10** .... (similar amount to burglar alarm connection)

Grammar workshop

Cleft sentences

1 In which sentence of each pair is the information in italics focused on more strongly?

1 a We *provide a more complete service.*
  b What we do is *provide a more complete service.*
2 a All he or she has to do is *press a button.*
  b He or she only has to *press a button.*
3 a It's *that sort of situation* that we want to avoid.
  b We want to avoid *that sort of situation.*
4 a We don't want people to be *calculating the cost of calling for help.*
  b The last thing we want is people to be *calculating the cost of calling for help.*

21 **2 Which one of each pair did you hear in Rosa and Richard's conversation? Listen again to check.**

3 Rewrite these sentences starting with the words given.

1 We deliver the pizzas to your home.
  What …
2 You only have to provide the venue.
  All …
3 We find the paperwork too time-consuming.
  It's the …
4 You shouldn't settle the invoice before you've received the goods.
  The last thing …

page 63 (Cleft sentences)

Role-play 2

Work in pairs. Before you do the role-play, work with another partner who has the same role as you and prepare what you are going to say. Then do the role-play.

Student A: You are the sales manager for CSS Ltd. Turn to page 118.

Student B: You are the operations manager for TopPlant Repairs Ltd. Turn to page 119.

Speaking

Work in groups of three. Take turns to give a sales pitch for a product/service your company offers (or a product/service you know well).

Grammar workshop 3

Position of adverbs

- Adverbs can be one word (e.g. *yesterday, unfortunately*) or several words (e.g. *in the past, on the telephone*). There are three main positions for adverbs:
  - front (i.e. at the beginning of the sentence): ***Last year,*** *sales exceeded €100m.*
  - middle (i.e. between the subject and the verb [but after the first auxiliary]): *Microsoft have* ***recently*** *launched a new operating system.* or after the verb *to be* if it is the main verb: *He is* ***undoubtedly*** *the best-qualified candidate.*
  - end (i.e. after the verb [and the object if the verb has an object]): *Our advertising budgets have been cut* ***drastically.***
- Adverbs which can go in the front are:
  - linking adverbs: *However, Consequently*
  - time and place adverbs: *By next year, In a recent article*
  - comment adverbs: *In my opinion, Probably*
- Adverbs which can go in the middle are:
  - frequency adverbs: *usually, never*
  - degree adverbs: *totally, slightly*
  - these adverbs: *already, finally, now, recently, soon, still*
- Adverbs which can go at the end are (in this order):
  1 manner: *impressively, carefully*
  2 place: *in the boardroom*
  3 time: *in the last three years*

Notes

1 These are not absolute rules: adverbs can be placed in other positions, but these are the most usual ones.

2 Adverbs can also modify adjectives: ***extremely*** *difficult*

Rewrite the sentences in the letter at the top of the next column by putting the adverbs in brackets in the most likely positions in the sentence.

Dear Mike,

1 The advertising campaign which we carried out has proved a great success. (*last month / in major European newspapers*)
The advertising campaign which we carried out in major European newspapers last month has proved a great success.

2 Brand awareness rose. (*by 5% / in the first three months / interestingly*)

3 This is due to our having targeted our audience. (*very carefully / in my opinion / before we started*)

4 We have managed to meet our sales targets for several lines. (*already / consequently*)

5 Sales of our most popular brands have risen. (*spectacularly / for example / since we began advertising*)

6 Our top-of-the-range brands have not performed. (*unfortunately / so impressively / however*)

7 Sales of these have stayed, or dropped. (*even / slightly / at the same level*)

8 I think we should meet to discuss this. (*as a result / soon*)

9 We need to find a solution, although it shouldn't prove difficult. (*especially / urgently*)

10 Could you call me? (*later today / on my mobile*)

Thanks

Hans

Present perfect simple and continuous

- Both the present perfect simple and continuous talk about something which started in the past and
  - either has a result in the present: *He****'s lost*** *his job* (i.e. he's out of work now). *We****'ve been working*** *hard at the office this week, so we're feeling pretty tired.*
  - or is still happening now: *Nestlé* ***has been running*** *a publicity campaign on healthy eating* (and they are still doing so).
- Often they are interchangeable. However:

The present perfect simple	The present perfect continuous
• emphasises the result: *We've discussed the problem and this is our solution.*	• emphasises the activity: *We've been discussing the problem all day – we're finding it extremely complicated to solve.*
• says how much we have done: *We've sold over 100,000 units.*	• says how long we've been doing something: *We've been selling these machines for 40 years now.*
• may give the idea that something is more permanent: *I've always worked in sales.*	• may give the idea that something is temporary: *I've been working in sales since they moved me from accounts.*
• is used when we want to say how many times something has been repeated: *I've spoken to Anne several times, but she's still arriving late for meetings.*	• is used when we want to emphasise the process of change over a period of time and that these changes are not finished: *Have you noticed how the company has been changing since the new IT system was introduced?*

Choose the best alternative in each of these sentences.

1 The board *has just decided* / ~~*has just been deciding*~~ – they're transferring head office to New York.
2 *I've tried* / *I've been trying* to decide where to put the new workstation, but I can't make up my mind.
3 Since he graduated, *he's worked* / *he's been working* in 15 different companies.
4 He's our most successful graduate: *he's made* / *he's been making* a million dollars and he's only 25!
5 *Have you always occupied* / *Have you always been occupying* this office?
6 You *haven't sent* / *haven't been sending* me that report. What *have you done* / *have you been doing* all this time?
7 *I've worked* / *I've been working* from home while the offices are being redecorated.
8 *I've phoned* / *I've been phoning* your office about 20 times this week, but you're never in.
9 It's very encouraging how the staff *have got* / *have been getting* to grips with the new system. I'm sure they'll all be proficient in a couple of months.

Cleft sentences

- Cleft sentences are a way of adding emphasis to what we want to say.
- These are some ways of forming cleft sentences:
  They advertised on television. → *What they did was advertise on television.*
  I'd love a job in sales. → *What I'd love is a job in sales.*
  I don't understand the theory. → *It's the theory that I don't understand.*
  I was persuaded to buy it by the discount. → *It was the discount that persuaded me to buy it.*
  It just needs time. → *All it needs is time.*
  She definitely doesn't need her workload increased. → *The last thing she needs is her workload increased.*

Change these sentences to cleft sentences, starting with the words given.

1 The CRM system had a positive effect on sales.
What had ...*a positive effect on sales was the CRM system.*...
2 They outsourced their production to Indonesia.
What they did …
3 They sold paper products.
What …
4 The problem is the time it takes.
It's …
5 Our biggest problem is Internet fraud.
It's …
6 He does nothing but complain.
All …
7 This shop only sells paint.
All …
8 I really don't want your advice.
The last thing …

UNIT 13

Forecasts and results

Getting started

Discuss these questions in small groups.

1 How can each of these help companies to make sales forecasts?
   1 computer projections
   2 predictions about interest rates
   3 reports from sales teams
   4 intuition
   5 the political situation
   6 the success of competitors' products
   7 past experience
   8 the marketing budget

2 Which factors, in addition to the sales forecast, will help the finance team produce a profit forecast?

Gloomy sales forecast mirrors the weather

Forecasting sales

Listening

You will hear five different people talk about how they contribute to their companies' sales forecasts and why the forecasts turned out to be inaccurate.

22 1 **Listen and look at the elements listed in *Getting started* above. Which of them does each person contribute to the sales forecast? Complete the first column of the table.**

	Contribution	Reason for inaccuracy
Olivia		
Jaime		
Gary		
Sylvie		
Nesreen		

22 2 **Look at the events in the 'Reason for inaccuracy' box. Listen again. Which reason does each person mention as to why the forecast was inaccurate? Complete the second column of the table.**

Reason for inaccuracy

a There was a shift in fashion.
b We were affected by a press report.
c There was an unexpected disaster.
d There was a lapse in quality control.
e Our advertising was poor.
f Our publicity was more effective than we expected.
g There was a change in government policy.
h We experienced a shortage of qualified staff.

Vocabulary 1

Match these phrasal verbs and expressions (1–7) from the listening exercise with their definitions (a–g). If necessary, look at the transcript for track 22.

1	catch on	a	approach (a task/problem)
2	up-and-coming	b	be successful/profitable
3	fall short of	c	become fashionable/popular
4	talk someone into	d	fail to reach a target
5	pay off	e	persuade someone
6	go about	f	refuse/reject
7	turn down	g	successful, likely to be successful

Talking point

Work in groups of three. Your company has sent you to a seminar on predicting business trends. The speaker at the seminar has asked you to work in small groups and discuss how businesses can improve their sales forecasts. Work together and decide:

- what things can make sales forecasts inaccurate
- what problems can arise from inaccurate sales forecasts
- what general advice you can give for companies to improve their predictions

You can include ideas you heard during the listening exercise if you wish.

UNIT 13

Reading

1 Work in small groups. Discuss whether you agree or disagree with the following statements (and give reasons why).

1 'Business people find it difficult to make pessimistic forecasts.'

2 'Making business forecasts should be a group activity, not the responsibility of a particular individual in the organisation.'

3 'Computers are better than people at forecasting sales.'

4 'The main problem with making forecasts is predicting what your competitors will do.'

2 Scan the article below to locate opinions about the four points you have just discussed. What is said about each of them?

FORECASTING DISASTER

Have you imagined some of the ways your company might go bust? Not likely. Most companies create forecasts that reflect rising sales, docile competitors, happy customers. "It's emotionally difficult for people to do negative scenarios," says Chris Ertel at Global Business Network (GBN). 1 .H.. When they don't achieve them, it damages morale as well as the stock price.

Creating rainy-day scenarios and knowing when to implement them is a rare but essential competency in unpredictable times. In the past six months, companies that never expected an earthquake have been wrecked by economic tremors. 2 ...... While even the best economists can't spot turning points in the country's economic direction, forecasting experts do have advice that can help produce clearer views in cloudy times and backup plans for dealing with unexpected twists.

3 ...... However, John Vanston, chairman of Technology Futures, says that it is useful to bring together people from various departments who think about the future in different ways. His company has identified five different approaches to thinking about the future. Extrapolators see the future as a logical extension of the past. Pattern Analysts look for similar situations from the past and try to apply those to the future. Goal Analysts identify powerful entities with the ability to influence the future. 4 ...... Counter Punchers seek a high degree of flexibility and responsiveness, and Intuitors gather as much information as they can and then depend on their subconscious mind for useful insights. "You want all five types of people involved in your forecasting because that produces much higher-quality results," Vanston says.

Most companies use forecasting software to visualize possible changes in demand, and most say the software is most accurate when trying to chart sales of existing products in stable markets. "We compare the machine forecasts to the human forecasts every month," says Jeremy Wise, a senior forecast analyst at Callaway Golf. "5 ...... If they're not, Wise wants to know why. But when in doubt, he says the human forecast, derived from a broad cross-section of employees in sales, production, and finance, wins.

Scenario-planning is different from traditional forecasting. 6 ...... The goal is a number of stories and scenarios, along with a sense of their relative likelihood, that can help a company be more flexible and resilient when it encounters challenging situations.

"The challenge of getting people to do negative scenarios," says Ertel of GBN, "is to find opportunity when you're at a disadvantage. 7 ...... Ertel prods them instead to look for ways they can take advantage of competitors' inactivity or retrenchments. The goal isn't to predict what's ahead precisely but to imagine both positive and negative outcomes, understand what might prompt them and consider how you might handle each one. "You're never going to make uncertainty go away," says Teplitz. "But you can certainly improve your warning systems and your ability to deal with it."

From *Darwin Magazine*

3 Choose the best sentence (A–H) for each gap in the text on page 65. There is one sentence you will not need.

A This has led to sweeping changes in the way businesses operate.
B It's designed to get groups to imagine dramatic discontinuities and tell stories about how they would react.
C Most companies have relatively narrow forecasting teams, if they have them at all.
D The numbers have got to be in sync with each other.
E They then try to understand their objectives.
F They've announced earnings shortfalls, layoffs, and reorganisations.
G When you get managers together, they look for the axe first.
H The result is that companies continue to operate on optimistic projections that they can't possibly meet.

Task tip

When you have finished the task, read the whole text again with the sentences you put in the gaps. Does it read logically? If not, think again!

Vocabulary 2

Find words or phrases in the text which mean the following.

1 go bankrupt
2 share price
3 lower-than-expected profits
4 redundancies
5 correspond with each other
6 typical sample
7 sudden changes in business trends
8 able to recover quickly
9 encourages
10 economies, reductions

Speaking

You have been asked to give a short presentation to students visiting your company from a local business school.

1 Work in pairs. Prepare a short presentation on one of these topics:

- Finance: How to prepare a sales forecast
- Finance: The importance of accurate sales forecasts for managing a company

2 Change partners and take turns to give your presentation to another student.

Useful language

It's particularly useful / absolutely essential / vital + infinitive
It's of prime importance to + infinitive
Accurate sales forecasts are essential/vital/crucial/critical/key because …

Task tip

- Structure your talk by introducing your points with *firstly*, *secondly*, *finally*.
- Conclude your talk by saying *In conclusion, …*
- Instead of repeating *important* several times, vary your vocabulary by using alternatives from the Useful language box.

Grammar workshop

Conditional sentences

1 Read paragraph 3 of the article *Forecasting disaster* again. Work in small groups and match each of these types of forecaster (1–5) with the statements made by each one (a–e).

1 Extrapolators

a 'According to my sources, Paltech, the American producer, are thinking of breaking into the European market, and I think they're chasing our business. Unfortunately, I don't have information about what their strategy will be, but <u>if they were to start a joint venture with Swanson's, it could seriously affect our market share.</u>'

2 Pattern analysts

b 'I think that there are a series of circumstances which could reduce our sales: new products from our rivals, a change in interest rates, the political situation overseas and a change of government at home. We have to have strategies in place to react to all these possibilities. I mean, as things turned out, <u>if we'd planned for a rise in property prices last year, we could have almost doubled our turnover.</u>'

3 Goal analysts — c 'If you look at sales for the last three years, you'll see they have risen by an average of 10%. If that trend continues, next year we'll be looking at sales in excess of three million euros.'

4 Counter punchers — d 'There are a whole range of factors to take into consideration and it's almost impossible to reach an accurate figure just by analysing them. I would guess, though, that the key factor will be the emerging markets in South America, which will have an extremely positive effect on our sales in the next five years. I mean, if in the last five years we'd been cautious about emerging markets in Asia, we'd have missed a major opportunity.'

5 Intuitors — e 'When we introduced the RD10 in 1995, it had sales of 50,000 units by the end of its first year. The RD20, which we launched in 2001, had sales of 55,000 after one year. I know circumstances are rather different now, but if we followed a similar strategy for the RD30, by my estimate we'd be selling in the region of 50–55,000 units by the end of next year.'

UNIT 13

2 Study the underlined conditional sentences in the statements above.

1 Which refer to past time and which refer to present/future time?
2 Which combination of tenses are used in conditional sentences which talk about the past?
3 Which combination of tenses are used in conditional sentences which talk about the present or future?

page 80 (Conditional sentences)

Talking point

Discuss these questions in small groups.

1 Which type of forecaster do you think you are / would be? Why?
2 Which type of forecaster would you pay most attention to if it was your responsibility to make the final sales forecast?

Reporting results

Vocabulary

1 Complete the accounts of Presto Bearings, a company which supplies machine parts, using the words/phrases in the box.

debtors · dividends · equipment · equity · liabilities · ~~loss~~ · pre-tax profits · profit and loss for the period · turnover

2 Find words in the accounts on the right which mean the following.

1 Buildings and land used by a company
2 Loss of value of an asset such as machinery over a number of years
3 Money borrowed from a bank
4 Part of a company's profit which is not distributed to shareholders as dividends
5 Things belonging to a company which have a value
6 Supply of components or raw materials kept by a company to be used in manufacturing their products
7 The value a company has in addition to the value of its assets, e.g. from its reputation

Profit and 1 *loss* account

	€m
2 .... (sales)	840
Cost of sales	(360)
Depreciation	(110)
Operating cost	(100)
Operating profit	270
Interest payable	(35)
3	235
Tax	58
Profit after tax /net profit	177
4	(100)
5	77
Retained earnings	89
Shareholders' 6	166

Balance sheet

	€m
Cash in bank	140
Stock	22
7	55
Total current assets	217
Premises	2,450
8	480
Total fixed assets	**2,930**
Goodwill	320
Total assets	**3,467**
Creditors	(27)
Overdraft	(420)
Total current 9	(447)
Total assets less liabilities	**3,020**

Talking point

Discuss the following questions in small groups.

1 What should companies take into account when deciding what dividend to pay shareholders?
2 What can companies do to reduce their tax liability?
3 Why is goodwill such an important asset?

Financing the arts

Getting started

Discuss these questions in small groups.

1 Which of these arts have to be subsidised in your country in order to survive?
• classical/traditional music • pop/rock music • theatre • cinema • painting • dance

2 Do you think artistic activities should be subsidised, or should they be subject to the laws of the market place? Why? / Why not?

The theatre business

Listening

The marketing director of Continental Bank, a large international bank with its head offices in London, has asked the marketing team to investigate the possibility of financing an arts activity, such as a theatre production.

You will hear Philip Franks, an actor and theatre director, talking about the theatre business in Britain.

1 Before you listen, match each item of theatre vocabulary (1–6) with its definition (a–f).

1 cast	a furniture and other scenery used in a play to make it seem realistic
2 choreographer	b objects used by actors during plays
3 set	c person who plans the movements dancers make
4 costume	d the actors in a film, play or show
5 props (properties)	e clothes worn by an actor
6 repertory house	f theatre where one company of actors performs a number of different plays

23 **2 Listen to Philip Franks and choose the best answer, A, B or C, to each of these questions.**

Task tip

Take some time before you listen to read each of the questions and underline the key words.

1 In what way is the theatre business different from other types of commercial activity?
   A It needn't be a product that people want.
   B It's not subject to the same criteria for success.
   C It needn't make a profit.
2 What is mentioned as a good way of guaranteeing commercial success?
   A having a well-known actor or actress in the cast
   B having a small cast
   C having a well-informed audience
3 How can you reduce the risks involved in putting on a new play?
   A by choosing the theatre carefully
   B by restricting the length and size of the production
   C by keeping actors' salaries low
4 What, according to Philip, are 'running props'?
   A the length of time the play runs
   B things which must be replaced with each performance
   C the costs of lighting and heating the theatre
5 What is the main danger of firing actors you've hired?
   A They may take you to court.
   B The cast may go on strike.
   C They may refuse to work with you in future.
6 How might 'angels' help finance a production?
   A by providing a theatre which belongs to them
   B by guaranteeing a loan from a merchant bank
   C by putting their own money into the production
7 Why is theatre production so risky?
   A The majority of productions are unsuccessful.
   B It takes a long time for a play to break even.
   C It is almost impossible to keep a production within budget.

Vocabulary

1 Match these words and phrases from the listening (1–8) with their definitions (a–h). If necessary, look at the transcript for track 23 at the back of the book.

1 break down	a cover costs, start to make a profit
2 running costs	b money you need to spend regularly to keep a system or organisation functioning
3 sue	c group of people who give financial support to something
4 put up (money)	d a wealthy person who invests money in new business projects
5 backers	e provide or lend an amount of money for a particular purpose
6 angel	f separate figures into different parts so that the details can be understood
7 flutter	g small bet
8 break even	h take legal action against a person or organisation

2 Complete these sentences with the words or phrases from Exercise 1.

1 How do the costs .... ? I want to see exactly how the money will be spent.
2 Electricity and actors' wages are .... and will form the main part of our expenditure.
3 If you're going to put on a commercial production, you will need some rich .... who you will need to ask to .... the money for the play.
4 The play will have to run for at least ten weeks in order to .... ; otherwise it will run at a loss.
5 They are liable to .... you if you don't honour the terms of the contract.

Sponsoring the arts

Talking point

Work in pairs or groups of three. As members of Continental Bank's marketing team, discuss these questions.

1 How can sponsorship promote a company's image?
2 What artistic activities are most suitable for this type of sponsorship?
3 Are there any risks for the sponsors of arts events?

Grammar workshop

UNIT 14

Infinitive and verb + *–ing*

One of your colleagues has found this proposal from a company she worked for previously.

1 Scan the proposal to find out the following things.

1 Why the company should sponsor the festival
2 What sponsorship would involve

2 Put the verbs in brackets into the correct form: infinitive or verb + *–ing*.

Proposal for Sponsorship of the Wimborne Theatre Festival

Fendara *International*

INTRODUCTION

Fendara International has been approached by the organisers of the Wimborne Theatre Festival with a view to our **1** *sponsoring* (*sponsor*) the festival next July. The purpose of this proposal is **2** .... (*examine*) the benefits and feasibility of **3** .... (*do*) so.

BENEFITS

The Wimborne Theatre Festival is a high-profile event dedicated to **4** .... (*promote*) the work of promising young writers and actors. It attracts a wide range of audiences from all over the region, while the national media tend **5** .... (*give*) it wide and favourable coverage. By **6** .... (*back*) the festival, we will improve our image as a company which participates in the local community and gives opportunities to talented and creative young people.

COSTS

7 .... (*sponsor*) the festival would be relatively economical. The festival organisers have budgeted for costs of approximately £30,000. These costs include **8** .... (*hire*) the theatre, actors' wages, publicity and miscellaneous running costs. A breakdown of their projected income reveals that they expect **9** .... (*receive*) approximately £15,000 from ticket sales and £5,000 from advertising. **10** .... (*cover*) the deficit, they would therefore require us to invest a total of £10,000.

SPONSORSHIP PUBLICITY

In return for our investment, Wimborne Theatre Festival would undertake **11** .... (*include*) our name and logo on all their publicity material and theatre programmes. Our logo would also appear at locations **12** .... (*be agreed*) in the theatre itself.

CONCLUSION

I recommend that we should agree **13** .... (*fund*) this festival because it represents a relatively low-cost opportunity **14** .... (*enhance*) our image both locally and nationally. What is more, it is possible **15** .... (*offset*) our sponsorship against tax, and it therefore represents a relatively economical marketing activity.

3 Check your answers in the key at the back of the book. Then work with a partner and find the following.

1 four examples of a verb + *–ing* following a preposition
2 one example of a verb + *–ing* as the subject of the sentence
3 one example of a verb + *–ing* following another verb
4 four examples of a verb + infinitive
5 two examples of the infinitive used to express purpose
6 one example of a noun + infinitive
7 one example of the infinitive used to express something which will happen in the future

page 80 (Infinitive and verb + *–ing*)

Listening

You will hear an interview with Paul Keene, an expert on arts sponsorship, who talks about corporate sponsorship of arts events.

24 **Listen and choose the best answer, A, B or C, for these questions.**

1 What, according to Paul, is the main advantage of arts sponsorship for large companies?
- A They have parts of buildings named after them.
- B They improve their reputation.
- C They reach a wider audience.

2 Why, according to Paul, do companies sponsor operas?
- A Members of the board enjoy them.
- B It is good for brand image.
- C They hope it will boost their share values.

3 What recent development has encouraged greater corporate sponsorship in Europe?
- A lower government funding for the arts
- B changes in tax rules
- C more aggressive fund-raising

4 Companies nowadays are more interested in sponsoring
- A art exhibitions.
- B classical music concerts.
- C theatre.

5 The main reason large arts organisations tend to attract more sponsorship is because
- A they are situated in the capital city.
- B they are more widely known.
- C they employ more people to obtain finance for their activities.

6 What, according to Paul, is the main advantage of arts sponsorship for smaller businesses?
- A It improves their image in their local communities.
- B It ensures better treatment by local authorities.
- C It promotes staff loyalty.

7 According to Paul, an organisation needing sponsorship should approach businesses with
- A a brief statement of their aims and financial requirements.
- B a folder containing high-quality publicity material.
- C a personal letter from their chief executive.

8 Paul says organisations should sponsor events which
- A fit their corporate image.
- B attract large numbers of people.
- C attract good press reviews.

Role-play

You are going to hold a meeting to discuss sponsoring a series of modern-art exhibitions.

1 **Work in pairs or groups of three. Each pair/group should choose Role A or Role B.**

Role A: You are the Marketing Team at Continental Bank. Turn to page 118.

Role B: You are the Exhibition Organisers at the Tate Modern gallery. Turn to page 119.

Study your role carefully and work together for about ten minutes to prepare for the meeting.

2 **When you are ready, hold a meeting with students who have chosen the other role. One of the students who chose Role A should act as chair.**

Tate Modern

Writing

1 **Work in pairs. Read the following writing task and discuss what information and ideas you could use.**

> Your CEO is interested in using sponsorship as a way of promoting your company and its products. He has asked you to make a recommendation about how this can be done. He would be interested in sponsoring either an arts or a sports event.
>
> Write a proposal for the CEO including the following information:
>
> - the type of activities which might be suitable
> - the benefits of this type of sponsorship for your company
> - the costs involved
> - your recommendation.

2 **Write your proposal. Use the proposals on pages 37 and 70 as models.**

UNIT 15

Late payers

Getting started

Discuss these questions in small groups.

1 Why do you think some companies are habitual late payers?
2 What are the effects on a business of customers who are late paying their invoices?
3 If a business pays its suppliers late, how does this affect the business relationship?
4 How can suppliers deal with late payers?

"There's an error in my bill. You accidentally sent it to someone who has no money."

Late payers and small businesses

Vocabulary

Match these words and phrases (1–11) with their definitions (a–k).

1 bank charges	a calculation of someone's ability to pay back money which they have borrowed
2 bookkeeping	b amount of money that a bank customer with an account is temporarily allowed to owe the bank
3 cash	c amount which is less than the level that was expected or needed
4 credit limit	d amounts of money that regularly have to be spent
5 credit worthiness	e money which is immediately available
6 debtor	f operating a business while not having enough money to pay creditors and employees
7 factoring	g someone who owes money
8 outgoings	h sums of money paid by a customer for a bank's services
9 overdraft	i system of buying debts for less than they are worth and then obtaining payment for them from the debtors
10 overtrading	j the job of keeping a record of the money that has been spent or received by a business
11 shortfall	k the maximum amount of money a bank will allow you to borrow

Reading

1 **Work in pairs. Each pair should read Text A, Text B or Text C. Work together and make sure you understand the main points of your text.**

2 **Form groups of three with students who have read the other texts. Explain the main points of your text to your partners.**

3 **When you have finished, check together what the texts say in answer to the questions in *Getting started*.**

4 **Find words or phrases in the three texts with these meanings.**

1 things which limit your freedom of action (text A)
2 without official permission (text A)
3 charges which are used to punish someone (text A)
4 to a level which is more than is necessary or reasonable (text A)
5 in advance (text A)
6 late (text B)
7 organised (text B)
8 reasons for something bad (text C)

UNIT 15

Text A

The impact of late payments on small businesses

1 Late payment continually features in the list of top constraints on business, and the problem is on the increase. If you are on the receiving end of late payment, it cannot only have a significant impact on your cashflow, leading to unauthorised overdrafts and punitive bank charges, but it can also eat into your precious time and cause undue stress.

2 But what if you regularly make a habit of paying late? What are the impacts on your business? Research shows that more than one in ten (13%) of all businesses that have experienced late payment would never do business with that customer again. Furthermore, 17% would only do repeat business if they were to receive cash upfront and a further 2% would have less trust in the late payer in the future. A staggering 52% do nothing – not out of choice but because the clients' business is too big and important for them. The message is clear – if you are paying your suppliers late, you stand a very good chance of losing their supplies.

Text B

What can you do if you are suffering from late payment?

1 Make sure that you have a process for checking the credit worthiness of new and existing customers. A simple and cheap solution is to use a credit-checking service which, for a small fee, will enable you to assess the financial standing of your customers.

2 Set credit limits for your customers.

3 Have effective processes in place for sending out invoices and monitoring payment from your debtors. In fact, around a third of small businesses only look at their overdue debtors every month. A simple and cost-effective way to put your finances in order is to automate your bookkeeping.

4 Work out what would happen to your cashflow and overdraft if your customers were to pay you late – could your business afford it? Keep your bank informed, as they may be able to help, either by providing an overdraft or suggesting an alternative way of financing your debtor, such as factoring.

5 Have sound procedures in place to recover overdue debts. When you contact your customers, record what has been agreed – when they will pay and whether you are going to charge interest. If they fail to pay, consider using a debt-collection service.

Text C

What should you do if you are a late payer?

1 Paying late generally arises from either lack of cash or poorly managed finances. If you are having difficulties with financial management, talk to your accountant.

2 If you do not have the money, then you need to look at the root causes as to why you do not have the cash. These might be:

- suffering from late payment yourself
- falling order book. You need to look at how you can reduce your outgoings.
- suffering from overtrading. If your business is experiencing rapid growth, then you may not be able to generate cash quickly enough to pay your bills. Talk to your bank, as they may be able to provide overdraft financing.

3 Talk to your suppliers. If you cannot pay, give your suppliers a realistic time when you will be able to pay.

4 Ensure you have budgets and forecasts in place, as these will show you in advance when you may run out of cash. Contact your bank early to seek funding to cover your cash shortfall.

All texts from http://www.clearlybusiness.com

Letter to a late payer

15 UNIT

Talking point

Discuss these questions in small groups.

1 How should you deal with late payers?
- by telephone
- by email
- by letter
- through a lawyer

2 When should you do so?
- immediately a payment becomes overdue
- after a few days
- after a month or two

Listening 1

You will hear Astrid Kloof, a credit controller, talking to her opposite number in another company.

2 **1 Listen to the conversation and complete her notes below with up to three words in each gap.**

Rajiv Narayan
- Reason for non-payment: 1 .... haven't paid – has 2 .... as a result.
- Informed him we have asked for an extension of 3 ....
- His company has reached its 4 ....
- Is sending written commitment by 5 .... today.
- Will pay within 6 ....

2 Discuss these questions in small groups.

1 How effective do you think a phone call like this is?
2 If Rajiv doesn't pay, what should be the next step?

Grammar workshop

Complex sentences

1 Complete the letter on the right using the words or phrases from the box below.

~~according to~~	and that	as
as a consequence	but also	however
not only	since	which	with whom

2 Join the sentences below using the words given in brackets.

1 The bank has agreed to extend our overdraft for another month. They normally handle our transactions. (*which*)
2 I regret to inform you that we keep a list of late payers. We share this information with other suppliers. (*not only / but also*)
3 We may have to put this matter in the hands of our lawyer. We would regret having to do this. (*which*)
4 We shall not be supplying you with any further goods. I informed you about this in my previous letter. (*as*)
5 We should set a credit limit of £5,000. My accountant tells me this. (*according to*)

page 81 (Complex sentences)

Dear Mr Narayan,

I am writing to remind you that payment on our invoice no. 472/f for the amount of £3,760 is still outstanding.

1 *According to* my notes on our telephone conversation three weeks ago, you explained to me that your company was itself suffering from cashflow problems and awaiting payments from some of your suppliers. 2 .... , you assured me that you expected payment shortly, 3 .... would mean that you would be in a position to settle your account with Prudhomme Ltd by the end of the month at the latest.

Unfortunately, that deadline has now passed, and your failure to pay is beginning to cause our company serious problems. 4 .... I indicated during our telephone conversation, the costs to us of your non-payment have included taking out an overdraft, with the resulting bank charges and interest. 5 .... , I have no choice but to inform you that 6 .... do we expect prompt payment of the invoice, 7 .... you will have to pay interest of 3% per month on all unpaid debts with our company until the invoice is paid.

I deeply regret having to write to you in this way, 8 .... , until now, you have always been a valued customer 9 .... we enjoyed a mutually profitable working relationship. I sincerely hope that this temporary unpleasantness can be resolved 10 .... we can return to normal business dealings shortly. Until such time, I regret to inform you that we are unable to supply you with any further goods.

Yours sincerely,

Astrid Kloof

Astrid Kloof
CREDIT CONTROLLER

Vocabulary

The underlined words and phrases in the letter are formal expressions. Match them with the following, more informal meanings.

1 able ... *in a position*
2 am very sorry ....
3 awkward problem ....
4 good for both of us ....
5 more ....
6 pay what you owe to ....
7 promised ....
8 quick ....
9 said ....
10 soon ....
11 unpaid ....
12 waiting for ....

Listening 2

You will hear William Brook-Hart talking about late payers at Gifford Engineering Consultancy.

3 **Listen and complete these notes by writing up to three words in each gap.**

- Concentration on late payers in order to reduce problems with **1** ....
- Customers contacted and told to **2** ....
- Other methods used when they have **3** .... for late settlement of debts
- The people who remind late payers are members of the **4** ....
- Some companies have **5** .... for withholding payment, e.g. because not **6** .... job Gifford has done.

Speaking

Your manager has asked you to give a short talk (of about one minute) to the finance department of your company on one of these two subjects:

1 How to deal with late payers
2 How to avoid taking on clients who are late payers

1 **Work with a partner. Choose one of the subjects and together prepare what you are going to say.**

2 **Change partners and give your talk to someone who has prepared the other subject.**

Writing

Work in pairs.

1 **Study Astrid's letter on the opposite page again. In which paragraph does she:**

1 state the reason for writing?
2 refer to a previous phone call?
3 outline Rajiv's excuses and promises?
4 explain how Rajiv has broken his promises?
5 explain the consequences for Prudhomme Ltd?
6 explain the consequences for Rajiv's company?
7 express the wish to continue working with Rajiv's company?

2 **Study the following writing task. Discuss which of the points in Exercise 1 you could make in this letter and what details you will have to invent.**

> You work for a company which produces ready-prepared food for restaurants. On several occasions recently, one of your main customers has been late in settling their account. This has caused your company cashflow and other problems. Write a letter to the customer:
>
> - complaining about the late payment
> - explaining the consequences for your business
> - saying what you will do if payment is not made.

3 **Make a brief plan for the letter in note form.**

4 **Work alone and write the letter.**

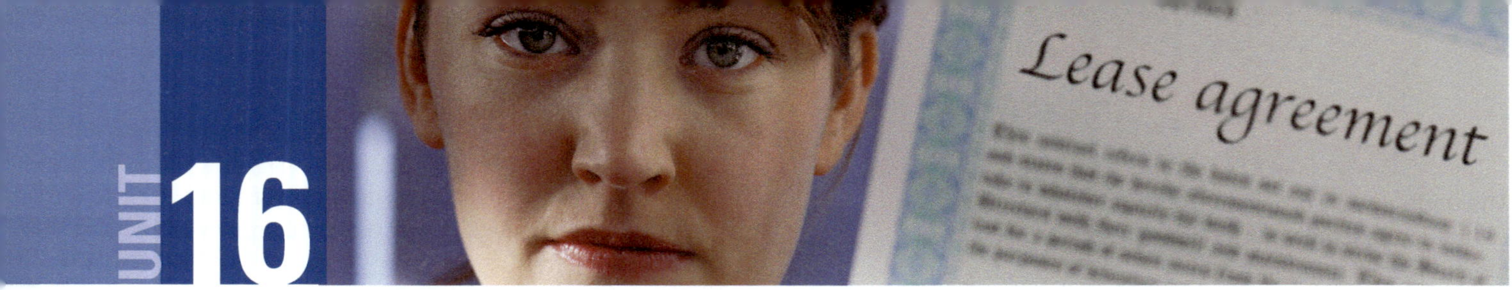

UNIT 16

Negotiating a lease

Getting started

1 Work in pairs. Discuss one of these questions. Take notes.

What would it be useful to know and how can you prepare before negotiating:

- your salary at a job interview?
- a lease on office space for your company?
- a sales target for your team with the sales manager?
- a production target for your factory with the CEO?
- a sales agreement with a customer?

2 Work in groups of three with people who chose other questions. Give one another a brief presentation of what you discussed and decided.

Hard bargaining

Listening

You will hear five people on a training course talking about their experiences of negotiating business agreements.

4 **Listen and complete the table to show:**

- which type of negotiation each of them mentions
- what problem arose during the negotiation.

Choose your answers from the boxes below.

	Type of negotiation	Problem
Vasili		
Melinda		
Glenn		
Carla		
Naomi		

Type of negotiation

A terms of a joint venture
B a distribution agreement
C a discount on a purchase
D a service agreement
E terms of payment for a purchase
F method and frequency of deliveries
G a leasing agreement
H penalty clauses in a contract

Problem

I They were unwilling to commit to a delivery date.
J They had to consult with head office.
K They were in too much of a hurry.
L They were too inflexible.
M They were not ready to sign an agreement.
N They did not state their terms clearly.
O They did not understand our situation.
P They set their demands too high.

Vocabulary

Match these words and phrases from the listening (1–8) with their definitions (a–h). If necessary, check with the transcript for track 4 at the back of the book.

1	compromise	a	an agreement in a negotiation in which the people involved reduce their demands or change their position in order to agree
2	the bottom line	b	a point in a discussion on which it is not possible to reach an agreement
3	sticking point	c	a situation in which agreement in a negotiation cannot be reached because neither side will change its demands or accept any of the demands of the other side
4	deadlock	d	negotiation which requires bargaining and each side reducing their demands
5	bargaining point	e	power to influence people and get the results you want
6	horse-trading	f	something which controls what you do by keeping you within particular limits
7	constraints	g	something which someone else wants that you are willing to lose in order to reach an agreement
8	leverage	h	the lowest amount acceptable in a negotiation

Talking point

Discuss these questions in groups of three.

1 What sort of things do you have to negotiate / have you had to negotiate? (If you don't work, these could be, for example, the rent of a flat, something at the place where you study, or an arrangement with your family.)
2 What problems tend to arise during these negotiations? Give examples.
3 What advice would you give to people who are new to negotiating?

Leasing office space

Reading

1 Discuss this question in pairs.

What issues should a company consider before negotiating to lease office space (e.g. length of lease)?

2 Read the following legal advice about leasing office space. How does the advice compare with the issues you suggested in Exercise 1?

Negotiating your office lease

Your lease of office space will have a large 1 ..impact.. on the future of your business. While you will need something that 2 .... your current needs, keep the future of your business in 3 .... as well. Take 4 .... of your present requirements and your plans for the future.

Think about the 5 .... of your lease. Do you want to 6 .... in stability of location and possibly price by negotiating a long-term lease? Or do you need the flexibility to move to a bigger, better location? How much of a(n) 7 .... to your business would a future change in location cause? Thinking about your business plans for the future, is there any time that would be better or worse for your lease to 8 .... up for renegotiation?

Make sure you know exactly what you are leasing. You will want to measure the office space for yourself to make sure you have envisioned it accurately. What kind of parking is there and how much of it is included? Who will be responsible for the costs of repairs or renovations? What, if any, are the 9 .... on your use of the property?

When it 10 .... to renewals, you want to avoid any terms that give the landlord 11 .... ability to increase your rent. If your business becomes very successful and would suffer from a change of location, the landlord will have a lot of 12 .... to raise your rent at renewal time. Instead, try to negotiate a formula for increases upfront. This will give you added stability and predictability.

From http://www.alllaw.com

3 Complete the advice above using the words in the box.

come	comes	~~impact~~	interruption	leverage	lock
meets	mind	restrictions	stock	term	unlimited

Listening

You will hear part of a conversation in which the company secretary and the regional director of an insurance company are discussing a prospective landlord's conditions for leasing office space in Warsaw.

5 **Listen and complete the regional director's notes with up to three words in each gap.**

Landlord's conditions:

- six months' rent as **1** ....
- no change of **2** .... without landlord's written permission
- annual revision of rent in line with **3** ....
- leaseholder must pay cost of **4** ....
- terms of lease **5** .... after five years
- option to lease **6** .... beneath building

Grammar workshop

Conditional sentences: alternatives to *if*

5 **1 Listen to the conversation again and complete these extracts with one word for each gap.**

1. '.......... we offered them two months and settled for three, do you think they'd accept that?'
2. '...we'll have to keep to the same commercial activity .... we obtain the owner's approval in writing.'
3. 'I mean, we're an insurance company, and .... we continue to be an insurance company, we won't have anything to worry about.'
4. 'We'll need a thorough survey, and we can only agree to this .... we're given a fairly long lease.'
5. 'In fact, I'd only take the lease .... we had a ten-year agreement.'

2 Complete these sentences in any way you like.

1. Supposing that our competitors lowered their prices. ....
2. Imagine .... How would you react?
3. We'll give you a five-year guarantee on condition that ....
4. .... as long as you sign a four-year contract.
5. We'll pay you a 10% bonus on condition that ....

page 99 (Variations on conditionals)

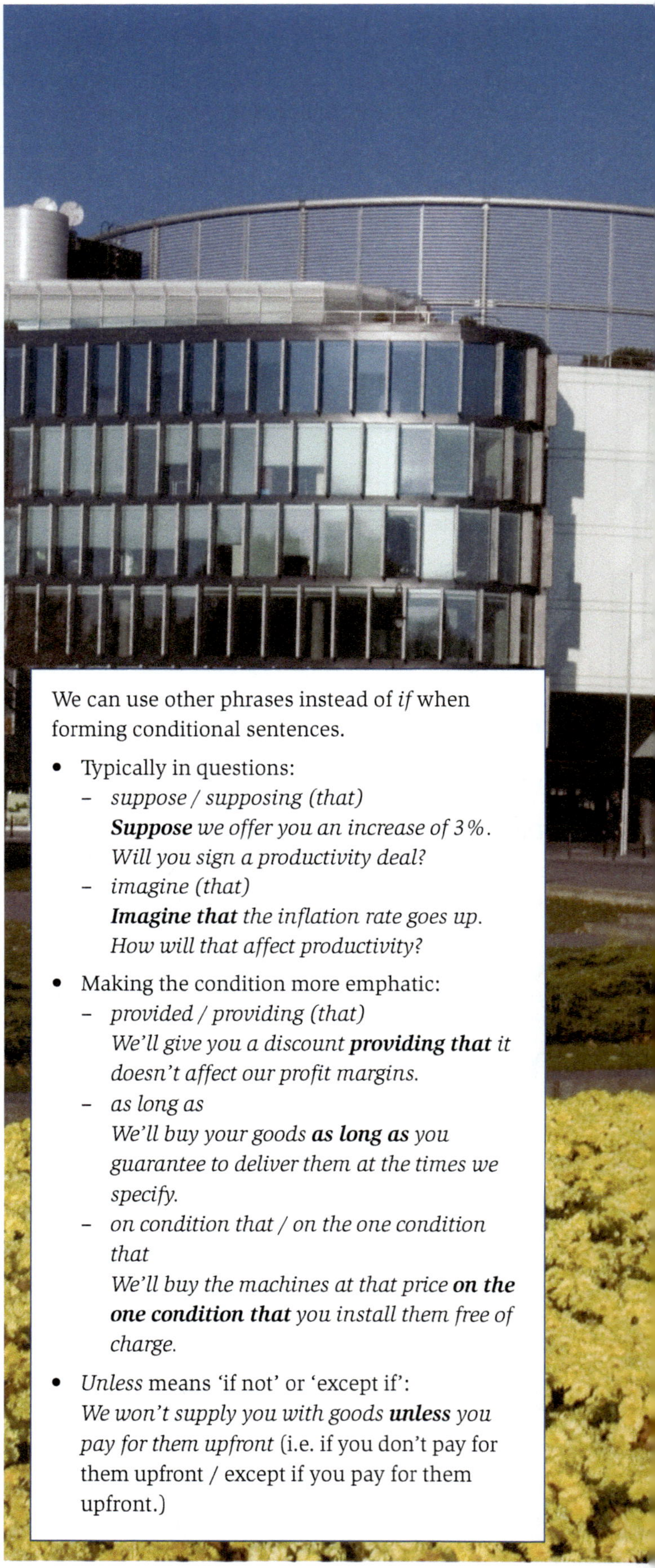

We can use other phrases instead of *if* when forming conditional sentences.

- Typically in questions:
  - *suppose / supposing (that)*
    Suppose *we offer you an increase of 3%. Will you sign a productivity deal?*
  - *imagine (that)*
    Imagine that *the inflation rate goes up. How will that affect productivity?*
- Making the condition more emphatic:
  - *provided / providing (that)*
    We'll give you a discount ***providing that*** *it doesn't affect our profit margins.*
  - *as long as*
    We'll buy your goods ***as long as*** *you guarantee to deliver them at the times we specify.*
  - *on condition that / on the one condition that*
    We'll buy the machines at that price ***on the one condition that*** *you install them free of charge.*
- *Unless* means 'if not' or 'except if':
  We won't supply you with goods ***unless*** *you pay for them upfront* (i.e. if you don't pay for them upfront / except if you pay for them upfront.)

Role-play

1 Work in pairs. Here are some typical stages in a negotiation (1–7). Which phrases might you use in each part of the negotiation? Choose from the list on the right (a–o).

1 meeting and small talk
2 agreeing an agenda
3 stating and finding out positions
4 bargaining
5 clarifying positions
6 reaching agreement
7 summarising agreement

a I think that's too high. That wouldn't give us enough profit. How about …?
b I'd be happy with that. What about you?
c I've drawn up a rough agenda for discussions. Is there anything you'd like to add?
d Let's see if I've got this straight. You want us to pay £500 upfront and the rest in a month's time.
e Now, let's see what we've got to discuss. I jotted down a few things here. What about you?
f Good to see you again. Did you have a good trip?
g OK. So let's just go over the points of our agreement again.
h Perhaps we'd better get down to business. Would you like to state your requirements first?
i So, let's see. What have we agreed?
j So, the first thing we have on our list is the price. We want £60 per unit. How do you feel about this?
k So, what you're saying is an increase in rent for this year, but nothing next year. Am I right?
l How was your summer?
m Suppose we paid the price you're asking. Would you be prepared to give us a discount if we place an order of more than 1,000 units?
n We'll give you that increase, as long as it's part of a two-year agreement.
o Well, it's not ideal, but I think we could do it.

2 Add one more phrase or sentence of your own to each stage.

3 You need to negotiate an agreement for leasing office space in the centre of Warsaw. You should work in negotiating teams of two or three and take the roles of either landlords or leasers.

Landlords: Turn to page 119.
Leasers: Turn to page 120.

Read your role card and spend some time preparing.

4 When you are ready, work with another team and negotiate the leasing agreement. Go through the seven stages outlined in Exercise 1.

Writing

1 Write an email to your colleagues (business partners or fellow managers) summarising what you agreed in your negotiations. You can start your email:

Dear colleagues,
I am writing to inform you about the results of …

2 Compare your email with other teams' emails. Decide who got the best deal.

Grammar workshop 4

Conditional sentences

- **first conditional:** *If* + present tense, future tense / modal verb (*can, might, should, must*, etc.)
  *If the Central Bank **raises** interest rates, that **will affect** the exchange rate.*
  The first conditional is used to talk about real, possible or likely events, in present or future time.
- *Unless* means 'if not'
  *Our sales **may** fall **unless** we develop some new products. (= … if we don't develop some new products.)*
- **second conditional:** *If* + past simple/continuous, *would/could/might* + infinitive
  *If we **had** a fire in one of our factories, we **would** almost certainly **have** difficulty meeting our orders, and this could adversely affect our market share.*
  The second conditional is used to talk about imaginary, hypothetical or less likely events, in present or future time.
- **third conditional:** *If* + past perfect simple/ continuous, *would/could/might have* + past participle
  *If we **had paid** attention to our computer forecasts, we **would not have had** such a large production shortfall this year.*
  The third conditional is used to talk about things which did not happen in the past.

Complete these sentences using the correct form of the words in brackets.

1 If, as seems likely, our competitors ..launch.. (*launch*) an updated version, we .... (*almost certainly lose*) market share.

2 It's never happened before, so I don't think this is very probable, but if the prices of our raw materials .... (*go*) down, we .... (*be*) able to reduce prices for our customers.

3 If we .... (*not run*) such a disastrous advertising campaign last year, we .... (*might/meet*) our sales targets – but we didn't.

4 You know, it doesn't necessarily follow that if our turnover .... (*increase*), our profits .... (*rise*) as well.

5 If we .... (*be*) more successful breaking into the Far Eastern market, we .... (*could/make*) record profits last year.

6 It's almost impossible to recruit trained staff, but if we .... (*can*) recruit them, the company .... (*be*) far more efficient than it is.

Infinitive and verb + *–ing*

- Infinitives are used:
  - to express purpose:
    *The purpose of this proposal is **to examine** the feasibility of sponsoring an arts festival.*
    *They sold the land **to finance** the building of a new factory.*
  - after adjectives:
    *The New Theatre have indicated that they would be **delighted to accept** our sponsorship.*
  - after *too* and *enough*:
    *It's **too** far in the future **to decide** yet.*
    *The offer is not high **enough** for us **to accept**.*
  - in a formal way, after the verb *to be*, to say something will happen in the future:
    *Volkswagen **are to open** a new factory in Romania next month.*
  - after certain verbs, including *afford, agree, aim, appear, arrange, ask, attempt, choose, dare, decide, demand, deserve, expect, fail, happen, help, hesitate, hope, intend, learn, manage, mean, neglect, offer, plan, prepare, pretend, promise, prove, refuse, seem, tend, threaten, volunteer, wait, want, wish*:
    *Don't **hesitate to contact** me if you require assistance.*
- The verb + *–ing* form is used:
  - after prepositions:
    *They are looking **into expanding** their operations in the Middle East.*
  - as a subject or object of a sentence:
    ***Financing** the arts is an expensive form of publicity.*
    *They fixed **breaking** into the Japanese market as their main objective.*

- after certain verbs, including *admit, appreciate, avoid, celebrate, consider, contemplate, delay, deny, dislike, enjoy, face, fancy, finish, imagine, involve, keep, mention, mind, miss, postpone, practise, report, resent, resist, risk, suggest*:
  They ***postponed launching*** *their special offer until after the holiday season.*
- after *while, after, before* and *when*:
  After completing *his MBA, he got a job in a bank.*
  When implementing *a new project, it's important to keep to budget.*

Complete these sentences using the correct form of the verbs in brackets (infinitive or verb + *-ing* form).

1 ..*Going*.. (*go*) into business involves .... (*take*) a certain amount of risk.
2 That production method is not cost-effective enough .... (*continue*) with; we risk .... (*go*) bankrupt unless we modify it.
3 He was quick .... (*spot*) the mistake in the accounts, and without even .... (*run*) them through the computer.
4 .... (*discourage*) their workers from .... (*go*) on strike, Fendara has been threatening .... (*close*) its Italian operation.
5 Do you happen .... (*know*) if Mr Woodward is considering .... (*visit*) Zurich during his European trip?
6 Could you arrange .... (*hold*) the meeting after .... (*complete*) the proposal?

Complex sentences

There are many ways of writing complex sentences. You can:

- include a relative clause (see Grammar workshop 1 on page 26)
- include a subordinate clause, e.g.:
  - a conditional (see page 80)
  - a concessive clause
    Although the shareholders were against it*, they decided to reinvest most of the profits.*
  - a time clause
    We'll order the goods ***as soon as we receive your cheque****.*
  - a clause giving a reason / expressing a consequence
    He failed to gain promotion ***as he lacked the financial acumen****.*
    We didn't meet our sales targets, ***so we were forced to lay off a number of staff****.*
- add a prepositional phrase
  Under the new tax regulations*, we have to declare all income paid within the European Union.*
- use an infinitive phrase
  We'd be happy ***to supply you with the goods you require****.*
  He flew to Dubai ***to see whether he could land a lucrative construction contract****.*
- use a participle phrase
  They returned all the goods ***damaged in transit****.*
  He met her ***working in the accounts department****.*

Write one complex sentence containing all the information in the following groups of sentences. Make any changes to vocabulary you think are necessary.

1 We experienced a shortfall in earnings last year. We lost one of our most important customers. This customer started buying from our principal competitor.
We experienced a shortfall in earnings last year as a result of losing one of our most important customers, who started buying from our principal competitor.
2 I'm writing to thank you. You dispatched goods to us last week. They arrived at our warehouse in record time. This means that our production is now ahead of schedule.
3 Martin Peters has decided to leave the company. His appraisal was not very satisfactory. You may remember this. Therefore, we will have to start recruiting a replacement. We must do this as soon as we can.
4 I was travelling home last night. I came up with a brilliant solution to our staffing problems. I'm going to put this in an informal proposal. The proposal will be circulated among senior managers.
5 Tasker Ltd will never manage to reach a productivity agreement. To reach a productivity agreement they will have to offer their employees more attractive financial incentives. The productivity agreement would put them ahead of the competition.
6 There's a shortage of skilled workers. The shortage is in the chemical industry. It's because there are insufficient numbers of young people. They don't study science subjects at school.
7 Redland Electronics have announced record profits. This is the fourth year running. It is because of their partnership with Kawasaki Electronics. This is a firm from Japan.

UNIT 17

Workplace atmosphere

Getting started

Work in small groups. Say whether you agree or disagree with these statements.

1 'Paying people at the same level in the company at different rates of pay introduces competitiveness and raises productivity.'
2 'Job insecurity encourages people to work harder.'
3 'People want to feel their job is important.'
4 'Few people are capable of managing themselves. They need firm management from above.'
5 'People need continuous praise and encouragement to prevent them from slacking off.'
6 'Peer-group recognition means more to people than management recognition.'

Motivating employees

Reading

1 **Skim the article in two or three minutes. Which of the things in *Getting started* do you think David Sirota would agree with?**

2 **Read the article again and check your comprehension by choosing the best answer, A, B, C or D, for each of these questions.**

1 In paragraph 1, what effect of high morale is mentioned?
A Employees stay with the company longer.
B Employees work harder than their counterparts in other companies.
C Companies produce better results than their rivals.
D Companies with high morale are more respected.

2 Which of these does Sirota suggest is a good reaction for a company with financial problems?
A reducing the workforce
B outsourcing to reduce costs
C reducing the rewards packages
D transferring employees to other jobs

Giving employees what they want:

The returns are huge

David Sirota, co-author of *The Enthusiastic Employee: How Companies Profit by Giving Workers What They Want*, finds that firms where employee morale is high tend to outperform competitors. He told us: "People at work have various basic goals. First, they want to be treated fairly. Employees want to know they are getting what is normally defined as competitive pay. If I feel underpaid, there is not much an organisation can do to boost my morale. Second, employees want a sense of achievement from

3 How did Toyota motivate workers on assembly lines?
A by asking managers to rotate workers
B by letting groups of workers make decisions on their work organisation
C by allowing teams to take over the whole process of production
D by rewarding them for achieving their production targets

4 How should bonuses be awarded, according to Sirota?
A They should be decided by people at the same level in the organisation.
B They should be given on a monthly basis.
C They should be based on routine work.
D They should be awarded as a result of evaluation from line managers.

5 What, nowadays, is the typical management–worker relationship?
A one where workers have to be cared for by their managers
B one of hostility
C one which is purely economic
D one of co-operation on equal terms

work. The key element is to be proud of your job and proud of the organisation for which you are doing it. The third element is camaraderie. This is also not mentioned much in our field, but it's key – not only in the sense of having a friend, but working well together as a team.

And, he says, there are a number of other things companies can do to boost morale: "First, provide security. Laying off people should be the last resort, not the first thing you do. Some companies use a ring of defense. If the business is having difficulties, they retrain workers or bring work inside from subcontractors. There are a number of steps you can take before making people redundant.

"Second, where there are difficulties in getting work done, we suggest self-managed teams. Toyota, which has been an incredibly successful company, is an example. In the 1970s, Toyota wanted to know how to enrich the job of assembly workers and thought about having groups of employees build an entire car. But that would have been so inefficient. Toyota said instead it could have a team of workers manage part of the assembly line. The team could look at quality and at what kind of maintenance and support were needed, and it could decide how to rotate workers. As opposed to the usual top-down management, this approach is tremendously satisfying for workers, and thus reduces the need for bureaucracy because the people essentially are managing themselves.

"Recognition is also important. Employees do not have to be told that you love them, but you want to be appreciative of good work. People need this kind of feedback. A lot of rewards don't work, including the employee-of-the-month one. Organization-wide awards should be like the Nobel Prize, where peers are involved in the selection of the individuals who receive the award for outstanding achievement, not day-to-day work.

"The traditional merit pay systems with an appraisal and pay increase are quite negative. Workers feel no relation between what they do and their pay increase. A reward has to be felt as such. Research has verified a system such as 'gain sharing', in which a group of workers judges its performance over time. If productivity goes up 20% and the workforce increases 10%, then that means there is greater efficiency. That result should be shared with the workers 50% and management 50%. This has a tremendous impact on productivity and morale.

"In the 1980s and 1990s, we had a reaction to particular forms of management. We talk about four kinds: the first one is paternalism, where workers are treated as children. Then there is adversarial, where workers are the enemy. Then there is transactional, where workers are like ciphers. Management does not know what they are like as individuals. The attitude is, 'We paid you, now we are even. We don't owe you anything.' That's where most companies have gone today. Loyalty is dead.

"The fourth is what we have been talking about, which is the partnership organization. It does not mean that because I paid you, we are now even. You don't treat partners that way because you might need them to help you out sometime, and they might need you. It's more like a relationship between mature adults – not like children or enemies, but allies."

From http://www.knowledge@wharton

Talking point

Discuss these questions in small groups.

David Sirota talks about four types of management–employee relationship: paternalistic, adversarial, transactional and partnership. Which:

- is typical of the organisation where you work (or one you know well)?
- would you feel most comfortable with?
- would you find least comfortable?
- is most likely to cause conflict, and which is least conflictive in your opinion?

Grammar workshop

Reference devices

1 Study these two extracts from the text. What do the underlined words refer to?

1 *The third element is camaraderie. This is also not mentioned much in our field, but it's key – not only in the sense of having a friend, but working well together as a team.*

2 *Some companies use a ring of defense. If the business is having difficulties, they retrain workers or bring work inside from subcontractors.*

2 **Work in pairs. Read the text on pages 82–83 again and say what each of the underlined words or phrases refers to.**

3 **Which of the underlined reference devices in the text is/are:**

1 relative pronouns?
2 pronouns referring to something in the previous sentence?
3 a verb referring to an action mentioned previously?
4 a pronoun referring to something which occurred in the past?
5 a noun phrase which refers to a way of doing things mentioned previously?
6 a word which means 'in this way'?
7 words and phrases which are reference devices within a list?
8 a way of avoiding repetition of the same noun in the same sentence?

page 98 (Reference devices)

Stress in the workplace

Reading

1 **Work in pairs. Study the charts below and discuss what they show.**

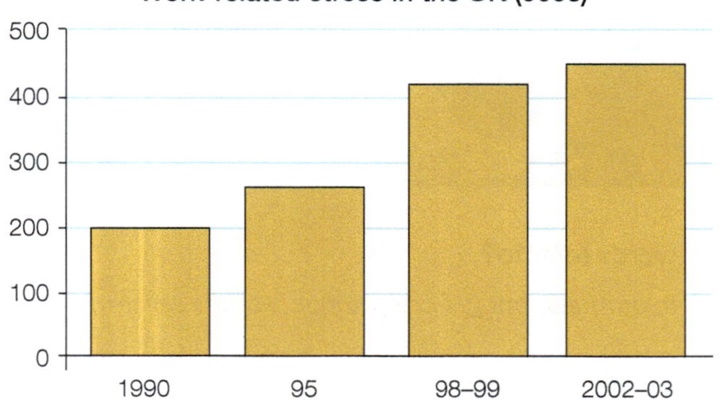

2 **Complete this report using the reference devices from the box.**

the following	the former	the same
themselves	they	this

This report summarises trends in fatal workplace accidents and work-related stress during the period 1990–2003; while **1** .... fell in Britain from 350 in 1990 to 180 in 2003, the latter rose during **2** .... period from 200,000 cases in 1990 to 450,000 in 2003. The most pronounced decrease in accidents occurred between 1990 and 1995, when only 190 took place. During **3** .... years until 1998, they underwent a slight increase to reach 205, before falling to an all-time low of just 160 deaths in 2000. **4** .... then rose to 210 in 2001, before decreasing to 180 in 2003.

Work-related stress, on the other hand, underwent a constant increase during **5** .... period and shows no signs of peaking. The largest increase occurred between 1995 and 1998–9, when the number of cases climbed from 260,000 to 420,000.

In conclusion, the two charts show that, while British workplaces are becoming safer, employees feel **6** .... to be under greater pressure.

3 **Find words or phrases in the text which mean the following.**

1 general developments or changes
2 very noticeable
3 experienced
4 small
5 the lowest it has ever been
6 reaching its highest point

Talking point 1

Discuss these questions in small groups.

1 Are the trends in accidents and stress similar in your country, do you think?
2 What do you think are the main causes of work-related stress, and what can employers do to reduce it?
3 How do you think stress affects business performance?

Listening

You will hear a television programme in which an occupational psychologist, Mariella Kinsky, is interviewed about work-related stress.

6 **1** **Listen to the interview and take notes on what she says in answer to Question 2 in *Talking point 1* above.**

6 2 Listen again and check your understanding of the details by choosing the best answer, A, B or C, for questions 1–8.

1 Which workers are most likely to suffer from stress?
A shopfloor workers
B non-managerial white-collar workers
C managerial staff

2 According to Mariella, what is the principal problem doctors have with stress?
A It's hard to diagnose.
B It's hard to treat.
C It's hard to cure.

3 What indicator of stress has been increasing in recent years?
A staff turnover
B absenteeism
C workplace sabotage

4 According to Mariella, what is the principal cause of the increase in stress?
A longer hours in the office
B increased management supervision
C increased workloads

5 According to Mariella, which of the following was the main reason why people suffered less from stress in the past?
A a friendlier working atmosphere
B a better work–life balance
C stronger unions

6 What contemporary social circumstance has probably increased stress levels?
A richer lifestyles
B reduced family sizes
C higher expectations

7 According to the speaker, why has stress become 'respectable'?
A It doesn't reflect on your ability to do your job.
B It doesn't show you have a weak character.
C It reflects the importance of the work you do.

8 According to the government, what is the most effective way for employers to reduce stress?
A by offering counselling
B by involving employees in decisions affecting their working lives
C by organising employees in teams

Talking point 2

Work in small groups. Which of Mariella's statements (1–3) do you agree/disagree with? Why?

1 Negative stress comes … from a perception one has of lack of control over one's life.
2 … work-related stress has become an acceptable, even a respectable thing to complain about.
3 … we have more time to worry …

UNIT 17

Writing

A recent survey of managers revealed the following information.

1 Work in pairs. Study the charts and say what they show. Are there any statistics which surprise you?

Effects of stress on organisations

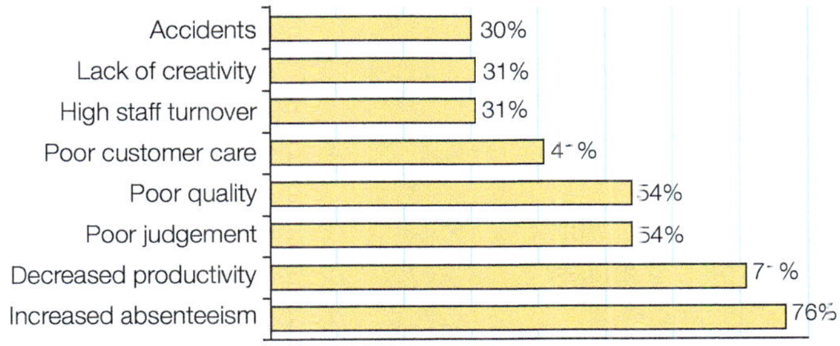

Annual cost of absenteeism per employee to small businesses

2 Your human resources director has asked you to write a brief report (120–140 words) based on these statistics. Before you write, study the Useful language box and discuss with your partner how you should structure your report.

3 Work alone to write your report.

Useful language

Expressing causes and results

- X *causes* + noun/pronoun + infinitive:
  Excessive stress causes employees to make poor decisions.
- X *leads to / gives rise to* Y:
  Excessive stress leads to / gives rise to poor decision-making.
- Y *(often) arise(s) as a result of* X:
  Wrong decisions often arise as a result of excessive stress.
- Y *is/are a frequent consequence of* X:
  Wrong decisions are a frequent consequence of excessive stress.

UNIT 18

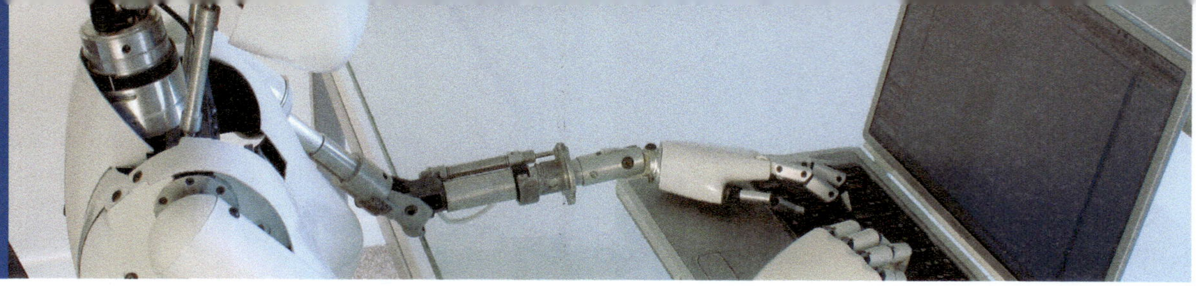

The workforce of the future

Getting started

1 Work in pairs. Match the types of worker (1–10) with their definitions (a–j).

1 shop-floor worker
2 blue-collar worker
3 project manager
4 freelancer
5 knowledge worker
6 self-employed person
7 semi-skilled worker
8 union rep
9 temp
10 white-collar worker

a person employed to work for a short period, while another person is absent or when there is extra work
b person who works in an office, doing work that needs mental rather than physical effort
c person whose work requires specialist knowledge
d person who coordinates and supervises different elements of a job
e worker elected by other workers in a factory or business to represent them in discussions with the management
f worker in a factory
g worker who does not work for an employer but finds work for himself/herself or who has his/her own business
h worker who does particular pieces of work for different organisations, rather than working all the time for a single organisation
i worker who does physical work rather than office work
j worker who has or needs only a small amount of training

2 Discuss this question in small groups. Give reasons for your opinions.

Which of these types of worker do you think there will be more of in the future, and which will there be fewer of?

Useful language

Giving tentative opinions

I imagine/suppose/guess that …
It could/might be that …
It's a possibility / It's (very/quite) possible that …
… are likely to …

The millennium generation

Reading

1 Work in pairs. Decide which of these statements you agree/disagree with, and why.

'Young people joining the workforce now …

1 are likely to take a short-term view of work.' ..E..
2 are more entrepreneurial.'
3 are not so worried about job security.'
4 find it easy to fund their own business ventures.'
5 identify with their own abilities rather than their employment situation.'
6 may continue their formal education when they are older.'
7 may have little time for people who avoid working with the new technologies.'
8 take advantage of work opportunities where they arise.'

2 Read the five extracts (A–E) from an article about how young people entering the workforce now, or in the next few years, are different from older generations. Decide which paragraph each of the statements on the left refers to.

Vocabulary

Find words or phrases in the extracts which mean the following.

1 fewer commitments (text A)
2 extremely active, excited or uncontrolled (text A)
3 not in use any more, having been replaced by something newer and better or more fashionable (text D)
4 present or noticeable everywhere (text B)
5 especially values (text E)
6 move with no particular aim (text E)
7 growing quickly (text C)
8 starting doing something new, independently of other people (text C)

A

Young adults are by nature well-suited for the unpredictable workplace of the future. They have less baggage and can therefore afford to take risks. People today get married later, and women have children three years later in life than their mothers did. Each generation is born into an era of more rapid change than their parents, making them ever better adapted for the frenetic world they are about to enter.

B

One of the most pervasive business trends of the past decade has been the rise of the 'free agent', caused both by the breakdown of the social contract between companies and employees, and by the growing share in the workforce of knowledge workers with portable skills. They define themselves by their skills, not the firm they work for. 'The overwhelming majority of graduates see their career at graduation not as a straight line of advancement in one company but as a zigzag path from company to company, job to job, skill to skill,' writes author Meredith Bagby.

C

With a booming economy, capital for the taking and unprecedented technological opportunity, it is no surprise that more young people have been striking out on their own. Rebecca Smith explains that when she arrived in New York last year, she had to choose between a job with a prestigious advertising firm and one with a tiny dotcom start-up. She chose the start-up, even though it paid $10,000 a year less. 'It was a choice between being someone's assistant or getting real responsibility and challenges,' she says. 'I think that a lot of people in my generation are going to smaller companies that allow them to grow much faster.'

D

Where years of education, training and experience were once necessary to succeed, now they are increasingly seen as irrelevant, even a liability. This trend is already showing up in teenagers with self-taught technical skills. They know that they will never again be as quick-learning and full of energy as they are now. These young programmers are starting to question the point of university. In a technology industry changing so rapidly, goes the thinking, skills quickly become obsolete, and in this market four years of studying history – or even computer science at an academic pace – is just four years wasted. 'You can always go back to college, but you can't regain your youth,' says one.

E

According to Bruce Tulgan: 'All they've known is a technology-based economy that moves quickly, downsizes constantly and places a premium on change.' The daily *USA Today* makes a similar point: 'Raised on a diet of MTV and video games, young managers are quick to roam from job to job, hungry for quick results, willing to do things differently and intolerant of technophobes.' Margaret Reagan, a consultant, predicts that barely one-third of young people will take steady staff jobs with companies. Instead, most will freelance, work under contract or part-time.

From *The Economist*

Job sharing

UNIT 18

Talking point

1 Match these ways of working (1–6) with their definitions (a–f).

1 flexible working
2 part-time working
3 home working/teleworking
4 job sharing
5 freelancing
6 temping

a doing part of a job with someone else, so that each person works part-time
b doing particular pieces of work for different organisations, rather than working all the time for a single organisation
c working at home, while communicating with your office by telephone, fax or computer
d working for a short period, especially in an office, while another person is absent or when there is extra work
e working for only some of the day or the week
f working without strict times for starting and finishing

2 Discuss these questions in small groups.

1 Which of these ways of working do you think will become more common in the future?
2 Which of these ways of working would you welcome?

Useful language

Giving strong/direct opinions

It's quite clear that …
I've no doubt that …
One thing for certain is that …
It/He/They is/are sure to …

Listening

You will hear an expert in organisational management giving a lecture about job sharing.

7 **Listen and complete these notes by writing up to three words in each gap.**

Advantages of job sharing for employees
- Provides **1** .... for employees with other interests
- Flexibility for workers with **2** ....
- Gives people who have given up working opportunity to **3** ....

Disadvantages for employees
- Have to **4** .... on a joint basis
- Receive **5** .... , as this is more costly for two people
- Not eligible for **6** ....

Advantages for employers
- Two part-time employees **7** .... than one full-time employee
- Reduction in **8** ....
- **9** .... also reduced

Disadvantages for employers
- Less continuity of **10** ....
- **11** .... between supervisors and job-share partners
- Training – though can be done by the **12** ....

Speaking

1 Work in groups of three or four. Discuss the advantages/disadvantages of one of these subjects for employees and employers.
- teleworking
- flexible working
- freelancing

2 Prepare a short talk on the subject.

3 Change groups and give your talk to your new partners.

How people feel about their jobs

Listening

You will hear part of a radio programme in which five people talk about how they view their present job and what their hopes for the future are.

8 **1 Listen and complete the table for each person using the lists below.**

	Views of the present	Hopes for the future
Lechsinska		
Ganesh		
Francesca		
Darron		
Irenke		

Views of the present

A not enough job security
B not trusted enough
C bad workplace atmosphere
D underpaid
E no career advancement
F too much stress

Hopes for the future

G to be self-employed
H to start own company
I to take a career break
J to retrain
K to go part-time
L to be given a permanent contract

2 Discuss this question in pairs.

Whose ambitions do you think are the most realistic?

8 **2 Check your answers by listening to the recording again.**

3 If you are working, tell your partner which sentences are true for you and why, and which are not true for you and why. If you are not working at the moment, talk about a relative or someone you know well.

Vocabulary

1 Work in pairs. Complete the sentences below using the words from the box.

~~apart~~ cut dire go going good run stuck taken

1 Basically, I like my job, apart from the smell.
2 I'm hardly getting what's the .... rate for my job in this part of the world.
3 I feel I'm .... in a rut and stagnating.
4 I'm on the .... all the time and don't get much chance to wind down.
5 The job is pretty high pressure, and I sometimes worry that in the long .... , it will affect my health.
6 The place I'm working at the moment is pretty .... , actually – I mean, no one seems to speak to anyone.
7 My dream is to get .... on by the Royal Shakespeare Company.
8 The money's .... because we get a .... of the profits.

Speaking

1 Think about these questions and prepare answers for them.

1 If you are working at the moment, how do you feel about your present job? What things do you like about it, and what things dissatisfy you?
2 What would you like to be doing in the future, say in five or ten years' time?

2 Work with a partner. Interview him/her and ask the questions above which apply. Follow them up with extra questions where necessary.

UNIT 19

Productivity

Getting started

Discuss these questions in small groups.

1 What is productivity?
2 What factors do you think have affected productivity in your country in recent years?
3 How would what is happening in the picture on the right affect productivity?
4 Is productivity always a good indicator of a company's performance?

Productivity at Magro Toys

Speaking

Magro Toys S.A., based in Villena, Spain, is the Spanish subsidiary of a leading European toy manufacturer. Below are four charts which show aspects of Magro Toys' performance over the last five years.

1
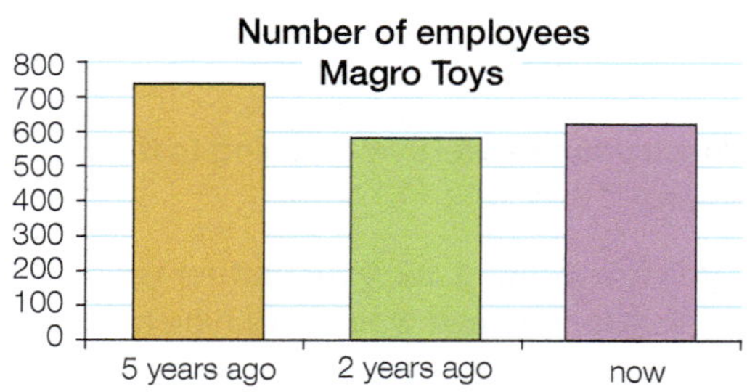

2
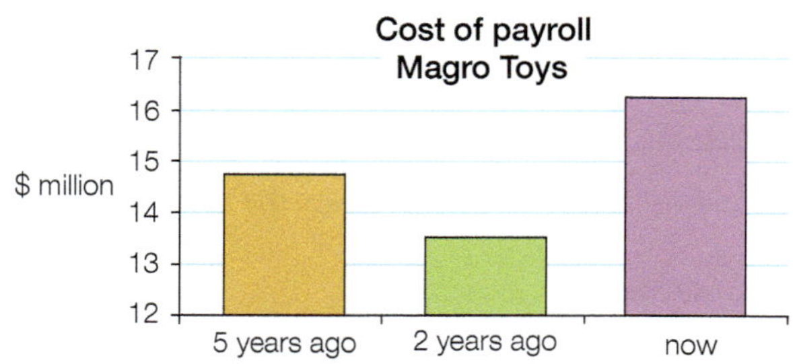

3
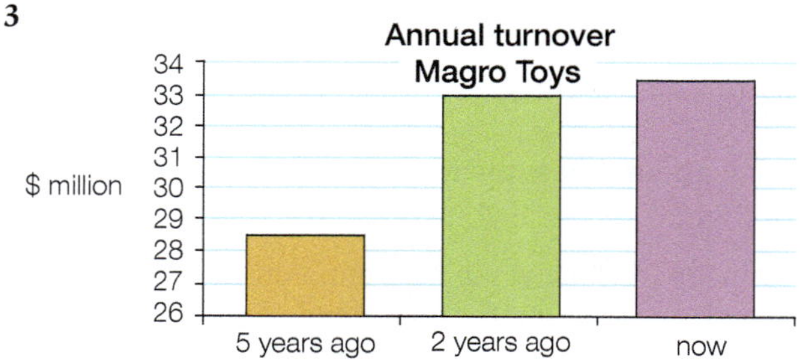

4
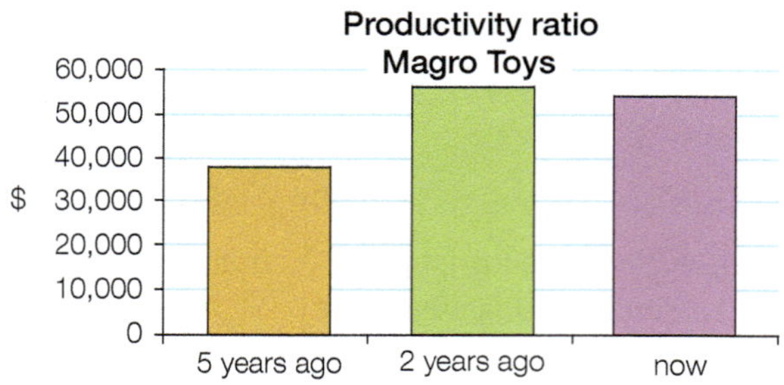

1 Work in pairs and discuss these questions.

1 What do the charts show?
2 What might have happened in this company to produce these results?
3 What other information would you need in order to have a more complete picture of the company's performance?

2 Change partners and present your conclusions to your new partner.

Useful language

Speculating

They might have …
They could have …
Maybe what happened was (that) …
Perhaps they …
It's possible that …
It could/might be that …

page 98 (Modal verbs to express degrees of certainty)

Reading

1 Read this report to find out what happened at Magro Toys to produce the results shown in the charts on page 90.

2 In most lines of the report, there is one extra word. However, some lines are correct. Find the extra word or put a tick (✔) if the line is correct.

3 Read the report again and find examples of these features of a formal style of writing.

1 use of the passive
2 using noun phrases instead of verbs (e.g. *an increase in turnover* instead of *turnover increased*)

Magro Toys – Report on productivity

The purpose of this report is to summarise changes in productivity at 1 ✔
our Spanish subsidiary, Magro Toys, over the last ~~of~~ five years and to 2 of
suggest reasons why productivity gains were achieved up until two 3 ......
years ago have not been maintained yet. 4 ......

Automation

Five years ago, it was decided to reduce the payroll costs by automating 5 ......
our labour-intensive manufacturing facilities where possible and 6 ......
thereby in shedding workers. The implementation of this decision 7 ......
had involved reducing our labour force through natural wastage and a 8 ......
voluntary redundancy scheme. This was carried out over a three-year 9 ......
period.

Financial performance

The automation of our Villena plant resulted in a reduction of payroll 10 ......
costs of an 8.7%. Furthermore, a vigorous marketing campaign, aided 11 ......
by a booming world economy, which gave rise to a 15.7% increase in 12 ......
turnover, though interest payments and capital depreciation costs 13 ......
resulting from the automation programme kept profits low. 14 ......
Productivity, however, rose up by 15.3% over this period. 15 ......

Labour costs

One consequence of our successful marketing campaigns it has been a 16 ......
considerable increase in sales. This, in turn, has meant that we have had 17 ......
to hire on more staff, especially, due to the increased automation of our 18 ......
production facilities, are more technically qualified and therefore more 19 ......
expensive staff. While the sales have remained buoyant and 20 ......
profitability has improved, productivity has undergone a slight 21 ......
decrease.

Conclusion

Productivity is forming only one measure of our company's 22 ......
performance. Financially, and in marketing terms, our company 23 ......
continues to perform ahead of the competition companies. While we 24 ......
should be continue to look for ways to streamline production, this 25 ......
should not be allowed to interfere with our broader objectives. 26 ......

Grammar workshop

Expressing causes and results

1 Underline the two phrases in these sentences which express causes and results.

The introduction of a new computer system led to an initial decrease in productivity. However, as a consequence of an intensive staff training programme, productivity soon rose to record levels.

2 Find and underline other phrases and expressions in the report which also express causes and results.

3 Match these causes (1–6) and results (a–f).

Cause	Result
1 higher interest rates	a 50% increase in sales
2 incentive scheme for sales staff	b cashflow problems
3 market research	c higher shop-floor productivity
4 new environmental regulations	d more efficient use of computer systems
5 new machines in the factory	e products more suited to our customers
6 staff training programme	f reduced pollution from our plants

4 Write sentences to express each cause and result using a variety of phrases from Exercises 1 and 2.

Higher interest rates have resulted in cashflow problems.

Productivity concerns

UNIT 19

Vocabulary

Match these words and phrases (1–10) with their definitions (a–j).

1 assembly line	a ability of a factory to produce more than it actually does
2 churn out	b activities are determined by the requirements of the product (as opposed to customer-led)
3 erode the manufacturing base	c amount produced by a person, machine or factory
4 excess production capacity	d build up a large store of goods which have not been sold yet
5 hire and fire	e employ and dismiss
6 output	f series of machines and workers in a factory where a product is built as it moves along
7 product-led	g produce large amounts of something quickly, usually of low quality
8 retool	h reduce the factory facilities in a region or country
9 stockpile	i replace machinery in a factory
10 technical glitch	j small problem or fault that prevents something from working well

Listening

You will hear a television interview in which three production managers, Lee Kah Seng, Ferenc Kovács and Mike Drewer, talk about issues of productivity.

9 **Listen and choose the best answer, A, B or C, for each of these questions.**

1 Why, according to Lee, did productivity in his company fall?
   A There was a decrease in orders.
   B There was an interruption in the supply chain.
   C There was an improvement in product quality.

2 Which of these factors make traditional productivity measures unreliable in his company?
   A variations in the prices of components
   B variations in lead times of manufacturing products
   C the complexity of factory systems

3 Which measure does Lee consider most useful when compared to traditional productivity measures?
   A the cost in man-hours of making a product
   B the speed at which customer orders can be met
   C the value added to each unit produced

4 Why, according to Ferenc, are traditional productivity measures wasteful?
   A They record past performance.
   B They require specialist personnel to record them.
   C They result in misguided decisions.

5 What does Ferenc say is the major pitfall of automation?
   A It makes the production process more expensive.
   B Machines tend to break down.
   C It does not result in a reduction in staff costs.

6 What does Mike say is the danger of industry concentrating too much on productivity?
   A It may lead to a drop in consumer demand.
   B It can adversely affect the morale of the workforce.
   C It can make companies too reliant on technology.

7 Why, according to Drewer, are productivity measures irrelevant in his company?
   A Work is largely outsourced.
   B Products are modified too often.
   C His production facilities are more modern than others.

8 What does Ferenc say is likely to drive productivity improvements in the future?
   A moving production to cheaper locations
   B the emergence of new technologies
   C more flexible labour laws

Speaking

You have decided to attend a symposium on productivity in your industry and to make a short presentation at the symposium.

1 **Work in pairs and choose one of these topics.**

1 **Productivity**: the importance of increasing productivity in a company
2 **Productivity**: the dangers of making productivity the central goal of your business strategy
3 **Productivity**: strategies for higher workforce productivity

Then work together and:

- brainstorm two or three ideas you want to express
- brainstorm vocabulary to use
- think of (or invent) reasons and examples to back up your ideas.

2 **Change partners and work in groups of three. Take turns to make your presentations. While you are listening to other students' presentations, think of one question to ask them at the end.**

Manufacturing and services

Speaking

You and your partner work as production manager and human resources manager in your company. The company needs to raise its productivity to remain competitive in your industry. Your managing director has asked you to suggest ways in which this can be done without creating unnecessary conflict with staff.

Work in pairs to discuss and decide:

1 what steps you can take to raise productivity with the co-operation of the staff
2 how you can communicate these proposals to staff.

Writing

1 **Work in groups of three or four. Read the task in the white box and discuss these questions.**

1 What changes could you mention and what reasons could you give for them?
2 Who will read the report and how will this determine the style you use?
3 What details could you include in your report to give it authenticity?

The division of the company where you work has recently made changes which have resulted in spectacular gains in productivity. Your manager has asked you to write a report for the board of directors of your company so that they can implement similar changes in other divisions of the company.

Write the report for the board of directors and include the following information:

- what changes you made and the reasons for them
- the results of your changes
- your recommendations for other divisions in the company.

2 **Write your report.**

Task tip

Before you start writing:

- study the report on page 91. Underline any words or phrases you think would be useful. When you write your report, try to imitate the style.
- revise reference devices on pages 83 and 98 and see if you can use some in your report.

UNIT 20

Staff negotiations

Getting started

Discuss these questions in small groups.

1. When a company is considering reorganising its operations, which of these considerations should be foremost in its thinking, and why?
   - shareholders' interests
   - employees' needs
   - customers' interests
   - pressure from the competition
   - public opinion
2. Which of these elements should be given the lowest priority?
3. How should companies consult staff when, for example, they are thinking of closing a factory or relocating people to offices in other parts of the country?

Travelsafe Insurance

Listening

Travelsafe Insurance is a small insurance company specialising in travel insurance with 450 employees based in Norwich, UK. You will hear Peter Fletcher, a trade-union representative, collecting opinions from staff members before a meeting with managers to discuss working conditions.

1 Work in pairs. Study the staff complaints and demands below and:

- (if you are working) say which ones you think also apply to you
- (if you are studying) discuss which are the most serious complaints, and which are the most reasonable demands.

Complaints

A I want to be sure I won't be relocated.
B I'm not trusted enough.
C I feel I'm not being treated fairly.
D I'm not being paid a competitive salary.
E I'd like a more transparent career structure.
F I would not know what to do in an emergency.
G I'd like a reduction in my workload.
H I'm not given enough recognition for what I do.

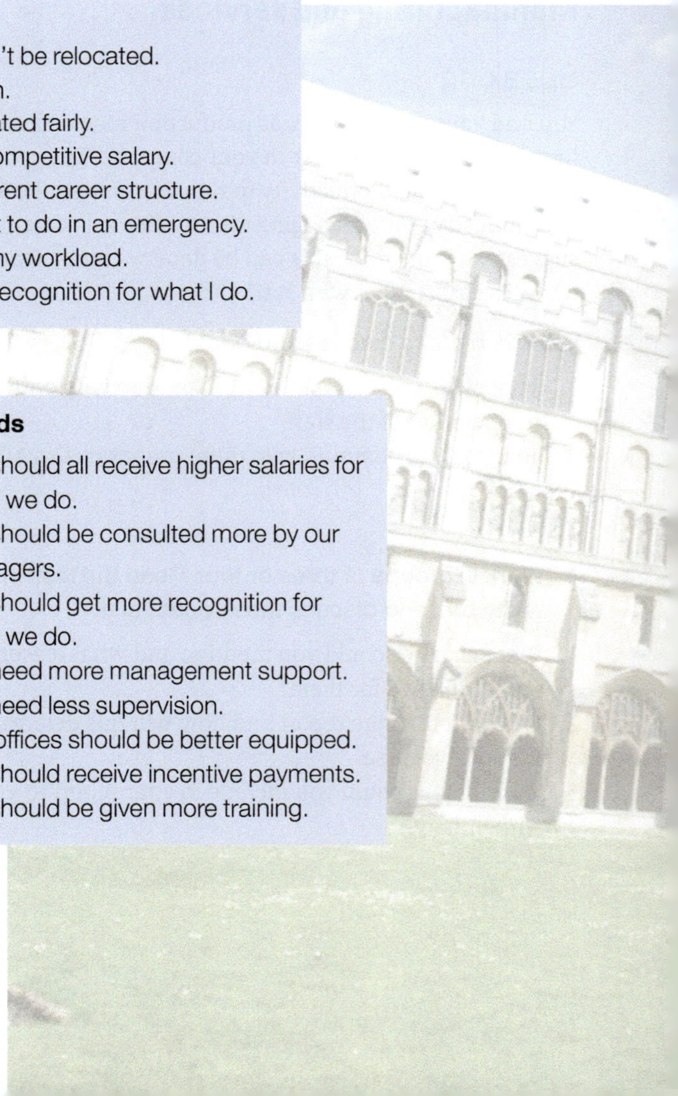

Demands

I We should all receive higher salaries for what we do.
J We should be consulted more by our managers.
K We should get more recognition for what we do.
L We need more management support.
M We need less supervision.
N Our offices should be better equipped.
O We should receive incentive payments.
P We should be given more training.

10 2 **Peter talks to five people. Listen and decide which complaint (A–H) and which demand (I–P) each of the five people makes.**

	Complaint	Demand
Wendy		
Demitri		
Naline		
Claudio		
Toya		

UNIT 20

Vocabulary

10 **Match the phrasal verbs and expressions (1–8) with their definitions (a–h). Then check your answers by listening again and reading the transcript for track 10.**

1 round the clock
2 get hot under the collar
3 picked on
4 put their money where their mouth is
5 passed over
6 breathing down my neck
7 get on with
8 up to scratch

a chosen frequently and unfairly to do something unpleasant
b all day and all night
c become angry about something
d continue doing work
e ignored
f of an acceptable standard
g show by spending money that they believe in something
h watching everything someone does

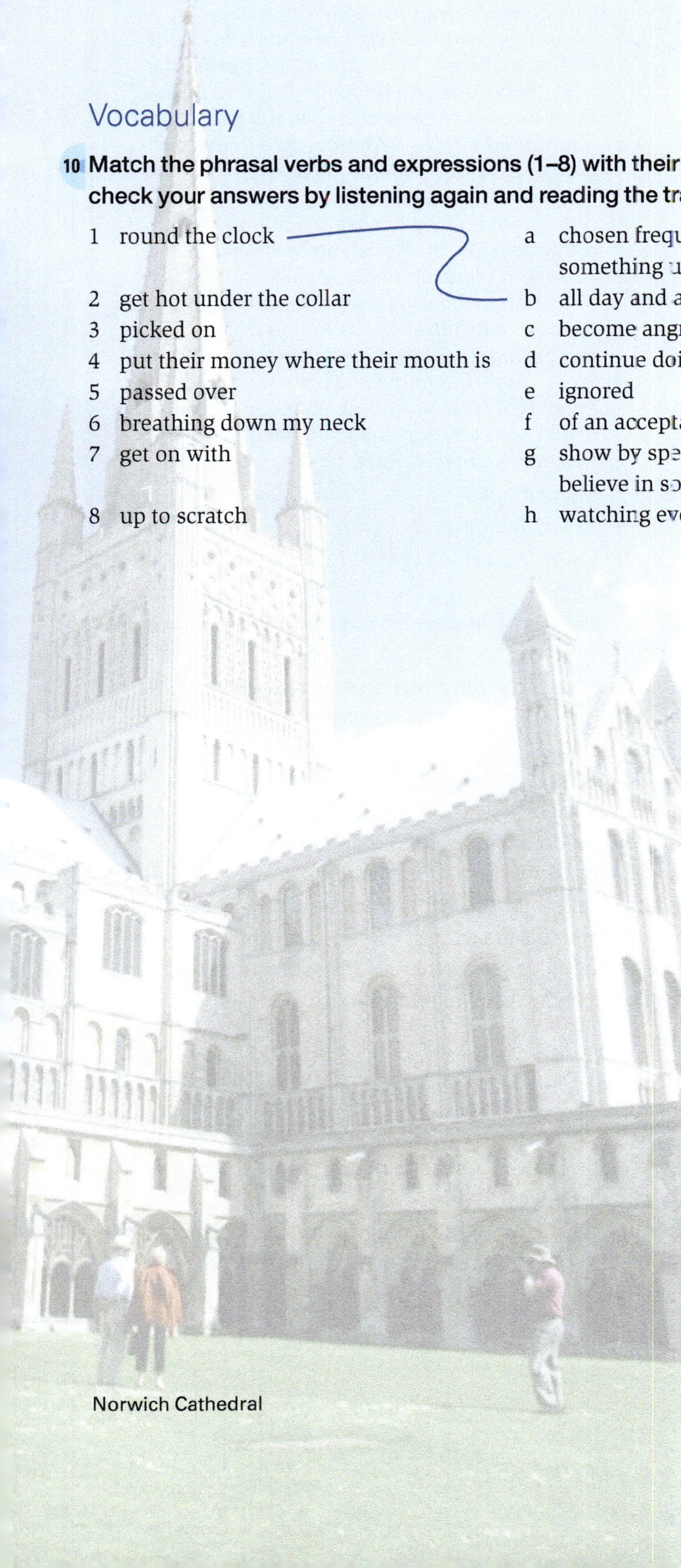
Norwich Cathedral

Grammar workshop

Variations on conditional sentences 1

Study these sentences from the listening activity and answer the questions below.

a *... if it weren't for us, this company would fold overnight.*
b *... had the bosses spoken to us about this possibility, I'd have told them what I thought.*
c *... what would we do in the event of a fire?*
d *I'd be happy to do all this, provided other people were being asked to do the same amount.*
e *... if they were to say something, then they'd have to put their money where their mouth is and give us a bonus.*

1 Which sentences are second conditional (➔ page 44)?
2 Which is third conditional (➔ page 44)?
3 Which words or phrases are used instead of *if*? Can you think of other words or phrases which can replace *if*? (➔ page 99)
4 Which sentence contains the following construction: *if it weren't for* + noun/pronoun?
5 Which puts the auxiliary verb before the subject to replace *if*?
6 Which sentence contains *were* + infinitive?

➔ **page 99** (Variations on conditionals)

20 UNIT

Reading

1 Read the memo opposite which the CEO of Travelsafe Insurance sent to all the staff. Briefly discuss these questions with a partner.

1 If you received a memo like this in your place of work, how would you react?
2 What demands would you make to your representatives if you were a member of staff affected in this way?

2 Complete the memo by writing one word in each gap.

Memo

To: All staff
From: CEO

As **1** .part. of our expansion plans, and with a **2** .... to closer contact with our key markets, we are planning to open new offices in Glasgow, Liverpool and Plymouth. **3** .... decision will involve reducing the size of our Norwich office **4** .... about 20% during the next 18 months and relocating staff to form a nucleus of experienced staff in the new offices mentioned **5** .... We hope to achieve our goal of 20% staff reductions **6** .... Norwich by providing incentives **7** .... early retirement and, if necessary, voluntary redundancies. Staff wishing to know **8** .... about our plans and how we aim to reformulate the organisation should consult the company intranet. We shall also be discussing our plans with staff representatives **9** .... a forthcoming staff–management meeting. If you would like to ask any questions or **10** .... any comments, please don't hesitate to send me an email.

Many thanks

Frank Mason

Frank Mason

CEO

Grammar workshop

Variations on conditional sentences 2

Several people at Travelsafe Insurance expressed disquiet about the company's plans for relocation.

1 Match phrases 1–8 with phrases a–h to make sentences said by Travelsafe's employees.

1 Had I known about the company's plans,
2 I guess several people in my department would be interested in relocating if
3 I'd jump at the chance to move,
4 I'd regard this as a great opportunity to go to a big city with more scope
5 I'll happily move back to Liverpool,
6 I'll only move to Glasgow on condition
7 If it weren't for my wife's job,
8 In the event of my entire department being relocated,

a as long as I'm given a section supervisor's job.
b providing I was offered some sort of permanent contract.
c I wouldn't have bought a new house here just six months ago.
d I'd consider moving as a possibility.
e I'll move with them to stay with the team.
f if it weren't for the fact that I have all my friends and family in this area.
g that they give me a generous resettlement package.
h the company were to offer the right package.

11 **2 Check your answers by listening to what the speakers actually said.**

3 Complete these sentences in any way you want. Then compare your ideas with a partner.

1 She would have left the company had she …
2 I'll change jobs providing …
3 He wouldn't stay late at the office if it weren't for …
4 Many staff will be made redundant in the event of …
5 I'll go on the training course on condition that …
6 He's happy to accept more responsibility as long as …

Talking point

Discuss these questions in small groups.

1 Would you be prepared to relocate? Under what circumstances?
2 Which reasons for relocating / not relocating given in the listening exercise do you think were best?

Horse-trading at Travelsafe Insurance

Listening

You will hear Travelsafe Insurance's CEO, Frank Mason, talking to Peter Fletcher, the staff representative.

12 **Listen and complete Peter's notes with up to three words or a number.**

Management offer

1 Reduction in staff numbers at Norwich office:
  1 .... , i.e. 90 employees
2 Maximum of 60 staff to relocate – encouraged by
  2 .... :
  a 5% immediate 3 ....
  b £12,000 4 .... to cover cost of move.
  c two weeks' 5 .... at time of move.
3 Incentive to take voluntary redundancy: one month's gross salary in addition to each employee's
  6 .... and free 7 ....

Talking point

Discuss these questions in small groups.

1 How generous is the company's offer?
2 What actions can their employees take if they are not happy with the offer?
3 What could be the company's next steps if their employees don't accept the offer?

Role-play

You are going to negotiate an agreement between management and staff at Travelsafe Insurance, concerning the relocation of staff to new offices.

1 Divide into 2 groups.

Group 1: You represent management. See page 120.
Group 2: You represent staff. See page 120.

2 Complete the Useful language box by writing phrases 1–15 in the appropriate spaces.

1 Another thing we/our staff want is …
2 For us, the most important thing is …
3 Here's another possibility. How about …? Why don't we …?
4 Yes, I guess that's acceptable. (However, if …)
5 I'm afraid … is out of the question. On the other hand, we could …
6 No, I'm afraid we couldn't possibly accept that. What we want is …
7 Now, let's just check I've got this right: what you want is …
8 Yes, that's fine. No problem.
9 OK. Let's just make sure we agree.
10 That's an interesting possibility. Can we come back to you on that?
11 We can't answer that one straight away.
12 What we'd like first of all is …
13 We'd have to consult on that one.
14 Yes, that would be OK (but only if …)
15 You're saying that if we …

UNIT 20

Useful language

A Introducing demands or proposals
Here's what we suggest:
....
....
....

B Buying time
Well, we'd have to think about that.
....
....
....

C Rejecting offers/making counter-proposals
We're not prepared to accept … However ….
....
....
....

D Agreeing/accepting (with conditions)
I'll have to think about that, but I think it's all right.
....
....
....
....

E Summarising
So, what you're saying is ….
....
....

3 Form groups of four, with two management representatives and two staff representatives. Take fifteen minutes to negotiate an agreement for the relocation of staff. Try to reach an agreement.

4 Compare your agreements with those of other groups. Decide who negotiated the best agreement.

5 Work in pairs with your partner from your negotiating team and follow the instructions below.

Management representatives: Write a brief memo to the board of directors outlining the agreement you reached.
Staff representatives: Write a memo to all staff summarising the agreement you reached.

Grammar workshop 5

Reference devices

- *This*, *that* and *it* can be used to refer to the things last mentioned, though *this* and *that* are more emphatic:
  Our employees have been asking to participate in management decisions. ***It/This/That*** *is something we will have to consider.*
- *This* is usually preferred if you want to add something new to your argument:
  We have decided to involve our employees in management decisions. ***This*** *will mean us having to supply them with more information.*
- *One* is used to refer to singular countable nouns from a group. *A(n) … one* is used with an adjective:
  Several companies are active in this field. ***One*** *is Vodafone.*
  There are a number of reasons for making the investment. ***An important one*** *is to stay ahead of the competition.*
- *Another* is used if you are adding to a list started with *one*:
  Several companies are active in this field; one is Vodafone and ***another*** *is Nokia.*
- *The other* should be used if there are only two things on the list:
  Two companies have been trying to dominate the market; one is BT and ***the other*** *is Telefónica.*
- *Do* is used to refer to a previous verb:
  I know our suppliers are going to raise their prices, and when they ***do****, we'll drop them.*
- *Do so* is used to refer to a previous verb and a complement (i.e. the words following the verb):
  Please contact the production manager, and when you ***have done so****, ask her why she missed the meeting.*
- *Thus* means 'in this way':
  They raised prices and ***thus*** *increased their per-unit profit.*
- *The former* and *the latter* can be used to refer to two things mentioned together:
  Both Ford and Nissan are active in the lucrative Brazilian market. ***The former*** *has a joint venture with a Brazilian company.* ***The latter*** *has opened a factory near São Paulo.*

Use reference devices from the box on the left to complete these sentences (you may need more than one word).

1 He hasn't emailed me yet, but when he *does*, I'll let you know.
2 He made a number of interesting points during his presentation. A particularly interesting .... was about the consequences of an increase in value-added tax. .... concerned our suppliers' different invoicing systems.
3 Many of our customers have threatened to change providers, but so far few have ....
4 The company decided to stop television advertising and increase its Internet advertising, and .... target potential customers more exactly.
5 There are two scheduled airlines flying to Cape Town from here. .... is South African Airlines and .... is Iberia. .... leaves at 10 p.m., so you fly overnight. .... leaves in the morning, so you arrive quite late in the evening.
6 We are moving a lot of our resources into e-commerce. .... is a comparatively new area for us and we have a lot to learn.
7 We are undertaking a company-wide drive to reduce absenteeism. .... is something which, if successful, will greatly improve our bottom line.

Modal verbs to express degrees of certainty

Present/Future time

- *May* and *might* mean 'it's possible, but not certain':
  You'd better leave early because the traffic ***might*** *be very heavy.*
- *Must* means 'I think this is true because I have evidence':
  The company ***must*** *be profitable because their market share has reached 50%.*
- The negative of *must* is *can't*:
  They ***can't*** *be losing money when they're selling so much.*
- *Should* means 'I expect this is true':
  You ***should*** *find your new job very enjoyable – it's totally suited to you.*

- *Could* usually means 'this is a remote possibility':
  I don't know where the key is. It ***could*** *be at home, but I don't think so.*

Past time

The past of all these modal verbs (with these meanings) is formed by *have* + past participle:

- *may* → *may have*:
  She ***may have been*** *delayed.*
- *might* → *might have*
- *must* → *must have*
- *can't* → *can't have*
- *should* → *should have*
- *could* → *could have*

Complete these sentences using a modal verb from the box above and the verbs in brackets in the correct form. (In some cases, more than one modal verb is possible.)

1 It's strange there's no one in the boardroom. The meeting *can't have been cancelled* (*cancel*) as it was extremely urgent.
2 Is the Japanese delegate here? He .... (*arrive*) by now because his train was due in half an hour ago.
3 There's a rumour going round that they're going to close this office, so this .... (*be*) our last week here.
4 I wonder why they're going to close this office. We .... (*lose*) money – after all, we had record profits last year.
5 Well, if the meeting hasn't been cancelled, they .... (*hold*) it in another room because it should have started ten minutes ago.
6 I think I .... (*dial*) the wrong number. I'm supposed to be calling Germany, and they keep answering in Spanish!
7 You can't assume that everyone has read your report. Some people .... (*not have*) time.
8 You .... (*find*) your trip to Switzerland very interesting. I found it fascinating the last time I was there.

Variations on conditionals

Here are some other ways of expressing conditional sentences:

Second conditional

- *If it weren't for* + noun / verb + *–ing*, *would* + infinitive
  If it weren't for the price*, we would buy one immediately.* (= If the price were lower ...)
- *If* + subject + *were* + infinitive, *would* + infinitive
  If they were to pay *a more competitive wage, I wouldn't think of leaving.*

Third conditional

- *Had* + subject + past participle, *would have* + past participle
  Had they sent *the goods on time, we would have been able to meet the deadline.*

Any conditional

- *In the (unlikely) event of* + noun / verb + *–ing*
  In the event of the workforce going *on strike, we'll have to offer them a wage increase.*
- *provided/providing (that)*
  I'd change offices, ***provided*** *I was given promotion.*
- *as long as*
  We'll continue with this product line ***as long as*** *no one complains.*

For questions

- *Suppose/Supposing (that)*
  Suppose *we close this office, will we lose any customers, do you think?*

Rewrite these sentences starting with the words given. Make any necessary changes to keep the same meaning.

1 If we had a good view, these offices would be perfect.
If it weren't *for the view, these offices would be perfect.*
2 If the transport costs were lower, I'd place an order.
If it ...
3 If the staff went on strike, the company would go bankrupt.
If the staff were ...
4 There would have been no problem if management had been ready to negotiate seriously.
Had management ...
5 If our supply chain is interrupted, we'll need to be able to source alternative parts quickly.
In the event ...
6 I'll do the extra work on Saturday morning if you pay me overtime.
Providing ...
7 The customer has promised not to complain unless we refuse to replace the part.
As long as ...
8 How would you react if they raised the price?
Supposing ...

UNIT 21

Corporate ethics

Getting started

Discuss this question in small groups. You can use ideas from the box if you wish.

What responsibilities do you think large companies have to ...

- their shareholders?
- their stakeholders (their customers, employees and suppliers)?
- society in general?

continuity	ethics	loyalty	profit	safety	tax

Useful language

They have a duty to ...
One of their main/prime responsibilities is to ...
They must not, under any circumstances / on any account ...
An area of particular interest (to shareholders) is / would be ...

Corporate Social Responsibility (CSR)

Reading

1 **Read the article on the opposite page about Corporate Social Responsibility carefully, ignoring the gaps for the moment, and note in just a few words the main idea of each paragraph. When you have finished, compare your notes with a partner.**

Paragraph 1: Large companies must be socially responsible, not just profitable.

2 **Work in pairs. Looking *only* at your notes, speak together and reconstruct the argument of the article.**

3 **Complete the article by choosing one sentence (A–H) for each gap.**

A Thus, making money serves a social purpose.
B They, at least, are accountable to voters.
C The problem is that the profits of private enterprise go exclusively to shareholders.
D One solution many companies have adopted is the appointment of so-called 'ethics managers'.
E The policy may in fact harm precisely those it is supposedly intended to help.
F However, the one thing that all these ideas have in common is that they are based on a faulty analysis of the capitalist system they are intended to cure.
G But that does not fully discharge the enlightened company's debt to society.
H Companies at every opportunity now express agreement with the principles of corporate social responsibility (CSR).

Task tip

Paying careful attention to the subject of each paragraph (as you did when you took notes) should help you to choose the right sentence. Also, look at clues within the sentences which link to what comes before and after.

CSR – worthy cause?

It will no longer do for a company to go quietly about its business, telling no lies and breaking no laws, selling things that people want and making money. That is so out of fashion. Today, all companies, but especially big ones, are expected to worry less about profits and be socially responsible instead. **1** ..H..

The practices that caring, progressive CEOs mention come in all shapes and sizes. Treat your employees well; encourage loyalty among your customers and suppliers; avoid investing in 'unethical' industries, or in countries where workers are paid low wages or denied decent benefits; take care to save energy and recycle used envelopes. **2** ......

Simply put, advocates of CSR work from the premise that basic capitalism fails to serve the public interest. **3** ...... What about the public good? Only if corporations recognise their obligations to society – to 'stakeholders' other than the owners of the business – will that broader social interest be advanced. Often, governments can force such obligations on companies, through taxes and regulation. **4** ...... For that, one requires CSR.

The goal of a well-run company may be to make profits for its shareholders, but merely in doing that, the company is doing good works. Its employees willingly work for the company in exchange for wages; the transaction makes them better off. Its customers willingly pay for the company's products; the transaction makes them better off also. All the while, for strictly selfish reasons, well-run companies will strive for friendly long-term relations with employees, suppliers and customers. **5** ...... The standard of living people in the West enjoy today is due to little else but the selfish pursuit of profit. This is the very reason capitalism works.

Unfortunately, in the name of socially responsible conduct, some multinational firms have withdrawn from investments in developing countries where labour practices fall short of Western standards. **6** ...... It deprives people in the poor countries concerned, who would have benefited either from employment at higher wages or from the knock-on economic effects of inward investment.

All things considered, there is much to be said for leaving social and economic policy to governments. **7** ...... Lately managers have found it a struggle even to carry out their obligations to shareholders, the people who are paying their wages. If they want to make the world a better place, they should concentrate on that.

From *The Economist*

Vocabulary 1

Match the words and phrases from the article with their definition.

1 benefits
2 premise
3 discharge a debt
4 stakeholders
5 better off
6 strive for
7 fall short of
8 knock-on effects

a idea or theory on which a statement or action is based
b indirect results of other events or situations
c try very hard to make something happen
d people such as employees, customers or citizens who are involved with an organisation and therefore have an interest in its success
e richer
f things such as medical insurance that employees receive in addition to money
g fail to reach a desired standard
h pay a debt completely

Talking point

Discuss these questions in small groups.

1 Do you agree that …
- companies have a debt to society apart from paying taxes and obeying the law?
- by concentrating on making profits, companies are contributing enough to society?
- managers should concentrate on making profits rather than CSR?

2 What relationship do you think there is between CSR and corporate culture?

Vocabulary 2

1 Study these adverbs and adverbial phrases from the article, which are used to signal how the argument is being developed. Then answer the questions below.

all the while   all things considered
at least   merely   simply put
supposedly   thus   unfortunately

Which adverb / adverbial phrase …

1 is used to emphasise that something is good in a bad situation?
2 is used to emphasise that you mean exactly what you are saying and nothing more?
3 is used to indicate what should happen, but in fact does not?
4 means 'at the same time'?
5 means 'for this reason'?
6 means 'taking everything into account'?
7 says 'I'm going to express something complicated in an uncomplicated way'?
8 signals that the sentence which follows will express some bad effects of a situation?

2 Complete these sentences using an adverb/adverbial phrase from the box on page 101. (In some cases, more than one answer is possible.)

1 .... , capitalism is a system based on the private ownership of property and the pursuit of profit.
2 He seemed to be an excellent team worker, but we didn't realise that .... he was passing our company secrets to a competitor.
3 The government's job is to ensure that companies adhere to regulations. .... , there are too many companies which consistently try to evade their legal responsibilities.
4 Our financial results look remarkably healthy, ... I mean, with the economic downturn and rising energy costs, it's surprising we managed to break even.
5 The government is .... working for the benefit of its citizens, and not .... to keep itself in power!
6 .... our customers are happy, even if our employees complain!
7 We sold our factory in Hanover and .... we were able to reduce our losses.

Fair trade

Talking point 1

Discuss these questions in small groups.

FAIRTRADE Guarantees a better deal for Third World Producers ®

1 What does the logo on the right represent?
2 Which of these statements do you think companies should agree with?

> We always look for the highest quality at the lowest price from our suppliers.

> We like to work with our suppliers to improve the products they sell us.

> If a provider's quality slips, we'll give them one chance to improve, then we'll drop them.

> Our suppliers' economic situations interest us. Also, how much pay the farmers and workers receive and how they treat them.

> Our duty is to our customers – to give them the best deal possible.

3 What is 'fair trade' and how does it break with conventional business models?

Listening

You will hear an interview with Professor Bernard Hill on the subject of fair trade.

13 **1 Listen and take notes on the following.**

1 factors driving the growth of the fair-trade movement
2 benefits of fair trade for suppliers

13 **2 Listen again and choose the best answer, A, B or C, for these questions.**

1 How has the fair-trade movement benefited the Maraba region of Rwanda?
A Farmers get better prices from intermediaries.
B Farmers can raise money against future harvests.
C Farmers can buy equipment for schools.

2 Why, according to one large supermarket, have they started stocking fair-trade products?
   A to satisfy customer demand
   B to conform to corporate policy
   C to improve their image
3 What has been the fair-trade movement's most effective publicity tool?
   A advertising
   B word of mouth
   C television reports
4 What, according to Bernard Hill, is the main obstacle to the development of the fair-trade movement?
   A higher prices
   B lower quality
   C government policy
5 Why, according to Bernard, is it in the interests of the rich world to promote fair trade?
   A It involves consumers in aid programmes.
   B It will reduce conflict between rich and poor countries.
   C It promotes self-sufficiency in poor countries.

Talking point 2

Discuss these questions in pairs.

1 Are you prepared to pay extra for fair-trade products?
2 Why is it in the interests of big businesses to treat suppliers in poor countries well?
3 What is the connection between fair trade and CSR?

Grammar workshop

Articles

UNIT 21

Complete this text about the difficulties of engaging employees in ethics programmes by writing *a*, *an*, *the* or '–' (if you think no article is needed) in the gaps.

The effort of ethics

Critical to **1** ..a.. successful ethics programme is **2** .... leadership. It is surprising, then, to find only **3** .... quarter of chief executives consider themselves directly responsible for **4** .... ethical conduct of their companies. Another curious omission is **5** .... lack of relevant training for **6** .... staff, surely another obvious component to **7** .... effective implementation of **8** .... company's stated ethical policies.

9 '.......... companies find it surprisingly difficult to translate **10** .... standards in their codes into **11** .... case studies that **12** .... employees can take away and apply to their day to day existence,' argues Martin Le Jeune, head of corporate responsibility at communications firm Fishburn Hedges.

Despite **13** .... difficulties of engaging **14** .... employees in **15** .... ethics programmes, many companies continue to believe that **16** .... employee discretion is **17** .... more effective long-term tool than **18** .... mandatory compliance.

From *The Guardian*

page 116 (Articles)

A proposal

Writing

1 Read the task below and work in small groups to discuss these questions.

1 Who will read the proposal?
2 What style would be appropriate and why?
3 What details could you include/invent?

> Your manager has asked you to investigate CSR and in general how your company can generate a more ethical image. Write a proposal in which you:
>
> - suggest some ways in which your company can operate ethically (you can consider employment policies, environmental policies, treatment of suppliers and customers)
> - give reasons for a more ethical policy
> - recommend a plan of action.

2 Work alone and write the proposal in about 250 words. You can invent the details and you can invent the company. See Unit 7 for how to write proposals.

UNIT 22

Expanding abroad

Getting started

Discuss these questions in small groups.

1 Why, increasingly, do companies have to expand into foreign markets?
2 What are the advantages and disadvantages of each of the following methods of breaking into a foreign market?
- using a local agent or distributor
- starting a joint venture with a local company
- acquiring or taking over a local company
- marketing directly yourself without a local collaborator

3 How does the company you work for (or a company you know well) sell its products abroad?

Wolseley's strategy

Reading

You will read about Wolseley PLC, an international company which pursues a vigorous strategy of international expansion.

Company background **WOLSELEY**

Wolseley PLC operates in 14 countries in Europe and North America, employing over 67,000 people. Wolseley is the world's number one distributor of heating and plumbing products to the professional market and a leading supplier of building materials in the USA, the UK and Europe.

1 Skim the webpage (ignoring the gaps at this stage) to find out:

1 how Wolseley expands (two ways)
2 how different aspects of their business drive their expansion.

When you have finished, compare what you have found out with a partner.

Our strategy

The strategic direction of Wolseley is **1** ...B... to its future success. Here are the main drivers in that overall strategy.

Growing through acquisition and organic growth

Our target is double-digit growth, year on year. We aim to achieve this through a combination of organic growth, including new branch openings and acquisitions. We continually **2** .... and evaluate possible acquisitions, **3** .... particular attention to evidence of a **4** .... financial position and the ability of the **5** .... company to grow.

Continuous improvement

Although we set the highest standards in **6** .... of sustained growth and profitability, we are

2 Choose the best word, A, B, C or D, to complete each gap in the text.

1	**A** main	**(B)** key	**C** chief	**D** prime
2	**A** follow	**B** monitor	**C** track	**D** trace
3	**A** placing	**B** drawing	**C** directing	**D** paying
4	**A** correct	**B** proper	**C** feasible	**D** sound
5	**A** objective	**B** aimed	**C** target	**D** focused
6	**A** terms	**B** ways	**C** means	**D** types
7	**A** chase	**B** search	**C** pursuit	**D** quest
8	**A** line	**B** link	**C** sequence	**D** chain
9	**A** finding	**B** locating	**C** sourcing	**D** procuring
10	**A** reliable	**B** faithful	**C** trustworthy	**D** sure
11	**A** field	**B** location	**C** place	**D** ground
12	**A** promise	**B** commitment	**C** undertaking	**D** dedication

Vocabulary

Find words and phrases in the text which mean the following.

1 buying new companies
2 continuing for a long time

never complacent. The **7** .... of double-digit growth demands continuous improvement from all Wolseley businesses.

Leveraging our international position

With almost 4,000 branches in 14 countries, we have access to a tremendous pool of experience and expertise that we are increasingly leveraging in order to share benefits across the business. We plan to develop a diverse footprint through an international supply **8** .... , the establishment of synergies across our European businesses, increased global **9** .... and international purchasing.

Enhancing our business diversity

Construction, plumbing and heating professionals depend on Wolseley for the timely and **10** .... delivery of a vast range of products. We aim to increase their choice through a strategy of diversification: of geography; of lines of business; and of products and services.

Developing our human resources

We rely on people on the **11** .... to drive sales. We continue to expand our **12** .... to developing human resources, ensuring that we attract and retain the best and brightest people.

From http://www.Wolseley.com

3 so satisfied with our abilities or situation that we feel we do not need to try any harder
4 using, exploiting for our benefit
5 a varied or mixed presence or operation
6 the combined power of groups of things when they are working together which is greater than the total power achieved by each working separately

Talking point 1

1 Discuss this question in pairs.

What impression do you have of Wolseley from reading this webpage?

2 Review the vocabulary in the text and the exercises. Choose words and phrases you could use to describe the company you work for, or a company you know well. Describe the company to another student.

Listening

You will hear Richard Coates, the European finance director for Wolseley, talking about how and why Wolseley expands into new markets.

14 Listen and complete the notes below by writing up to three words in each space.

Wolseley:
- acquires people and companies **1** .... in sector they want to break into
- would avoid **2** ....
- speciality distribution, not **3** .... of products

Criteria for expansion:
- size of market
- its **4** ....

Criteria for buying companies:
- management's **5** ....
- quality of **6** ....
- speed of growth
- quality of **7** ....

Reasons for selling companies to Wolseley
- owners can **8** ....
- management can take advantage of **9** ....
- target companies gain know-how to expand in **10** ....

Talking point 2

Discuss these questions in small groups.

1 What do you think of Wolseley's expansion strategy?
2 Is this a strategy companies in your country use?
3 Do you think it is always a good strategy, or might it in some circumstances give rise to problems?

UNIT 22

Wolseley's Chief Executive

Reading

1 Before you read, work in small groups and discuss what qualities you would expect the CEO of a company like Wolseley to have.

2 Scan the article about Wolseley's Chief Executive, Charles Banks, to check your ideas.

Charles Banks's business is on a **non-stop expansion drive.** Its low-profile and mundane product range mask a **£6bn world-beater.**

i Banks has headed Wolseley, the British firm that has become the world's biggest plumbing-products distribution business, for four years. In that time, sales and profits have surged, and the share price – nearing £10 last week – has doubled, giving the company a market value of almost £6 billion. **1** ..G.. In fact, it owns the Plumb Center and Build Center chains in Britain, and similar operations in America and continental Europe, with a huge trade customer base. But previous bosses, while building Wolseley into a FTSE 100 world-beater, had decided that a low profile for the group was the smart approach.

ii 'I was told, "Charlie, if you stick your head up, people will want to shoot it off",' says Banks. '**2** ......' And the answer is: pretty good, at the moment. Sales topped £10 billion last year, and double-digit growth is promised by Banks for this year, as for every year since he took over. That is achieved through a mix of continual acquisitions – another four, costing £41m, announced last week – and organic expansion. **3** ......

iii Last month, Wolseley, which does two-thirds of its business in America, emerged in the top ten of Britain's most admired companies in a survey by *Management Today* magazine, and many now rate Banks among the most successful American bosses over here. **4** ...... Co-workers describe him as a hard-driving boss who has pushed his way up from the bottom and prides himself on his inquisitiveness, competitiveness and straight talking. There's an old-fashioned quality to his leadership, too: no computer on his desk, a reliance on one-to-one briefings.

iv Previously boss of Ferguson, Wolseley's American plumbing-supplies arm, he arrived here four years ago with a clutch of ideas on how he wanted to make the size of the group pay off, and practical experience of what annoyed him about reporting to a foreign head office. 'I didn't think we were creating enough value for the companies that were part of Wolseley,' he says. 'There had to be some value in putting it all together. **5** ......'

v Previous bosses had pulled Wolseley away from manufacturing so it could concentrate on distribution – getting plumbing and heating products and building materials to its trade customers, both big and small, at the right prices. **6** ...... And he has not stopped. 'Part of the key to our growth is that we have to do acquisitions, as that is the foundation for future organic growth, and it allows us to broaden our customer base, our geography and our products.'

From *The Sunday Times*

3 Choose a sentence (A–G) to complete each gap. There is one extra sentence you will not need.

A And the business world is beginning to take notice.
B Banks improved efficiency and started buying bolt-on acquisitions.
C But we have thousands of investors and we have an obligation to let them know how we are doing.
D His main objective is to make Wolseley a global distribution business.
E He brings an interesting mix of qualities to Wolseley.
F There was lots of talent here, creative ideas and buying power, but how do you go about it?
G Yet many outside the building trade have no idea what Wolseley does.

Vocabulary

Find words or phrases in the text which mean the following.

1 increased suddenly and greatly (paragraph i)
2 average of the prices of the stocks of the 100 largest companies on the London Stock Exchange (paragraph i)
3 exceeded (paragraph ii)
4 making other people work hard (paragraph iii)
5 meetings where information and instructions are given (paragraph iii)
6 group (paragraph iv)
7 produce success (paragraph iv)
8 acquire a wider range of customers (paragraph v)

Supervising overseas subsidiaries

Talking point

Discuss these questions in small groups.

1 What can parent companies do to supervise their subsidiaries?
2 How can they communicate their corporate culture to their subsidiaries?
3 In marketing, what advantages do local brands have over global or international brands?
4 What advantages do companies have when they expand or go global?

Listening

You will hear Richard Coates talking about the points you discussed above.

15 **1 Listen and take your own notes about what he says.**

2 Work in pairs and, from memory, complete these notes with up to three words in each gap.

Supervision of local managers
- meetings to 1 .... and evaluate performance
- managers submit monthly reports on 2 .... of business and operations

Implantation of company culture
- communicated to local managers by 3 ....
- meetings of European managers at 4 ....
- developed by recruitment through a 5 ....
- employees at 6 .... are moved to different posts across Europe

Promotion
- newly acquired businesses promoted through:
  – 7 .... (while keeping local brands)
  – marketing campaigns to raise 8 .... and create demand

Staying national or going multinational?
- staying national a possibility for 9 ....
- advantages of going multinational: 10 .... leading to lower costs
- Wolseley's success due to concentration on 11 .... rather than price

15 **3 Check your notes by listening again.**

Vocabulary

1 Put these adjectives/adverbs in order from the most frequent to the least frequent.

annual(ly) biannual(ly) daily every half hour every two months fortnightly hourly monthly quarterly twice weekly

2 Complete these sentences using the words and phrases from the box in Exercise 1.

1 We hold .... team meetings – on Mondays and Thursdays.
2 The .... sales conference always takes place in February.
3 The airport bus leaves .... – at ten to and twenty past.
4 Have you seen the .... sales figures? The January–March ones are particularly disappointing.
5 The trade journal comes out .... on the 1st and 15th of every month, which means I often don't have time to read it all.

Speaking

1 Your company is thinking of buying a foreign company as a subsidiary. Your managing director has asked you to investigate the opportunity. Work in pairs and discuss these questions.

1 What are the advantages of buying a company in order to expand into a new market?
2 What activities are useful when trying to incorporate a new company into your company's culture?

2 Change partners and take turns to present your conclusions to each other. Each of you should speak for at least a minute.

UNIT 23

An overseas partnership

Getting started

1 Work in pairs and spend a few minutes preparing a short (two-minute) presentation on one of these topics.

1 The problems of expanding into a new market
2 Advice for foreign companies thinking of expanding into your local market

Think about the following points:

- language
- laws and regulations
- local tastes and customs
- local collaborators and competitors
- finance

Task tip

- For each point you make in your presentation, give reasons and examples.
- Make brief notes and decide who is going to say what in the presentation. When you speak, use your notes but look at your audience.

2 Change partners and work with someone who prepared the other topic. Take turns to give your presentations.

Finding an overseas partner

Listening

Magiczne Lustra SP ZO.O. is a small Polish company which produces components for scientific instruments. It is currently interested in expanding its export market.

Marion Armley is British and works part-time as a PA for Aniela Polanski, CEO of Magiczne Lustra. You will hear a message which Aniela left on Marion's voicemail.

- Write **1** .... to people on list made last Friday
- Use their names where poss. and write in a **2** ....
- Tell them about product and include **3** .... for last three years
- Give info about improved **4** .... and summarise future plans
- Say we are seeking distributor or **5** ....
- Inform them Aniela going on an **6** .... next month
- Where possible, will get agency to **7** .... into other European languages

16 **1 Listen and complete Marion's notes with up to three words in each gap.**

2 Work with a partner and decide the following.

- Who will read the letter and why the style should be formal
- How many paragraphs the letter should have and what each paragraph should contain

3 Work together and write a plan for the letter.

Reading

1 **Complete Marion's letter by writing one word in each space.**

2 **Compare the plan you made with the letter you have just read.**

Dear Mr Lee,

We are a specialist producer of top-quality reflective optical components for microscopes and 1 *other* scientific instruments based in Lublin, Poland. **2** .... you may have read in the trade press, just over a year ago we patented an improved version of an extremely compact mirror which is **3** .... of reflecting almost 100% of the light it receives. Sales of this mirror (in **4** .... original form) to our customers in Europe and the US have risen from US $1m two years ago to just **5** .... US $4.5m last year.

6 .... to our excellent sales projections, based on market research in Europe and America, we have increased our production capacity by 100% and are now also **7** .... a position to begin supplying other markets with our products. Our plans, therefore, include an Asian presence, and **8** .... that objective in mind, we are seeking a distributor, **9** .... possibly a joint-venture partner in your country. Other products which we have in the pipeline and **10** .... we should be launching within the coming year include a refraction-free liquid lens for microscopes and a self-cleaning eye-piece suitable **11** .... a wide range of optical instruments.

Aniela Polanski, Magiczne Lustra's CEO, **12** .... be undertaking a tour of Asian countries next month, with a **13** .... to identifying possible sales partners, and would welcome the opportunity to meet with you to discuss our plans and demonstrate our products. Please **14** .... me know if this possibility would interest you and what dates would be the **15** .... convenient for you.

We look forward to hearing from you.

Yours sincerely,

Marion Armley

Marion Armley
PA to Aniela Polanski

UNIT 23

Grammar workshop

Complex sentences

1 **Find phrases in the letter which mean the following.**

1 situated in
2 it's possible you've seen this in specialist journals
3 the way it was designed at first
4 because of our favourable sales forecasts
5 can now also start
6 planning to achieve that aim or purpose
7 being developed
8 with the intention of

2 **Rewrite these sentences using the words in brackets.**

1 We are a large chemical company and our main offices are situated in Bahrain. (*based*)
We are a large chemical company based in Bahrain.
2 We are thinking of moving our offices to Abu Dhabi, and it's possible you heard this on the news. (*as*)
3 This book sold very successfully in the USA and Canada in the way it was designed at first. (*form*)
4 We are launching an updated version of this product because we have made some technological innovations. (*due*)
5 Our training budget has been approved, so we can now run the course. (*position*)
6 We are hoping to increase our sales in India, and, in order to achieve that purpose, we are launching a multi-million-rupee advertising campaign. (*mind*)
7 We have various new products being developed at the moment. (*pipeline*)
8 We shall be launching a new publicity campaign in order to increase our share of the North American market. (*view*)

A trade sales letter

Writing

1 **Work in pairs. Read this task and answer the questions below.**

Your company has a new product/service which is doing well in your existing markets. You are now planning to launch it in a new market and will have a stand at a trade fair for this purpose. Your manager has asked you to write a letter to prospective customers:

- giving them details of the new product/service
- describing its success in existing markets
- explaining your future plans for it
- inviting them to visit the stand and meet the marketing manager.

1 Who will read the letter and what style would be appropriate for these readers?
2 What points *must* you deal with in the letter?
3 What details will you have to invent in order to complete this task?

2 **Work alone and write the letter. Write about 250 words.**

23 UNIT

Going into new markets

Listening

You will hear five managers talking about their reasons for moving into new markets and the problems they expect will arise.

1 Before you listen, work in pairs and do the following.

1 Decide which words in the box below you might hear with each of the reasons on the right (A–H).
2 Write two words or phrases you think you might hear with each of the problems on the right (I–P).
3 Compare your ideas with the rest of the class.

> affluence   an approach   cut costs
> a gap in the market   global ambitions
> go into a whole new area   keep to targets
> meet targets   move a lot of product
> move upmarket   an opening
> spending power   spread risks
> undercut the competition
> write to accept   wage a price war

Reasons

A to achieve a corporate objective
B to achieve economies of scale
C to reach richer customers
D to confront their competitors
E to expand their sales areas
F to respond to an invitation
G to maintain sales levels
H to take advantage of an opportunity

Problems

I We'll face strong competition from local firms.
J We'll find it difficult to communicate with local managers.
K We'll find it difficult to recruit high-calibre personnel.
L We'll have to adapt to local working methods.
M We'll have to change the packaging of our products.
N We'll have to make a large capital outlay.
O We'll need a different advertising message.
P We'll need help from a local firm.

17 **2 Listen and, for each speaker, decide which reason and which problem they mention.**

Speaker	Reason	Problem
1		
2		
3		
4		
5		

Grammar workshop

Tenses in future time clauses

1 Put the verbs in brackets into the correct tenses. (All the sentences come from the Listening activity, but some have other possible answers.)

1 … when we .... (*get*) the whole operation going, we'll have taken one step further in satisfying the company's ambition of becoming a global presence.
2 And once the operation really .... (*get*) off the ground, there'll be plenty of profits for us there.
3 I'll show you one as soon as he .... (*send*) me a sample.
4 … when we .... (*sell*) our products there, we'll have to take account of the local culture.

17 **2 Check your answers by listening again.**

➔ **page 117** (Future time clauses)

Replying to Magiczne Lustra's approach

Speaking

Read Marion Armley's letter again (page 109) and discuss these questions in small groups.

1 Which of the points (a–j) on the right would it be appropriate to include if you were replying to Marion's letter?
2 Put the points you want to include in the order you would include them in the letter.

a details of who your other suppliers are
b a reference to Marion's letter and the date of the letter
c a summary of your company's activities
d an offer to arrange her accommodation during her visit
e how successful your company is
f that you would like a meeting with Aniela
g the purpose of Marion's original letter
h what type of working arrangement you think might be suitable
i when you could meet her
j who your main clients are

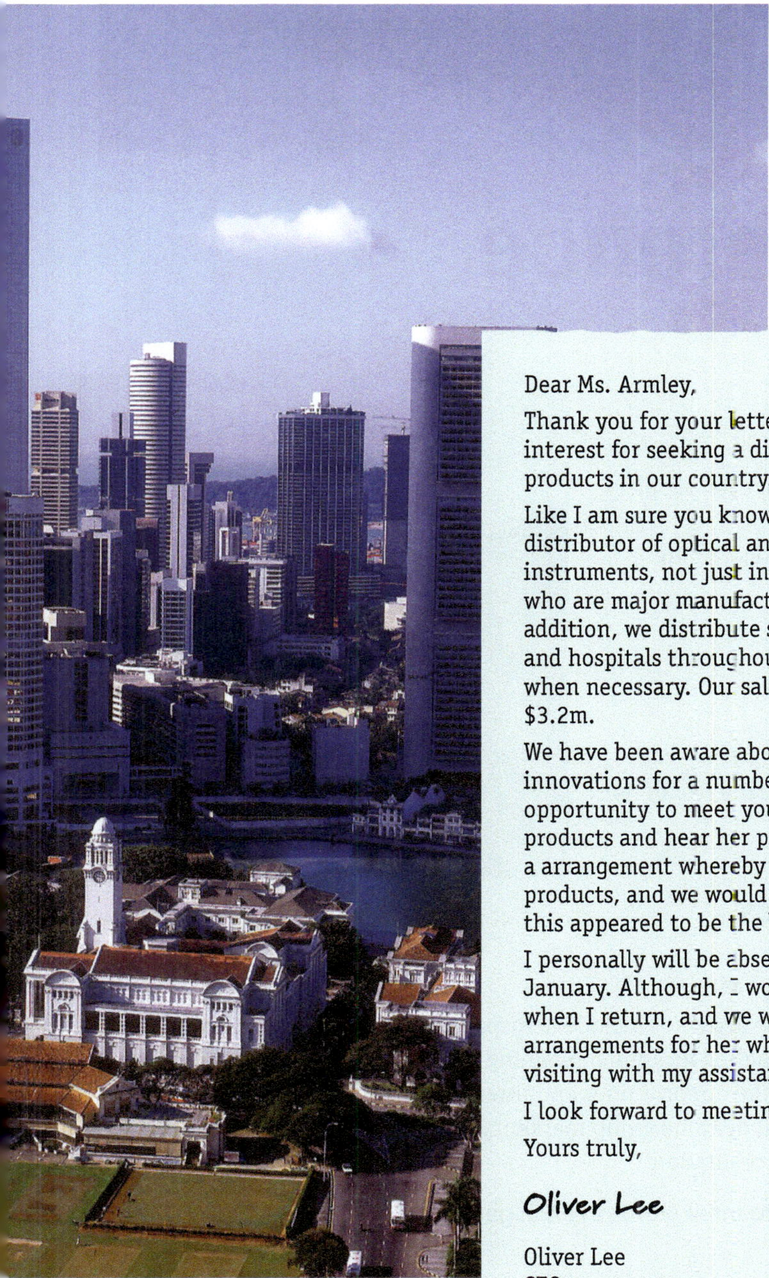

Singapore

Reading

1 Read the letter below. In what order does Oliver Lee mention the points a–j on page 110? (He does not mention all the points.)

2 In most lines, there is one wrong word. Delete the wrong word and write the correct word in the space provided. Some lines are correct. If the line is correct, put a tick (✔).

Dear Ms. Armley,

Thank you for your letter of December 8th in ~~that~~ you mention your 1 *which*
interest for seeking a distributor or joint-venture partner to market your 2 ....
products in our country.

Like I am sure you know, Singapore Instruments are the leading local 3 ....
distributor of optical and electronic components for scientific 4 ....
instruments, not just in this country but too in the region, for clients 5 ....
who are major manufacturers of scientific and medical apparatus. For 6 ....
addition, we distribute scientific and medical apparatus to universities 7 ....
and hospitals throughout the region, together with replacement pieces 8 ....
when necessary. Our sales in this sector last year are in the order of 9 ....
$3.2m.

We have been aware about your company and its ground-breaking 10 ....
innovations for a number of years now and could welcome the 11 ....
opportunity to meet your CEO, Aniela Polanski, seeing samples of your 12 ....
products and hear her proposals. We would certainly be interested in 13 ....
a arrangement whereby we acted as exclusive distributors of your 14 ....
products, and we would also consider the possible of a joint venture if 15 ....
this appeared to be the best way to proceed. 16 ....

I personally will be absence from the office during the first week of 17 ....
January. Although, I would be most interested to meet Ms. Polanski 18 ....
when I return, and we would be delighted to do the necessary 19 ....
arrangements for her while she is here. Please finalise the details of her 20 ....
visiting with my assistant, Miss Cheung. 21 ....

I look forward to meeting Ms. Polanski.

Yours truly,

Oliver Lee

Oliver Lee
CEO

Writing

1 Work in pairs. Read the writing task on the right and discuss what details you could include in your letter.

2 Work alone and write the letter. Write about 250 words.

An important foreign associate has written suggesting a visit to your company in the near future with a view to discussing a new business project which your companies could undertake together. Your manager has asked you to write a letter to him/her:

- welcoming the visit and expressing interest in the project
- summarising your company's activities and its performance
- suggesting how your companies could cooperate on the project
- proposing a convenient time for the visit.

UNIT 24

A planning conference

Getting started

Discuss these questions in small groups.

1 Which of the following do you think are good pieces of advice for people giving short business presentations?
- Avoid using PowerPoint or other visual aids, as they are distracting.
- It's all right to give your presentation sitting down.
- Make eye contact with your audience.
- Make two or three important points and repeat them.
- Rehearse your presentation in advance.
- Speak quickly and say as much as possible in the time.
- Start with a joke.

2 Write two or three other pieces of advice. Then read them to the rest of the class and see if they agree.

Making presentations to colleagues

Listening

Ascendor, a large multinational company whose activities include aerospace, electronics, consumer products, financial services and insurance, is holding its annual planning conference, where staff from different divisions and departments talk about the opportunities and threats facing the company and discuss solutions to various challenges. You will hear the group marketing director, Fedor Brodsky, giving a presentation on 'How to protect your brand's reputation'.

18 **1 Listen and complete these notes with up to three words in each gap.**

Brand reputations

Brands' reputations built by **1** .... and destroyed by **2** ....

Brands must be protected by
- continually meeting **3** ....
- strict quality control, where quality not affected by **4** ....
- ethical corporate behaviour, e.g. by not **5** .... , not outsourcing to companies which **6** .... , ignore safety rules, etc.

Best achieved in companies which are **7** .... , i.e. the health of brand the **8** ....

2 Study the transcript for track 18 and discuss in pairs whether these statements are true or false.

The speaker ...

1 makes a brief introduction.
2 makes a joke.
3 says how many points he is going to make.
4 illustrates all his points with an example.
5 says which point he is making before making it.
6 gives reasons for everything he says.
7 includes statistics where appropriate.
8 finishes with a brief conclusion.

3 Find phrases in the transcript which have a similar meaning to these phrases.

1 The subject of my talk today is …
2 I'd like to start off by saying that …
3 I'd like to make three main points …
4 The first one is that …
5 My third and final point is …
6 To conclude, …

For other useful language for presentations, see Unit 8 (**page 41**).

Grammar workshop

Concession

- *Although / Even though / Even if* + subject + verb
  Although they spent *millions on advertising, the brand never took off.*
  She wasn't interested in the job, ***even though the money was*** *good.*
- *In spite of / Despite* + noun / noun phrase / verb + *-ing*
  Despite his producing proof of his identity*, she refused to give him details of his bank balance.*
- *However / No matter how* + adjective/adverb
  However hard *I work, I never manage to reduce my inbox.*
  However safe *the investment seems, don't risk all your money on it.*
  No matter how expensive *it is, we need that machine.*
- *Whatever* + noun
  Whatever the risks*, we are determined to implement the proposals.*
- *Whatever / No matter what* + subject + verb
  Whatever you do*, don't press the red button.*
  No matter what the risks are*, we are determined to implement the proposals.*

Rewrite these extracts from the presentation, starting with the words given.

1 … however good a brand reputation is, it can be ruined overnight by critical media coverage …
Even if a brand …has a good reputation, it can be ruined overnight by critical media coverage.…
2 Despite pressures from shareholders, the customer comes first in any business …
Although there may …
3 … although your finance department may want to implement cost-cutting exercises, brand quality should never be compromised.
Despite your finance department …
4 … people will just stop buying them, even though you spend millions on advertising.
People will just stop buying them, however many …
5 … whatever you do in whatever area of corporate activity, you should first consider whether this could affect the health of the brand …
No matter …

page 117 (Concession)

Speaking

1 Work alone. Choose one of these presentation topics and prepare a short talk (with a brief introduction, two or three points and a brief conclusion). If possible, give examples from the place where you work or describe how your company deals with these things.

Ascendor PLANNING CONFERENCE

PRESENTATIONS AGENDA

1 **Staff management:** How to optimise the performance of your staff.
2 **Corporate Social Responsibility:** Companies' responsibilities to the community.
3 **Customer relations:** How to maintain customer loyalty.
4 **Marketing:** The factors involved in deciding how to price products and services.
5 **Advertising:** How to choose the most effective advertising medium for your products.
6 **Sales:** Methods of motivating sales staff.
7 **Finance:** How to ensure a healthy cashflow.
8 **Exporting:** How to identify potential new markets.

2 Work in groups of five or six. Take turns to give your presentations. While you are listening to your colleagues' presentations, think of a question you can ask about it at the end. Follow up each presentation with a question-and-answer session.

Risk management

Talking point 1

At the planning conference, you have been asked to discuss various eventualities using your previous experience.

Work in groups of three or four and discuss this question.

Which of these risks does a company you know well, or a company you have worked for, face? How could they affect the business?

- industrial accidents
- negative publicity
- innovations by competitors
- changes in the world economic situation
- mistakes made by people in the company
- hacking and industrial espionage
- others (please specify)

Useful language

An industrial accident such as a(n) ... is a risk because it could ...
We are not at much risk from competitors' innovations because ...
The chances of ... affecting our business are high/low/remote because ...
One/Another thing which could damage our business is ...

Reading

1 Work in pairs. Look at these statements and decide which ones you agree with and which you disagree with. Give your reasons.

1 'Businesses face many more risks now than in the past.'
2 'Damage to a rival's reputation can also damage yours.'
3 'Damage to the company's image is one of the biggest risks.'
4 'It is important to have contingency plans in place for the various risks a business faces.'
5 'Preparing for risks can be costly and the cost may appear unjustified.'
6 'Risk management is more complex than other management issues.'
7 'It is much easier nowadays to discover damaging information about companies.'
8 'One area of risk concerns businesses you employ to do part of your work.'

2 Work alone. Read the five extracts from articles about risk management. Match the statements in Exercise 1 with the extracts. Some extracts match more than one statement.

A

Managing risk is one of the things that bosses are paid for. Yet risk is trickier to handle than mergers or product launches. It does not lend itself to forecasts or plans, but requires managers to look at a range of possible outcomes. Most people who run companies would be more comfortable with a single figure to aim for, even if in the end it turns out to be wrong. Financial tools such as derivatives have enabled them to trade away many risks, but there are plenty left that are simply part of doing business.

B

Darrell Rigby of Bain, a management consultancy, explains that managers now have to be prepared for a range of risks that were unthinkable not long ago. Global supply chains expose them to potential calamities, not only in their home country but all over the world. These disasters can range from forest fires in California to dock strikes, power cuts, Internet attacks and even top managers' hands in the till. The traditional advice to managers is simple: identify your risks. Be prepared for each of them individually, and for the possibility of many of them occurring at the same time. Monitor and track your risks as you go along. And when something untoward happens, make sure you move quickly to deal with it.

C

One reason why risk management is difficult to grasp is that it is, by its nature, defensive. In the late 1990s, companies spent millions on updating their computer systems to guard against the Y2K bug that was expected to create havoc on January 1st 2000. When nothing dreadful happened on the day, many felt duped. Managing risks can seem a waste of time and money – until something goes seriously wrong.

D

If a company suffers a blow to its reputation, it can collapse with astonishing speed. Arthur Andersen's clients deserted it long before the accounting firm had its day in court. When Putnam Investments, a mutual-fund company, came under scrutiny by Eliot Spitzer, New York State's attorney-general, its clients began to pull their money out of its funds literally overnight. Even if a company survives damage to its reputation, the loss of business can be devastating.

E

Companies have also become much more concerned about other reputation makers and breakers: the government, the public and the media, and, increasingly, the Internet, which has greatly improved transparency. Corporate secrets are becoming ever harder to keep. Businesses are now finding that, perhaps unfairly, they are being judged by the company they keep. As they rely more on outsourcing, they may be held responsible for the sins of their subcontractors. Wal-Mart, a giant American retailer, was recently sued by the government for illegally using foreign workers to clean its floors. They were working for a subcontractor without Wal-Mart's knowledge, but the company still got a bad press. More unfairly still, the misdeeds of one company can tarnish all its competitors as well.

From *The Economist*

Listening

You will hear Nicole Frère talking about risk in business.

19 **1 Listen and note down what factors she says have increased the risks businesses face these days and what factors have reduced the risks.**

19 **2 Listen again and check your understanding of the main points by choosing the best answer, A, B or C, to each question.**

1 According to Nicole, in what ways is the world riskier for business?
  A There are more natural disasters.
  B Businesses are more globalised.
  C News reports are more likely to alarm markets.

2 What has made doing business safer?
  A It's easier to quantify risks.
  B It's easier to spread risks.
  C The workplace has become safer.

3 What is the main obstruction to effectively dealing with risks?
  A Decision-makers do not have an accurate view of the risks they face.
  B Investors are increasingly risk-averse.
  C People tend to be slow to react to new situations.

4 What does Nicole say about computer models?
  A They cannot cope with the unexpected.
  B They tend to be inaccurate.
  C Business people are unwilling to trust them completely.

5 Why, according to Nicole, should business people accept a certain level of risk?
  A It creates profit.
  B It makes business more interesting.
  C It is unavoidable.

Talking point 2

In the third part of Ascendor's planning conference, you have been asked to work in groups and discuss different possible risks and scenarios which could affect the company.

1 Work in pairs or groups of three. Choose one of the scenarios below and brainstorm vocabulary connected with the topic.

2 Discuss the problem for three or four minutes.

3 When you have finished, report your conclusions to the whole class.

Staff retention

A number of key staff have left your company in recent months. You have been asked to recommend things the company can do to keep staff.

Discuss and decide:

- how losing staff can damage a company
- what makes an organisation an attractive place to work in
- what conditions your company can offer to keep staff.

Market share

A competitor has been waging an expensive advertising campaign in order to capture part of your market share. Your manager has asked for suggestions about how to deal with this threat.

Discuss and decide:

- why market share is an important measure of a company's success
- how the company should react to this challenge.

Grammar workshop 6

Articles

The definite article

- *The* is used:
  - with things we have mentioned before or when it's clear who/what we are referring to from the context
    We've found a new supplier. ***The*** *supplier is based in Malaysia.*
    Could you take these packets to ***the*** *post office, please?* (i.e. the post office near here)
  - with things which are unique
    the *Internet,* ***the*** *global economy*
  - when the noun is followed by *of*
    the *price of coffee*
  - when the noun is followed by a defining relative clause
    The profits we've made *have all been reinvested.*
  - with adjectives to express groups
    the *unemployed,* ***the*** *rich,* ***the*** *French*
  - with superlatives
    the *best,* ***the*** *longest*
  - with names of some countries
    the *United States,* ***the*** *Czech Republic*
  - with names of rivers, mountain ranges and seas
    the *Nile,* ***the*** *Alps,* ***the*** *Mediterranean*
- Do not use *the*:
  - when talking in general and in the plural
    Coffee farmers *are struggling with low prices.*
  - when using abstract nouns
    Trade *between our two countries is increasing.*

The indefinite article

- *A* or *an* are used:
  - with singular, countable nouns
    a *company car,* ***an*** *independent financial adviser*
  - to express rates
    50 kilometres ***an*** *hour, $50,000* ***a*** *year*
- *A* or *an* are **not** used with plural or uncountable nouns
  Companies *try to make profits.* ***Money*** *is the basis of business.*
- *An* is used instead of *a*:
  - before vowels
    an *email*
    but not when *u* or *e* produces a *y* sound
    a u*nion,* ***a E****uropean manager*
  - when *h* is silent
    an *hour,* ***an*** *honest man*

Complete this text using *a*, *an*, *the* or '–' if you think no article should be written.

Nestlé launch of fair-trade coffee divides company's critics

Nestlé, **1** ..*the*.. world's largest and most ethically questioned food-and-drink company, yesterday launched **2** .... fair-trade-certified coffee brand in Britain. But **3** .... initiative divided **4** .... company's critics, some of whom congratulated it for encouraging **5** .... growth of **6** .... fair trade, while others said it was **7** .... cynical attempt to improve **8** .... company's global reputation.
Nestlé, which has a turnover of $67bn and buys 750,000 tonnes of **9** .... coffee beans **10** .... year, refused to say how much **11** .... fairly traded coffee it was expecting to sell under its new Partners' Blend label, but said it was serious about wanting to improve **12** .... conditions of **13** .... small farmers in Africa and Latin America.
'This represents **14** .... fundamental, serious commitment to help some of **15** .... poorest farmers in **16** .... world. We want **17** .... whole fair-trade market to grow,' **18** .... company spokeswoman said yesterday.
Nestlé said it was spending £1m promoting its new brand and **19** .... similar amount supporting **20** .... health and education projects for its new suppliers in Ethiopia and El Salvador.

Future time clauses

- In time clauses which refer to future time, use a present tense (after *when, while, as soon as, until, after, before* and *as*)
  *I shall retire **when I am** 60* (**not** *when I ~~will be~~ 60*).
  - Use the present simple in time clauses for things which will happen
    - at a particular moment in the future
      *We'll start the meeting **when she arrives**.*
    - for the same length of time as something else mentioned in the future
      *I'll type the report **while you do** the graphics.*
  - Use the present continuous for something
    - which will happen for longer than something else mentioned in the future
      *I expect we'll reach agreement **while we're having** coffee after lunch.*
    - in progress at a time in the future
      *We won't be able to entertain visitors **while we are refurbishing** the offices.*
- Use the present perfect for things which have finished before a time in the future
  *Our output should double **when we've built** the new factory.*
  Note: In sentences like this, the present simple is very often also possible
  *I won't tell you the contents of my report until I **finish / have finished** writing it.*

1 Put the verbs in brackets into the present simple, continuous or perfect in these sentences. (In some cases, more than one answer is possible.)

1 When I *finish/have finished* (*finish*) this course, I hope my job prospects will have been greatly improved.
2 I won't have time for a holiday while I .... (*work*) on this project.
3 We won't come to any firm decision until the market research .... (*be completed*).
4 Why don't you drop by our office while you .... (*visit*) Hong Kong?
5 I won't be able to finalise the sales forecast until I .... (*speak*) to all our sales managers.

2 Complete these sentences in any way you think suitable.

1 I'll be happier with my work when …
2 I won't stop studying English until …
3 I hope to make my first million before …
4 Next year, while …

Concession

You will find some ways of expressing concession in Unit 24, page 113. Here are others:

- *Although* and *though* are conjunctions and are used to join sentences. *Though* is more informal than *although*.
  ***Although** I don't believe our costs are lower, we still manage to undercut our competitors.*
  *We managed to recruit someone pretty good, **though** there weren't many applicants for the job.*
- *However, nevertheless* and *though* are adverbs (compare this use of *though* with the one above). *However* and *nevertheless* start a new sentence; they refer to the sentence immediately before. *Though* is used at the end of the second sentence.
  *We're able to undercut our competitors. **However**, I don't believe our costs are lower.*
  *Our sales this year have not been encouraging. **Nevertheless**, we think next year will be better.*
  *We managed to recruit someone pretty good. There weren't many applicants, **though**.*
  Compare the use of *however* here with its use on page 113.

Join these sentences using the words given in brackets.

1 Profits are up. Productivity is down. (*though*)
Profits are up, though productivity is down.
2 We won't be able to meet the deadline. We'll work very hard. (*however hard*)
3 You can pay him a high salary. He won't work harder. (*no matter how*)
4 He made a good keynote speech. The shareholders voted him off the board. (*despite his*)
5 Interest rates are falling. Consumer demand is not increasing. (*even though*)
6 He may ask you anything. Don't reveal our commercial plans. (*whatever*)
7 We run excellent psychometric tests. We never manage to recruit the ideal candidate. (*in spite of*)
8 We have a very small budget. However, the project will go ahead. (*however small*)
9 Our model won an innovation award. Sales never really took off. (*despite*)

Communication activities

Unit 12

Cold-calling

Role-play 1

Student A

Sales Manager for CSS Ltd

Your company supplies satellite tracking devices for vehicles and for packages. By means of these devices, companies can instantly locate company cars and delivery vans, as well as individual packages or containers. This enables companies to check where their employees are and what they are doing. It also helps to prevent theft of valuable consignments.

You have decided to cold-call TopPlant Repairs Ltd to see if your devices would suit them. You want to try to set up a meeting where you can make your sales pitch.

Making a sales pitch

Role-play 2

Student A

Sales Manager for CSS Ltd

Prepare your sales pitch. Use the information below to help you. You want to sell satellite tracking devices for vehicles and for packages.

These can be used for:

- locating company vehicles and employees
- checking that employees are doing the job assigned to them
- tracking packages and equipment
- preventing theft.

You know that TopPlant Repairs Ltd has problems with:

- theft of equipment
- supervision of maintenance staff.

Charges

There are fixed monthly charges for lease of equipment.

Unit 14

Sponsoring the arts

Role A

Marketing Team, Continental Bank

You are members of the marketing team of Continental Bank. You have been approached by London's Tate Modern gallery to sponsor a series of high-profile modern-art exhibitions over the next three years. You are going to meet the exhibition organisers to explore the possibilities.

Before the meeting, work together and:

- discuss what possible benefits and dangers there might be for a well-known bank to sponsor modern art
- prepare a list of questions and discussion points to talk over with the exhibition organisers connected with
  - types of exhibition
  - image
  - visitor numbers
  - finances
  - publicity opportunities for the bank
  - other co-sponsors (their image / are they competitors?)
- other perks the exhibition organisers can offer, e.g. private viewings.

Unit 16

Leasing office space

Landlords

You have an office block with 2,000m^2 of office space which has now been unoccupied for 18 months, so you are keen to lease it.

These are the points you have asked for in the leasing agreement:

- rent: €550 per m^2
- deposit: six months' rent in advance
- annual revision of rent in line with index of rental prices in Warsaw area
- length of leasing agreement: five years
- no change of commercial activity without your written permission
- leaseholder must pay cost of alterations and repairs to property
- terms of lease to be renegotiated after five years

There is also the possibility of leasing space to park 30 cars in basement of building.

Discuss these terms with your partner(s) before you start the negotiation and decide how important each of these terms is and how much you are prepared to move on each.

Unit 12

Cold-calling

Role-play 1

Student B

Operations Manager for TopPlant Repairs Ltd

You run a highly efficient and profitable operation and you employ a team of highly trained technicians. However, instead of phoning them and interrupting their work whenever you need them, you would like to be able to locate them at the touch of a button. Also, on a few occasions, valuable equipment belonging to clients has been stolen from your company's vehicles, and you would be interested in ways of preventing this. However, you have to chair an important meeting in five minutes, so you don't have time for a lengthy phone call.

Making a sales pitch

Role-play 2

Student B

Operations Manager for TopPlant Repairs Ltd

Prepare questions to ask the sales manager from CSS. You are interested in equipment which will allow you to:

- track vehicles and maintenance staff at all times without having to ring them
- track equipment belonging to your customers.

You have had problems in the past with:

- theft of customers' equipment
- maintenance staff who have not been working when they should have been.

You are interested in how the equipment works and how much it costs.

Unit 14

Sponsoring the arts

Role B

Exhibition Organisers, Tate Modern

You are organising a series of high-profile modern-art exhibitions at Tate Modern gallery, London, over the next three years. You have approached the Continental Bank, a large international bank, to invite them to sponsor the exhibitions.

Before the meeting, work together and decide:

- the type of exhibitions, the amount of money you require from sponsorship, what other revenue you expect (from entrance fees, government grants, etc.) visitor numbers, etc.
- how the exhibitions will enhance the bank's image and contribute to their marketing effort
- what opportunities you can offer the bank for publicity, e.g. logo on the exhibition guides, a room of the gallery named after the bank, etc.
- other perks you can offer the bank, e.g. private viewings, etc.

Unit 16

Leasing office space

Leasers

You work for a large insurance company which wants to open an office in central Warsaw. At present, you need approximately 1,400 m^2 of office space, but you are expecting to expand and would be prepared to lease more.

The office block you have seen is in an ideal location but:

- the rent being asked is high – you have had other quotes for €450–€500 per m^2
- you would like to pay a deposit of two months' rent in advance
- you are prepared to pay rent increases in line with inflation based on the retail price index
- you would like the leasing agreement to be for ten years minimum
- you will need to make fairly extensive alterations to the property and you think some of the costs should be met by the landlord, since they will actually be improvements
- terms of the lease cannot be altered without both parties' agreement.

You understand there is the possibility of leasing parking space, and you would like to take this option if the price is right.

Discuss these terms with your partner(s) before you start the negotiation and decide how much you are prepared to move on each.

Unit 20

Horse-trading at Travelsafe Insurance

Group 1

Management

You should take about ten minutes to work together and discuss the following points.

- What are likely to be the staff's counter-demands to your offer (made in the listening activity)?
- What would be reasonable concessions to make during the negotiations? Prepare some fall-back positions.
- Which would probably be a more successful strategy in order to achieve your aims: incentives or coercion?

When you have finished your discussion, prepare your negotiating strategy.

Group 2

Staff representatives

Take ten minutes to complete the following three steps.

1 Read the counter-demands below, which you established at a staff meeting:
   - all 90 employees from Travelsafe Insurance should have the option of relocating if they wish.
   - incentives for relocation:
     - 8% increase in salary and promotion from current staff grade to next level.
     - £16,000 payment to cover cost of move + £1,000 for each family member who also relocates.
     - three weeks' paid leave at time of move.
   - guarantee that there will be no forced redundancy.
   - incentive to take voluntary redundancy: 3 months' gross salary in addition to employee's legal entitlement.

2 Discuss the following questions:
   - what would be reasonable compromises to reach between these demands and management's original offer (in the listening activity on page 97)?
   - what industrial action would it be reasonable to threaten in order to achieve your aims?

3 Prepare your negotiating strategy.

Exam skills and Exam practice

Contents

About BEC

Recognition of BEC is rapidly growing, as a number of companies are using the examination as a focus for in-company training courses. A list of companies that use the BEC examination for a variety of purposes including recruitment can be found on the BEC pages of the Cambridge ESOL website.

The BEC suite is linked to the five ALTE/Cambridge levels for language assessment, and the Council of Europe's Framework for Modern Languages.

BEC	Equivalent Main Suite Exam	ALTE Level	Council of Europe (CEF) Level
	Certificate of Proficiency in English (CPE)	Level 5	C2
BEC Higher	Certificate in Advanced English (CAE)	Level 4	C1
BEC Vantage	First Certificate in English (FCE)	Level 3	B2
BEC Preliminary	Preliminary English Test (PET)	Level 2	B1
	Key English Test (KET)	Level 1	A2

At all three levels, the 'business' aspect of this examination affects the vocabulary, the types of texts selected and the situations presented in the tasks. In addition, as in the Cambridge ESOL Main Suite exams, other skills, such as understanding the gist of text and guessing unfamiliar words in a listening situation are tested.

The table below shows the common characteristics at the different levels of BEC.

	BEC Preliminary	BEC Vantage	BEC Higher
Reading	• 7 parts/45 items	• 5 parts/45 items • 1 hour	• 6 parts/52 items • 1 hour
Writing	• 2 tasks • 1 hour 30 minutes • Reading *and* writing	• 2 tasks • 45 minutes	• 2 tasks • 1 hour 10 minutes
Listening	• 4 parts/30 items • about 40 minutes, including transfer time	• 3 parts/30 items • about 40 minutes, including transfer time	• 3 parts/30 items • about 40 minutes, including transfer time
Speaking	• 3 parts • 12 minutes • 2:2 format*	• 3 parts • 14 minutes • 2:2 format*	• 3 parts • 16 minutes • 2:2 format*

* two examiners, two candidates (2:3 format used for the last group in a session where necessary)

Reading Paper Part 1: Exam skills

Part 1 consists of:

- eight statements numbered 1–8, which appear before the reading texts
- five short texts lettered A–E on a related subject, or five paragraphs from the same text.

You must decide which statement refers to which extract.

You practised similar skills in Unit 5 (page 31).

In the exam, you should allow ten minutes to do this part. It tests your ability to:

- scan texts and identify relevant information
- locate information expressed in the numbered statements.

Suggested exam technique

1 Read the statements before the texts carefully first. This saves valuable time.
2 While reading the statements, underline key words or phrases. This helps you concentrate on their meaning.
3 Words in the statements are not repeated exactly in the texts, so think how they might be expressed in other words.
4 Read the texts carefully to locate the ideas in the statements.
5 Be strict about timing: take exactly ten minutes.

Exercises

1 Read these statements about business schools and underline the key idea(s) in each.

1 <u>Business schools</u> are partly <u>responsible</u> for <u>management's failure to evolve</u>.
2 Completing a business course is not so problematic as obtaining a place on the course.
3 During their courses, students' attitudes generally change in unintended ways.
4 Many business students are ill-equipped to take advantage of their courses.
5 Many courses do not teach the skills required for running businesses.
6 Students do not appear to benefit financially from obtaining business qualifications.

2 Work with a partner and use other words to explain the meaning of the statements in Exercise 1. This will help you imagine how the ideas might be expressed in the texts.

1 Management hasn't changed, and this is partly the fault of business schools.

3 Which text, A, B or C, does each statement in Exercise 1 (1–6) refer to?

A The most commercially wounding criticisms of business schools are those that appear to contradict the claim that an MBA enhances career prospects. There was uproar when, two years ago, Mr Pfeffer and Christina Fong argued in *Academy of Management Learning and Education* that there was little evidence that getting an MBA had much effect on a graduate's salary or career. 'Usually it just makes you a couple of years older than non-MBA peers,' one source told them. Of course, business schools may be important, mainly as a screening mechanism – their basic skill may be choosing students, not teaching them. Once in, and the vast bill paid, few are ever thrown out for failing their exams

B A different complaint is that business schools fail to teach their students the right things. The strongest advocate of this view is Henry Mintzberg, a professor at Canada's McGill University. In *Managers not MBAs*, a new book, he argues that conventional MBA courses offer 'specialised training in the functions of business, not general educating in the practice of management'. Their students are often too young and inexperienced to learn skills that, in any case, are often easier to acquire in the workplace than sitting in a classroom. Conventional MBA programmes, he complains, ignore the extent to which management is a craft, requiring zest and intuition rather than merely an ability to analyse data and invent strategies.

C Rakesh Khurana, of Harvard Business School, is writing a book on why management has failed to develop as a profession. He points out that other activities in which society prizes a sense of restraint, judgement and the pursuit of the common good, such as law, health care and religion, have evolved into professions. 'At the heart of professionalism is the renunciation of certain things,' claims Mr Khurana. Lots of business schools now offer courses on ethics, surely a key attribute of professionalism. Students are not always enthusiastic. In 2002, the Aspen Institute surveyed 2,000 MBA students and found that their values altered during the course. By the end, they cared less about customer needs and product quality and more about shareholder value.

To try a real exam task, go to page 124.

Reading Paper Part 1: Exam practice

Questions 1–8

- Look at the statements below and the five news reports about financial deals between companies.
- Which report (A, B, C, D or E) does each sentence 1–8 refer to?
- For each statement **1–8**, mark one letter (**A**, **B**, **C**, **D** or **E**) on your Answer Sheet.
- You will need to use some of the letters more than once.

Example:

0 The deal will allow the organisation to respond to the growing market for its products.

	A	B	C	D	E
0	☐	☐	☐	☐	■

1 This organisation has increased its share price by shedding one part of the company.

2 This organisation is in negotiation with possible buyers.

3 This organisation has no current plans to become multinational.

4 Companies with a vested interest in this organisation believe a takeover would benefit them.

5 This organisation's sales have undergone a significant downturn recently.

6 The purchase of shares in this organisation were not part of a takeover bid.

7 Although these organisations will combine certain operations, they will each keep their brand names.

8 The financial involvement of another organisation will not affect the way this organisation is run.

A The Optic Bank in Austria is open to buying another European bank if the price is right but such a move is not among its strategic priorities, according to its Chief Executive Martin Kale. 'Only if the sums are right and we can create value for our shareholders, will we do it,' Kale said in Saturday's edition of *The Investor*. The magazine said Kale had explained that the Optic Bank was really looking for organic growth domestically and therefore it had no plans to buy one of the larger listed banks. Kale said he thought it was very unlikely that his company would want to expand beyond national boundaries.

B UK technology group, Brinite, has become the second company to drop out of takeover talks with UK banking software firm BNS. However, an unnamed source has said BNS are still talking to more than one party. BNS's independent board of directors was believed to be holding out for an offer of around 145 pence to 160 pence a share in order to recuperate losses. Brinite's investment group, led by Mark Daly, is believed to be unwilling to offer more than 130 pence a share. Reports also claim that a consortium led by technology investor IPC Partners had already pulled out of the process. Suppliers are pushing for a decision in the hope that it will lead to increased sales.

C There have been attempts to allay UK fears over Credit of India's intentions towards DBD Technologies following the bank's acquisition of a 5% stake in the company. 'The 5% stake is not a sign of some sort of aggressive behaviour by the Indian side; it is a play on the share market and the Indian bank saw a favourable deal and took advantage of it.' DBD, which is 15% owned by the UK government, but controlled by British industrial interests, strongly defended its tightly held corporate structure last week after it was suggested that the Indian bank might seek greater control.

D Mak Kitchens has agreed to sell its retail operations to private equity group Triple Bond for a nominal one pound, sending its shares up over 12% on Friday. Mak said it would pay Triple Bond up to £74 million to take the retail division off its hands. Mak said it expected to incur a net loss of £65 million in the current financial year on disposal of the division. Mak's share price has fallen by around half over the past four years, as stiff competition and a slowdown in the UK housing market has meant a substantial reduction in its market share.

E Fulton Oils plans to buy a majority stake in one of South East Asia's top independent processing firms, the HD Group, which will make it number three in the world's second-largest market. It will quadruple Fulton's capacity and increase its global volume by 6%. This will mean it has a small amount of spare capacity for the next two years but will soon need to add additional plants to meet soaring demand for the refined product. Supply chains will be integrated, but the companies will continue to market Fulton's and HD's products separately, to help bolster growth in both premium markets where Fulton is strong, and the mainstream segment where HD has a larger presence.

Reading Paper Part 2: Exam skills

Part 2 consists of:

- one text of 450–500 words with seven gaps.
- eight sentences listed after the text.

You must fit the correct sentence in each gap.

The first gap is always done for you as an example using sentence **H**, and is numbered **0**, so:

- you will have six gaps to fill
- there is one extra sentence which you will not use.

You practised similar skills in Unit 1 (page 12) and Unit 10 (page 51).

In the exam, you should allow ten minutes to do this part. It tests your ability to:

- understand the global meaning of the text
- understand the organisation or sequence of information in the text
- relate sentences to the information which comes before and after them and to use the cohesive features in the text to help you fill the gaps.

Cohesive features

These are words or phrases in the text which relate to other parts of the text: for example, pronouns may refer to someone or something mentioned earlier in the text, adverbs such as *however* will refer to the previous sentence, etc.

Suggested exam techniques

1. Look at the sentence which was given in the example (H) and cross it off the list immediately.
2. Read the text carefully first. You should be able to follow a clear line of argument, even with the sentences missing.
3. Read the list of sentences carefully. As you are reading them, some answers may occur to you.
4. Read particularly the sentences before and after each gap. Does the sentence you want to put in the gap fit logically with them?
5. Underline the cohesive features. They provide useful clues.
6. Fill the gaps you find easiest first as this will reduce the choices for the gaps you find more difficult.
7. When you have finished, read the whole text again with your answers. Does it develop logically?

Examples

Especially when you are practising for the exam, it's a good idea to study the examples to see how the exam works. When you do the exam, you should read the sentence in the example to help you understand how the text develops.

Exercises

1 Underline the cohesive features in these sentences.

A <u>But</u> how do you measure the 'quality' of communication with workers or incentives for employees?

B For instance, under one heading, a British consumer-products firm whose managers' only meaningful performance target was volume (with no mention of quality or waste) scored 1.

C So, if poor management does not pay, why does it last?

D There is little evidence, though, that competition raises standards by forcing managers to work better.

E They ascribe some of the gaps to differences in the quality of capital equipment, or in the development and installation of new technology.

F Thus, even among competing neighbours, there was huge variation in management practices.

G A further reason appears to be connected with something economists call 'management culture'.

H In fact, the system is nothing like as ruthless as it is cracked up to be.

2 Choose the best sentence from Exercise 1 to fill each of the gaps in the article on page 126. There is one extra sentence you will not need.

Why do so many badly run companies survive?

To both its admirers and its enemies, the most awe-inspiring feature of capitalism is its ruthless efficiency. In theory, poorly performing firms are crushed and cast aside as fitter rivals come up with superior goods or cheaper methods of production. **0** ..H.. Plenty of suppliers fail to deliver goods on time. Many managers are hopeless at motivating their staff. And badly run firms survive, even in the same industry as state-of-the-art companies.

All of this has long had economists pondering two questions. First, why are there such wide differences in the productivity of competing companies? Second, why do these differences persist? **1** ...... But there has long been a suspicion that quite a lot of the discrepancy between fit and flabby firms has to do with the quality of management.

The difficulty lies in putting a number on it. If economists are to explain company performance in terms of management practices, these must somehow be quantified. **2** ...... An intriguing new study attempts to do just that, and goes on to examine why badly run firms survive.

The study is based on interviews with managers at more than 730 manufacturing companies in America, Britain, France and Germany. The answers were given a score between 1, the worst, and 5, the best, in each of 18 categories. **3** ...... A German industrial-goods firm that focused on market share and technological leadership (but did not make workers aware of these goals) scored 3. An American manufacturer that communicated financial targets by telling workers that they packed boxes until lunchtime to cover overheads and after that for profit scored a full 5.

The American companies came out on top, averaging 3.37, followed by the Germans (3.32), the French (3.13) and the British (3.08). However, in each country there was a wide range of scores: only 3% of the variation could be explained by the country of operation. One-fifth was accounted for by variation between industries. Three-quarters of it persisted among firms in the same country and industry. **4** ......

Differences in management practices do seem to matter. They account for 10–15% of the gap in total factor productivity between American and British firms. And higher management-practice scores correlated with higher returns on capital employed, sales per employee, sales growth and growth in market share. **5** ......

The study suggests three reasons. First is the degree of competition in an industry. In industries in which there are many rivals, management practices tend to be better. **6** ...... More important is the second explanatory factor: the age of companies. Competition works mainly by weeding out young, badly managed firms.

From *The Economist*

To try a real exam task, go to page 127.

Reading Paper Part 2: Exam practice

Questions 9–14

- Read this review of a business book about managing mistakes.
- Choose the best sentence from below to fill each of the gaps.
- For each gap **9–14**, mark one letter (**A–H**) on your Answer Sheet.
- Do not use any letter more than once.
- There is an example at the beginning, (**0**).

How to avoid the biggest mistakes

This book is about the avoidable traps that we set for ourselves as business people that lead to disasters. It is about what we can learn from the patterns of action or inaction that preceded disasters (sometimes called 'accidents') in a variety of business and non-business settings in order to avoid similar traps and patterns of mistakes.

This is not a book about crisis management. It is not about managing public relations, the victims, the lawyers, or the shareholders. (**0**) ..H... Even if you do not totally avoid such situations, knowledge of the typical patterns that occur should help you create an organisation that is observant enough to intervene early and minimise damage. (**9**) ...... But it could result in you never having to manage the aftermath of an unpleasant situation.

There are lessons to be learned from looking at the mistake patterns and commonalities in other organisations, especially since most organisations do not do a very good job of evaluating their own mistakes even though they have the most information. (**10**) ...... The reason we often fail to recognise what these can teach us is because we believe, 'Their situation was different – we don't have much to learn from them.'

The reality is very different because studies show that while the specifics may be different across industries and situations, the patterns of mistakes preceding accidents are quite similar. (**11**) ...... While these can teach you something, you can often learn more by looking at examples in an industry or situation that is markedly different from your own and recognising that there are great similarities in the patterns of actions and behaviours. (**12**) ...... You can therefore absent all the distracting details, and quickly see for yourself the problem, how it arose and the solution.

The mistakes identified are usually the result of direct action or inaction by humans. (**13**) ...... In other situations, the mistakes may have been in the design of systems or business procedures that were based on faulty assumptions. (**14**) ...... These initiating factors must be considered in decision-making when they are present because, although they are not always human in origin, they are a part of the chain of causes that leads to disasters where humans have an opportunity to intervene effectively or ineffectively.

Example

0	A	B	C	D	E	F	G	H
	☐	☐	☐	☐	☐	☐	☐	■

A Learning doesn't always come from the sources you expect, like your own experience, your own industry, or very similar companies.

B In many scenarios, the sequence was initiated with equipment malfunctions that were known but not taken into account in decision-making.

C Learning and implementing the lessons described here will not mean that you throw away your plans for handling problem situations.

D Learn from the mistakes of others and envision business success without mistakes, because your future may depend on your ability to do just that.

E Sometimes there were significant, uncontrollable initiating or contributing factors, such as equipment failure or a natural weather occurrence.

F We miss learning opportunities by not being curious enough to look deeply at our own failures, but we also miss a very rich set of opportunities when we do not look at the mistakes others have made, especially when they have been well documented.

G This is because without the burden of a set of assumptions around what you 'know' is the right or wrong way to do something, it is easier to observe the salient facts.

H Instead it is about discipline, culture, and learning from the experiences of others to improve the odds that you can avoid the things we label as accidents, disasters, or crises altogether.

Reading Paper Part 3: Exam skills

Part 3 consists of:

- one text of 500–600 words
- six multiple-choice questions where you must choose the best answer, **A, B, C** or **D**.

You practised similar skills in Unit 2 (page 15).

You should allow ten minutes for this part of the exam. It tests your ability to:

- read in detail
- interpret opinions and ideas expressed in the text rather than facts.

Skimming

Skimming consists of reading very fast to get a general idea of the meaning and contents of the whole text. This is an essential business skill: for example, you might get a long email marked 'urgent' just before you are going into an important meeting and you have to decide what action to take very quickly.

- When you see unfamiliar words or sentences you don't understand, do not spend time trying to understand them – continue reading.
- You should only work on difficult vocabulary or sentences if you think it will help you to answer a question.

Suggested exam technique

1. Skim the text first to get a quick, general idea of what it says. This way, when you read the questions, you will know roughly where to find the answers in the text.
2. Read the stem of the first question (the part before the alternatives A, B, C or D) and underline the key words.
3. Find where the question is dealt with in the text and read that part of the text carefully.
4. Then read the four alternatives and decide which matches the idea expressed.
5. Remember: the words of the text will not repeat the words of the question. You will have to find the same idea expressed in a different way.
6. Make sure there is evidence in the text to support your answer.
7. The answers to the questions come in the same order in the text, so when you have answered one question, move on to the next part of the text to answer the next question.
8. Be careful about time. If you take too long on this part, you won't have enough time for other parts.

Exercises

1 Skim the article 'Call centers' (it is about half the length of an exam text, so take a maximum of three minutes to do this), then say which paragraphs talk about:

1. problems for workers caused by customers
2. how workers' feelings may affect their work
3. which personalities are best for call-centre workers.

Call centers:
How to reduce burnout, increase efficiency

1 With an estimated 3% of the U.S. workforce employed in call centers, the emotional labor of dealing with customers can lead to employee burnout and high turnover rates, according to Steffanie Wilk, a Wharton management professor who has done extensive research on call centers. It's important, she said, to figure out ways to counter stressful situations so that employees "are not feeling overwhelmed by their work, so they are not building up more steam."

2 Nancy Rothbard, professor of management at Wharton, presented the results of research on workers' mood, performance, and burnout conducted by her and Wilk at a large property and casualty insurer. "When we think about call-center workers, one of the biggest challenges is remaining resilient to the anger and hostility that can come their way. That's the negative side," said Rothbard. "But what about the positive side? If a client is pleasant and cheerful, does that infuse you with energy in the way I found it does when a positive mood from home spills over?"

3 Earlier work, she added, shows an emotional spillover between home and work for employees. She suggested that problems at home do not necessarily lead to problems at work. "I found there was more evidence of enrichment – where positive emotions from home spilled over and caused people to be more engaged with work. Negative emotions also spilled over and caused people to be more engaged with their work. Employers fear spillover from home will cause workers to be disengaged, but people try to escape from a negative experience by throwing themselves into another role."

4 Preliminary results of the insurance-company call-center research show that workers' moods coming into the job surface throughout the day, Rothbard said. If workers arrived in a positive mood, they were likely to stay that way, and the same held true if they arrived in a bad mood. As for the contagion effect of customers, Rothbard said there is spillover, but more for positive interactions than for negative ones. "My guess is employees are skilled and able to segment that away from themselves, but they let in the positive if the customer is cheerful and happy … Perhaps it's a coping mechanism."

5 In focus groups, according to Wilk, call-center workers routinely say the hardest part of their job is that they know how to help the customer, but do not have the authority to take action, such as waiving a late fee. This forces the customer to get angry enough that he or she asks to speak to a person who has authority. "It's incredibly frustrating" for the initial call-center representative.

6 Malcolm McCulloch, senior research consultant at LIMRA International, suggested companies make a better effort to hire employees who will fit into the culture of their organization. McCulloch defined what he calls "person–organization fit" as the match between an individual's values and preferences and the characteristics of the work organization. He used the example of a claim center where accuracy and attention to detail are important. An individual who avoids risk and accepts supervision is likely to feel satisfied and comfortable in the job and develop a commitment to the organization. "On the other hand, a misfit at the claim center may have an entrepreneurial spirit. They're not going to be happy campers. They won't commit to the organization and they will soon leave."

To try a real exam task, go to page 130.

2 Answer the questions in six or seven minutes. Compare your answers with your partner, and highlight the evidence in the text which supports your choices.

1 According to Wilk, it is important to reduce stress in call centres so that staff:
   - A perform their job more efficiently.
   - B stay in the job for longer.
   - C treat customers more politely.
   - D make their organisation more profitable.

2 According to Rothbard, what is most likely to improve workers' feelings at work?
   - A awkward customers
   - B friendly customers
   - C a happy home atmosphere
   - D a friendly work atmosphere

3 How do difficulties at home affect workers' performance?
   - A They show more commitment to their work.
   - B They lose interest in their work.
   - C They transmit negative feelings to their customers.
   - D They start looking for another job.

4 According to Wilk, what is the main problem call-centre workers encounter in their job?
   - A difficulty speaking to their supervisors
   - B lack of empowerment
   - C not knowing how to help callers
   - D dealing with angry callers

5 Who does McCulloch say is more suited to working in a call centre?
   - A someone who likes to take the initiative
   - B someone who understands the aims of the organisation
   - C someone who wants to feel part of a larger team
   - D someone who does what their superior asks them to do

Reading Paper Part 3: Exam practice

Questions 15–20

- Read the following article about rewarding employees and the questions on the opposite page.
- For each question **15–20**, mark one letter (**A**, **B**, **C** or **D**) on your Answer Sheet, for the answer you choose.

We all have ideas about what employee rewards should be (more money, a bigger title, a bigger office) but how can managers provide meaningful incentives, and rewards, for star performers?

Management professor Anne Cummings recently spoke to an MBA student about an experience he had while working for an aircraft manufacturer. The student, then a full-time employee, had come up with an idea that over the long-term would save the company millions of dollars and also potentially save lives. For his effort he received a few stock options as a bonus. 'While this was some recognition from the company, the "reward" was, in fact, a big reason why he left the organisation,' says Cummings. 'He told me that what would have been more meaningful would have been an offer of more autonomy, or another project to work on, or to be given two incoming engineers to help him develop a new idea.'

Cummings' research looks at how managers can structure work so that creativity is both fostered and rewarded. 'I started looking at the models behind creativity, and at what managers can do to bring out employees' creative functions at work. We're all good at something, but we're not all good at everything,' she says. 'A manager's job is to identify those areas where their employees are most creative, most productive or most fulfilled, and then come up with ways to give them autonomy to pursue ideas in those fields. In the end, creativity leads to a better work environment. We are all more efficient and more productive when we are doing something we feel engaged by.'

As part of her research, Cummings has studied where truly innovative ideas in companies originate. 'Just because an idea is innovative doesn't mean it's good,' she says. 'It has to be useful, well thought out, grounded in a real context, and able to be implemented. But if there is a good plan going in, you reward that regardless of the financial outcome. You don't necessarily wait until you see a change in market share. During the process, you may choose to allot 40% of that person's time to the project rather than 20%, or to give him or her an additional person for the project team.'

Traditional companies need to offer a different culture if they are to prevent staff drifting to the more dynamic new dot.com companies, according to Cummings. It may be the opportunity to work for the company for a relatively long period of time during which the employee is supported, encouraged to grow and given the resources to try out new ideas. It may be life balance incentives, such as the opportunity to job share, to have flexi-time, to work offsite. It may also be age-related. 'Different incentives mean different things to a 27-year-old versus a 40-year-old,' Cummings says. 'The point here is that companies other than the "cutting edge" dot.coms can encourage and leverage employee creativity.'

Sometimes it's the little things that managers can alter that can improve work situations. For example, advantages may accrue from allowing employees to use personal stereo headsets on the job. Job productivity actually increases because employees can more easily shut out distractions and concentrate more fully on the project at hand. And when space is tight, Cummings suggests building in as much privacy as possible. 'Not everyone can have their own office but supervisors can arrange to have visible barriers set up, like partitions between desks. Both the sense of privacy and of being valued by one's supervisor can contribute positively to an employee's creative thinking.'

15 The story of the MBA student in the second paragraph illustrates that

A employees prefer company shares as a reward for coming up with new ideas.
B companies need to offer greater financial rewards to star employees.
C employees consider that rewards other than money can be more meaningful
D companies should recognise employees' contributions publicly.

16 Cummings claims one way a manager can help foster creativity is by

A understanding how individuals can perform at their best.
B correctly identifying which employees to support.
C demanding a more efficient work environment.
D allowing staff to work in different departments.

17 In the fourth paragraph, what does Cummings say companies should reward?

A projects which increase a company's market share
B the preparation and practicality behind a project
C the speed with which the project is completed
D the originality of a proposed project

18 What does Cummings say traditional companies need?

A a range of options which allow staff more free time
B a willingness to invest more in staff
C a broader approach to staff incentives
D an understanding of employees' domestic concerns

19 What is the purpose of the examples mentioned in paragraph six?

A Employees need privacy in order to work.
B Staff work better in quiet environments.
C Managers should be relaxed about office rules.
D Minor changes can improve employees' output.

20 What do you think would be the best title for this text?

A How Money Can Keep the Best Staff
B How to Develop Original Thinking in Employees
C Getting the Best out of your Staff
D Rewarding Innovation

Reading Paper Part 4: Exam skills

Part 4 consists of:

- one text of about 250 words
- ten multiple-choice gaps where you must choose the best word, **A, B, C** or **D**.

You practised similar skills in Unit 4 (page 23) and Unit 7 (page 37).

This part of the exam tests your knowledge of:

- vocabulary
- idiomatic expressions
- collocations
- dependent prepositions (e.g. *depend* ***on***)
- some grammatical structures which go with particular words (e.g. *make* + object + infinitive without *to*).

Collocations

Collocations are words that are often found together but which are not fixed expressions. Collocations may be:

- adjectives with nouns, e.g. *You will have to work to* ***tight deadlines****.*
- adverbs with verbs, e.g. *Prices have* ***risen sharply****.*
- verbs with nouns, e.g. *He was unable to* ***repay his debts****.*

Suggested exam technique

1 Before looking at the alternatives A, B, C and D, try to think which word will go in the gap.
2 The alternatives may have slightly different meanings: look for the word which best fits the context.
3 The alternatives may have similar meanings: look for a dependent preposition or a grammatical structure which only goes with one of the alternatives.
4 Look for possible collocations: do you *do, send, pass* or *provide* a service? (Answer: *provide*)
5 Does the gap seem to be part of a fixed expression? If so, can you remember it?
6 When you have finished, read the text again with your answers. Check and change anything which doesn't sound natural to you.

Extensive reading

Probably the best general preparation for this type of question is to read texts connected with business extensively – business books, articles from business magazines and websites, etc. This will build up the vocabulary knowledge needed to be able to deal with this part of the exam.

Exercises

1 Choose the best word for each of these gaps. In each case, the correct word is the only one which will go with the preposition. (Note that the preposition is not always just after the gap.)

Customer-service staff should make it their business to **1** .... to customer feedback immediately, especially when customers **2** .... to them about the quality of their product or service. Managers should **3** .... up guidelines so that all staff deal with these situations in roughly the same way.

1	**A** answer	**B** attend	**C** deal	**D** handle
2	**A** comment	**B** complain	**C** remark	**D** criticise
3	**A** write	**B** fill	**C** draw	**D** edit

2 Choose the best word for each of these gaps. In each case, the correct word will form a collocation.

Business people use quite a **1** .... variety of more or less reliable methods of making sales **2** .... The most popular way is to **3** .... figures based on reports from their sales **4** .... and to **5** .... these with computer extrapolations based on **6** .... years' results.

1	**A** vast	**B** different	**C** wide	**D** long
2	**A** forecasts	**B** previsions	**C** predictions	**D** expectations
3	**A** arrange	**B** collect	**C** add	**D** save
4	**A** group	**B** force	**C** workers	**D** resources
5	**A** combine	**B** join	**C** connect	**D** tie
6	**A** earlier	**B** past	**C** prior	**D** previous

3 Choose the best word for each of these gaps. In each case, the correct word will form part of an idiomatic expression.

Great leaders, we are told, are few and **1** .... between. But what makes that exceptional leader who **2** .... out from the crowd? Excellent interpersonal skills are one of the qualities, as is the ability to see the bigger **3** .... and provide a vision for their entire organisation.

1	**A** far	**B** long	**C** distant	**D** way
2	**A** steps	**B** picks	**C** makes	**D** stands
3	**A** view	**B** image	**C** picture	**D** panorama

To try a real exam task, go to page 133.

Reading Paper Part 4: Exam practice

Questions 21–30

- Read the article below about predicting the success of a product.
- Choose the best word from below to fill each gap.
- For each question **21–30**, mark one letter (**A**, **B**, **C** or **D**) on your Answer Sheet.
- There is an example at the beginning, (**0**).

How soon will your product sell?

Two Wharton researchers have developed a mathematical model that they say will (**0**) ..A.. companies, for the first time, to predict how fast new products will gain (**21**) ...... in markets where purchasing decisions by knowledgeable, influential customers influence the buying (**22**) ...... of others

Wharton marketing professor Christophe Van den Bulte and doctoral student Yogesh V. Joshi say their model can be put to use in industries as (**23**) ...... as movies, music, pharmaceuticals and high-technology. It is possible the model may also be a way to identify directors and actors who are ready to make the (**24**) ...... from small films to the Hollywood mainstream, they add.

According to Van den Bulte, chief marketing officers do not need to be maths experts to use the model. He and Joshi have developed a handy spreadsheet that (**25**) ..... a close approximation of the equations and does the (**26**) ...... for executives. Also, the model can easily be copied by employing SAS, a commercial software (**27**) ...... popular with market research analysts.

Companies wanting to understand how new products become popular are especially interested in markets that (**28**) ...... of two segments: 'influentials' (knowledgeable people who keep abreast of product (**29**) ...... and readily accept them) and 'imitators' (people whose purchasing decisions are swayed by their more knowledgeable counterparts). Targeting influential people who are more in (**30**) ...... with new developments than most people and converting them into customers, the thinking goes, allows companies to benefit from a 'social contagion' effect in marketing campaigns.

Example:

A allow **B** let **C** make **D** give

	A	B	C	D
0	■	□	□	□

21	**A** approval	**B** acceptance	**C** acknowledgement	**D** acquisition
22	**A** habits	**B** manners	**C** routines	**D** ways
23	**A** various	**B** numerous	**C** several	**D** diverse
24	**A** skip	**B** bounce	**C** leap	**D** spring
25	**A** involves	**B** incorporates	**C** covers	**D** unites
26	**A** previewing	**B** planning	**C** speculating	**D** forecasting
27	**A** package	**B** set	**C** collection	**D** combination
28	**A** form	**B** consist	**C** comprise	**D** contain
29	**A** changes	**B** alterations	**C** introductions	**D** innovations
30	**A** sense	**B** agreement	**C** touch	**D** unison

Reading Paper Part 5: Exam skills

Part 5 consists of:

- one text of about 250 words
- ten gaps which you must fill with one word.

You practised similar skills in Unit 6 (page 33).

This part of the exam tests your knowledge of grammar, sentence structure and cohesion. The words you will need are likely to be 'grammar' words, especially:

- prepositions,
- articles (*a, an, the*)
- auxiliary verbs
- pronouns
- relative pronouns
- grammar adverbs (*however, still, yet,* etc.)
- conjunctions.

What type of word?

The position of the word in the sentence will often tell you what type of word you need. For example:

- between the subject and the main verb, either an auxiliary verb, a modal verb or an adverb: *Many businesses .... formed by serial entrepreneurs.* (Auxiliary verb: *are*)
- before a noun, either a preposition, an article or an adjective:
  He noted that .... businesses are formed by serial entrepreneurs. (Adjective: *many*)
  Fewer than half of .... businesses formed by people under 25 are successful. (Article: *the*)
  Banks are ready to lend money .... businesses which have solid assets. (Preposition: *to*)

Suggested exam technique

1 Read the whole text first.
2 Then look at each gap, sentence by sentence.
3 Consider what type of word you need – this will depend on the position of the word in the sentence.
4 When you know what type of word you need, think of alternatives and try them in the space.
5 Look carefully at the other words in the sentence, e.g. .... *interesting than* – you must write *more* or *less*; *it will depend* .... – you must write *on*.
6 Read what came before the gap and, if necessary, previous sentences. Similarly, read the sentences after the gap.
7 If you can't think of a word, leave it and come back to it later.
8 Don't leave any spaces blank – if you can't think of the correct word, make an intelligent guess; think of the type of word you need and use one which sounds reasonable – you might be right!
9 When you have finished, read the whole text again: does it read logically with the words you have chosen?

Exercises

1 Read the following sentences with a partner and decide

a what type of word would fit each space
b what the correct answer is.

1 Companies .... employees get fewer than three weeks' holiday a year are more likely to go bankrupt than their more generous counterparts, according to a recent study.
2 They expanded their export market into South America .... the recession which was affecting all sectors of their industry.
3 Oil prices have been rising .... to increasing demand from emerging markets.
4 The company would probably .... required a loan from the bank to make the necessary investment.
5 Unfortunately, some borrowers are slower than they should .... at paying back the money they owe.
6 The implementation of the proposal was put .... for a year due to lack of funds.
7 Steve Marshall worked .... an investment manager in the late 90s.
8 Many managers expect to be promoted every three years. .... leads to short-term strategies rather than long-term decision-making.
9 Few people have had .... an impact on the computer industry as Bill Gates.
10 There are several reasons for the firm's underperformance. .... is lack of investment, while another is lack of commitment from the firm's owners.

2 **Write one word in each space below.**

Workshops miss their target

White-water rafting or going parachuting **1** .... part of a team-building strategy workshop is more fun than a normal day at the office for most managers. But such corporate away-days have no clear-cut impact on productivity or profitability, **2** .... to the UK's first ever study into their effectiveness.

A new study found that four in ten managers on such corporate outings believe that the rendezvous they attended had **3** .... any impact or a negative impact on a range of measurable business outcomes. The report reveals that **4** .... the expense and time spent **5** .... them, few companies measure the impact of these exercises. Estimates of **6** .... cost range from £10,000 to £50,000. The overwhelming majority last for two days (90%) and are held **7** .... from the office (73%); senior executives (61%) lead most of them.

Many of the 1,337 respondents also report that these away-days **8** .... short of expectations, with 10% of attendees polled saying their workshop failed to meet its basic objectives. Hardly surprising, since top executives lead two-thirds of such workshops and are rarely keen to entertain opposition to their plans.

The people who actually know **9** .... is going on, the frontline staff or line managers, are invited to fewer than a quarter of these strategy days. **10** .... is despite increasing evidence suggesting that wider participation in workshops can improve employee/management relationships and boost staff morale.

To try a real exam task, see below.

Reading Paper Part 5: Exam practice

Questions 31–40

- Read the article below about organisational change.
- For each question **31–40**, write one word in CAPITAL LETTERS on your Answer Sheet.
- There is an example at the beginning. (**0**)

Example:

0	AS		

A dynamic approach to change

Many mature organisations need reinvention. If you are helping your company reinvent itself (**0**) AS a dynamic organisation, you need to be more than just flexible and responsive. Reinventing a mature company often means changing its mental model, including its approach to customers, suppliers, employees, and everyday working habits. It means being (**31**) ...... of change instead of behind it.

There is a great untapped potential (**32**) ...... revitalising mature organisations within the private and public sectors and within civil society. If tapped, mature organisations could become more relevant and valuable to their customers. (**33**) ...... in turn, means they could enjoy greater growth and profitability, and they could create more and better jobs for their staff.

You may well be (**34**) ...... of the problem: are you so involved with your organisation's success that you have lost the ability to step (**35**) ...... a few paces and look upon your organisation at a distance? Managers in particular need to remind (**36**) ...... constantly that their mental model must never become (**37**) ...... of those which is based on tradition – it should be oriented toward the future instead of the past.

There are three factors that make mature organisations easy targets for the virus (**38**) ...... converts success into failure. The three factors are size, age, and success. (**39**) ...... an organisation's growth, it gets more management layers, they establish more departments, and they introduce more and more rigid procedures. If organisations go (**40**) ...... to enjoy success, they can become complacent, and even arrogant, eventually forgetting the needs of their customers that were the initial source of their wealth and success.

Reading Paper Part 6: Exam skills

Part 6 consists of:

- one text of 150–200 words
- 12 lines in the text with one extra, unnecessary word in most lines.

You practised similar skills in Unit 4 (page 25) and Unit 19 (page 91).

This part of the exam tests your:

- ability to identify and correct errors in texts
- knowledge of grammar and sentence structure.

Editing texts

Editing texts to find errors is an essential business skill. You do it every time you read something you have written in your own language. In business, you may have to do it with texts you have written in English and when checking colleagues' texts in English as well.

Extra words

Mostly you should look for small 'grammar words'. Here are some examples with the extra word crossed out:

- pronouns, e.g. *Launching a new product ~~it~~ is extremely risky.*
- articles, e.g. *Brand awareness is best raised by running ~~the~~ advertising campaigns.*
- conjunctions, e.g. *If a firm is unable to sell a product immediately, ~~and~~ it is likely to withdraw it from the market without hesitation.*
- auxiliary or modal verbs, e.g. *Over the years job cuts in the industry have ~~been~~ lowered morale among workers.*
- prepositions, e.g. *New technology is usually introduced ~~for~~ to make processes more efficient and lower costs.*
- small adverbs, e.g. *Running your own business is a ~~so~~ challenging job and should not be undertaken ~~yet~~ unless you are prepared for hard work.*

Suggested exam technique

1. Skim the text quickly to get a general idea of what it is about.
2. Although there is an extra word in most lines, **read the text by sentences** not by lines.
3. There will not be more than one extra word per line.
4. Remember that **some lines are correct**, but read each sentence carefully to make sure.
5. When you have finished, read the whole text again carefully to check that it sounds natural.

Exercises

1 Find the extra word in each numbered line of this text. The extra words are: an article, two adverbs, two auxiliary verbs, two pronouns and three prepositions.

New project teams

When you will plan a new project, one of the main questions you	1 ......
may have to face up is the composition of your project team. We	2 ......
help you to make the decisions which we will optimise your choice	3 ......
of team members. Often teams are being formed by those people	4 ......
whose departments have released them for the job without a regard	5 ......
as to whether they have either of the right competencies and skills	6 ......
for the job or whether their personality will then fit with the project in	7 ......
hand or with other team members. As in an outside consultancy,	8 ......
we will identify the individuals inside your organisation who they	9 ......
are suitable for the project you have in mind and so when necessary,	10 ......
negotiate their secondment to the team with their departmental heads.	

2 There is an extra word in most lines of this text. Two lines are correct.

Langloffan cheese

Leon Downey had been making cheeses for hardly 20 years when he	1 ......
set up his website in 1997. By that time, he still had built up a solid	2 ......
reputation as an independent producer when offering high-quality	3 ......
cheeses, so the website was forming a natural extension of his	4 ......
existing family-run business. The initial outlay was too small: the	5 ......
site cost £350 to set up, and at the beginning, ISP charges were only	6 ......
£300 a year. Downey got put in early – he was the first Welsh cheese	7 ......
maker, he says, to have a website, and he was astute enough to	8 ......
register for the domain name, reasoning that no one would have	9 ......
heard of Llangloffan cheese. 'If someone's been looking for Welsh	10 ......
cheese, they're going to put a "Welsh cheese" in the search engine.'	11 ......
The decision has paid off – the site now gets 29,000 hits once a	12 ......
month.	

To try a real exam task, go to page 137.

Reading Paper Part 6: Exam practice

Questions 41–52

- Read the text below about dressing casually for work.
- In most of the lines **41–52** there is one extra word. It is either grammatically incorrect or does not fit in with the sense of the text. Some lines, however, are correct
- If a line is correct, write **CORRECT** on your Answer Sheet.
- If there is an extra word in the line, write **the extra word** in CAPITAL LETTERS on your Answer Sheet.
- The exercise begins with two examples (**0**) and (**00**).

Examples:

0	A	R	E						
00	C	O	R	R	E	C	T		

Dressing casually for work

0 There is now a trend for dressing more casually in business. Employees are
00 accustomed to putting on suits and smart shoes (for men) or skirts and blazers
41 (for women) suddenly have to worry about their attire. I object so to the fact
42 that I now have to think about what kind of trousers, what kind of shirt; what's
43 acceptable and what's not. The limits of what is casual are as hard to define
44 and so are very ambiguous. It takes up considerable thought and
45 confidence to dress well casually. Then there is the question of how to
46 distinguish by yourself in a workplace where you want to be casual, but don't
47 want to look even like the person two floors below who earns one-third of your
48 salary. Also most people would admit that businesswear it is generally more
49 flattering than other styles. When suits and dresses hide a multitude of
50 imperfections that just don't get covered up by most casualwear. Personally, I
51 think people look good in suits. They have pockets to keep them things in. You
52 get better service when you wear one. Yet they can take you anywhere you want to go.

Listening Paper Part 1: Exam skills

Part 1 consists of:

- a monologue where a speaker gives information on such things as a meeting or an event. You may hear instructions, arrangements or programme details.
- You must complete notes with a maximum of three words or a number in the spaces.
- There are 12 spaces.
- You hear the monologue twice.

You practised similar skills in Unit 18 (page 88) and Unit 24 (page 112).

This part of the exam tests your ability to identify what information is needed and listen for it.

Predicting before you listen

This is an essential skill for all parts of the Listening Paper. In the time before the recording is played, you should try to predict:

- the type of information required
- how the information might be expressed
- the type of word(s) which would fit in the space, e.g. noun, verb, adjective, etc.

This will help you to focus on the task.

Suggested exam technique

1 Before you listen, read the question (the message, notes, etc.) and identify what sort of information you need.
2 The recording will not repeat the exact words of the question. However, the answers which you write in the spaces must be **exactly the words you hear**.
3 Remember: you must **spell your answers correctly**.
4 Check that your answer fits grammatically in the space and that it fits with the meaning.

Exercises

You will hear the managing director of Unipro, a consumer products company talking about how his company manages complexity.

1 **Look at the notes below and predict what information you will need to complete the spaces and what types of words (noun phrases, verb phrases, etc.).**

2 **Briefly discuss your ideas with a partner.**

2 3 **Listen to the talk twice and complete the notes by writing up to three words in each space.**

4 **When you have finished, check your answers by reading the transcript for track 2.**

Managing complexity

Why more complexity?

- Consumer demand the main driver of larger 1 ....
- Customers require more 2 .... products
- Complexity in Unipro also the result of recent 3 ....
- Unipro has to 4 .... in order to stay ahead of rivals
- By dropping product lines, companies in danger of 5 ....
- New product lines allow the company to 6 ....

Negative impacts of complexity

- Products can lose 7 ....
- 8 .... tend to become more complicated
- Tendency for 9 .... to take longer
- At Unipro, only a small proportion of products account for most of the 10 ....

Ability to manage complexity comes from:

- 11 .... of markets
- Culture of 12 .... processes

To try a real exam task, go to page 139.

Listening Paper Part 1: Exam practice

3 Questions 1–12

- You will hear a woman, Anna Grant, giving a talk about her recruitment company, PKS.
- As you listen, for questions **1–12**, complete the notes using up to **three** words or a number.
- You will hear the recording twice.

PKS: current position

1 Alan Murton is now a .... in PKS.
2 PKS's sales grew by .... last year.
3 PKS has several clients in the UK for whom it organises all .... staff recruitment.

PKS: operations & services

4 PKS is responsible for the .... up to the final recruitment decision.
5 PKS makes decisions regarding the .... for hiring staff.
6 PKS recruits a high proportion of people through ....
7 PKS is also usually responsible for assessing .... for roles.
8 PKS also helps people who lose their jobs through ....
9 PKS insists on having .... with their clients.

PKS: the future

10 PKS is discussing selling a share of the business to a ....
11 Anna Grant would like to reach the stage where she can .... the company.
12 Anna plans to increase business by expanding into an additional ....

Listening Paper Part 2: Exam skills

Part 2 consists of:

- five short monologues on a similar theme
- two tasks in which you must match the speakers to a list of eight alternatives (**A–H**).
- The two tasks may be a combination of things such as the following:
  - identifying the purpose of an action
  - a cause or a result
  - a problem
  - advice, etc.
- You hear the recording twice.

You practised similar skills in Unit 13 (page 64).

This part of the exam tests your ability to:

- infer meaning where things are not expressed explicitly
- understand the general idea of what the speaker is saying (the actual words of the correct answer will not be said)
- recognise functions such as complaining, greeting, apologising, etc.

Suggested exam technique

1 You will not be able to predict what the speakers are going to say, but read the alternatives. What sort of vocabulary might you expect to hear with each of them?

2 While you listen, note down (or make a mental note of) vocabulary which may give you clues.

3 Avoid stereotypes, e.g. don't assume that a PA will be a woman, a manager will be a man, etc.

Exercises

1 a **If you were listening, which of the words or phrases in the box would you associate with each of the problems (A–H) in Task 1, Exercise 2? (You may put the same words or phrases with more than one problem.)**

called in a maintenance crew disappointing at first
key brands key files missed a deadline
not much take-up running at a loss
slow off the mark system crashed the board
top customer vanished completely
went over to the competition
helpline never stopped ringing wiped off

b **With a partner, brainstorm more vocabulary you would associate with the problems.**

2 a **Read the instructions for the listening exercise below. Work in pairs and brainstorm vocabulary you might expect to hear for Task 2.**

4 b **Listen to these four speakers. Each speaker is talking about a problem. For Task 1, decide which problem is mentioned. For Task 2, decide which cause is mentioned.**

	Problem	Cause
Speaker 1		
Speaker 2		
Speaker 3		
Speaker 4		

Task 1

Problems

A Certain product lines were losing money.
B The directors responsible were slow reacting.
C The product sold slowly to start with.
D Customer complaints were increasing.
E The project was late starting.
F Vital equipment broke down.
G A key contract was lost.
H Confidential information disappeared completely.

Task 2

Causes

I There was over-manning of the assembly line.
J Someone with the wrong competencies was recruited.
K The project was underfunded.
L Quality control was poor.
M The sales forecast was inaccurate.
N A key supplier went out of business.
O The system was changed without warning.
P New staff were given insufficient training.

3 **Check your answers by reading the transcript for track 4. What words and phrases gave you the answers? What words and phrases might have distracted you from the correct answers?**

To try a real exam task, go to page 141.

Listening Paper Part 2: Exam practice

5 Questions 13–22

- You will hear five different people talking about their company's recent expansion.
- For each extract there are two tasks.
- For Task One, choose the way the company chose to expand from the list **A–H**. For Task Two, choose the challenge the company now faces from the list **A–H**.
- Do not use any letter more than once.
- You will hear the five extracts twice.

TASK ONE – METHOD OF EXPANSION (Questions 13–17)

- For questions **13–17**, match the extracts with the methods of expansion (**A–H**).
- For each extract, choose the way the company chose to expand.
- Write one letter (**A–H**) next to the questions (**13–17**).

13 ....
14 ....
15 ....
16 ....
17 ....

A by opening more retail outlets
B by increasing its product range
C by buying up a rival company
D by exporting goods to new markets
E by forming an alliance with another company
F by licensing its products
G by offering an online ordering service
H by setting up a franchise operation

TASK TWO – CHALLENGE (Questions 18–22)

- For questions **18–22**, match the extracts with the challenges (**A–H**).
- For each extract, choose the challenge the company now faces.
- Write one letter (**A–H**) next to the questions (**18–22**).

18 ....
19 ....
20 ....
21 ....
22 ....

A attracting adequate investment
B recruiting suitable staff
C finding a reliable supplier
D monitoring key projects
E improving distribution channels
F controlling production costs
G developing a training programme
H complying with government regulations

Listening Paper Part 3: Exam skills

Part 3 consists of:

- an interview, discussion or conversation with two or more speakers
- eight multiple-choice questions where you must choose **A**, **B** or **C**.

You practised similar skills in Unit 14 (page 69).

This part of the exam tests your ability to:

- listen for the gist or general idea of what people are saying, specific information and speakers' attitudes
- interpret what the speakers say in order to choose the correct alternative.

Multiple-choice questions in the Listening Paper

One particular problem candidates have with multiple-choice questions is that they have to read carefully and listen carefully at the same time.

The words you hear when listening may not be the same as the words you read, but the meaning will coincide with one of the options.

Something connected with each of the distractors is usually also mentioned, so you have to listen very carefully.

Suggested exam technique

1 Use the pause between hearing the instructions and listening to the recording to:
- read each question and underline the key words so that you know what you are listening for
- study the alternatives for the first few questions and predict how these might be expressed.

2 The speaker will probably say something about all three alternatives. Listen carefully to discard the wrong alternatives.

3 Remember: the speakers may not use the same words as are used in the questions – you will have to listen for the **same meaning**.

4 Use the pause between listening the first time and listening the second time to check the questions which give you problems.

5 The Listening Paper requires a lot of concentration. Make sure you keep concentrating hard until the end of the paper!

Exercises

1 You will hear an interview with Jeremy Pollock, a psychologist who has investigated decision-making in business. Before you listen:

- underline the key words in these questions
- check with a partner, and then discuss how Jeremy might express each alternative in the questions using other words.

6 **2 Listen and answer these questions.**

1 What is the result of over-optimism in decision-making?
A Managers generally perform better and produce better results.
B Managers concentrate on things they would do better to ignore.
C Managers underestimate the abilities of their company's competitors.

2 What example does Jeremy give of how Americans are over-optimistic?
A They overestimate their future incomes.
B They invest too heavily on the stock market.
C They pay more than the market value for their homes.

3 What influence does the 'anchor effect' have on business negotiations?
A Negotiators do not investigate beyond a narrow range of options.
B Negotiators tend to discuss the asking price rather than a realistic figure.
C Negotiators refuse to discuss compromise solutions.

4 According to Jeremy, why is having large amounts of information a problem for decision-makers?
A They find it hard to distinguish relevant from irrelevant information.
B They find it hard to reach a final decision.
C They spend too much time on small decisions.

5 How does stubbornness affect decision-making in pharmaceutical companies?
A They develop unsuitable products.
B They devote too much of their budget to research.
C They take on new members of staff.

6 How do bosses typically treat unproductive staff who they personally have recruited?
A They fire them.
B They pass them to another department.
C They keep them.

7 What is the negative effect of 'home bias' on investment decisions?
A Investors tend to invest in unprofitable ventures close to home.
B Investors do not spread their risks sufficiently.
C Investors invest too much in property and not enough in shares.

3 Check in the transcript for track 6 to see how each option is discussed and which one is correct.

To try a real exam task, go to page 143.

Listing Paper Part 3: Exam practice

7 Questions 23–30

- You will hear an interview with a consultant, Jason Copeland, on the competitiveness of small retail stores.
- For each question **23–30**, mark one letter (**A**, **B** or **C**) for the correct answer.
- You will hear the recording twice.

23 According to Jason, a retail store's success depends on
- **A** advertising the store effectively.
- **B** pitching products at the right price.
- **C** researching what kind of product mix is required.

24 Jason claims that smaller stores can compete with large chain stores by
- **A** giving exceptional customer service.
- **B** emphasising how unique the business is.
- **C** creating the right atmosphere for shopping.

25 Jason thinks stores should focus on low-spending but regular customers because
- **A** they are likely to recommend the store to others.
- **B** they spend more overall than the average shopper.
- **C** they may become big spenders in the future.

26 Jason thinks that retailing will remain competitive with online shopping as a result of
- **A** the delays encountered with online shopping.
- **B** concern about the security of online payments.
- **C** consumers' desire to touch merchandise.

27 Jason says that relocating a retail store can be beneficial as long as
- **A** you focus on retaining your existing customers.
- **B** your plans are designed to increase profit margins.
- **C** you advertise in order to attract new customers.

28 According to Jason, retailers' attitude to customers should be that
- **A** they are always right.
- **B** they should be made to feel important.
- **C** they are decision-makers.

29 Jason says that the best way to keep good sales assistants is to
- **A** motivate them through pay and promotion.
- **B** establish an appraisal system to identify their needs.
- **C** prepare a comprehensive training programme.

30 According to Jason, a small retail business can make large profits if you
- **A** make sure you are the sole owner of the business.
- **B** gain a reputation for specialising in certain products.
- **C** take risks in order to expand the business.

Writing Paper Part 1: Exam skills

Part 1 consists of:

- a short report in the form of a memo, an email or a report describing figures and making inferences based on information from a chart or table.
- Length: 120–140 words
- Time: maximum 25 minutes
- Marks: You are given marks out of 10 for this task. The writing paper carries 30 marks in total.

You practised similar skills in Unit 10 (page 53) and Unit 11 (page 56).

This part of the exam tests your ability to:

- describe the facts and figures commonly presented in graphs, bar charts, pie charts and tables in business contexts
- understand information presented in graphic form
- convey information clearly.

Line graphs, pie charts and bar charts

- **Line charts** are usually employed to show a trend and describe changes over a period of time. Line charts may contain several lines, in which case you will have to
  - describe the changes
  - compare or contrast the trends between the things shown by the different lines.
- **Pie charts** show how the whole of a category is divided. The complete 'pie' represents 100%. For example, a pie chart could be used to show a number of companies' market share. You may see two pie charts side by side, in which case you will have to:
  - say how much share each division of the chart has of the total
  - compare the information given in the two charts.
- **Bar charts** show totals for different categories, but not what would constitute 100%. You may have to:
  - describe trends or changes
  - compare facts and figures
  - say how much each bar represents.

Suggested exam technique

1 Read the instructions carefully and make sure you know whether you should write an email, a memo or a report.
2 Study the charts/graphs. Make sure you understand what the charts show.
3 Make a brief plan. In fact, you should be able to describe the information in the order in which it appears on the page. However, your first sentence should be an introductory sentence which says in general what the chart(s) show(s).
4 When you write, use linking phrases such as *on the other hand, although, in contrast, consequently,* etc.
5 Make sure you include **all** the important information.
6 When you have finished, check what you have written
  - for mistakes in your English
  - to make sure you have mentioned everything
  - to make sure it is written in a clear style which is easy to understand.

Exercises

1 Work in pairs. Study these three charts and discuss what each of them shows.

Chart 1

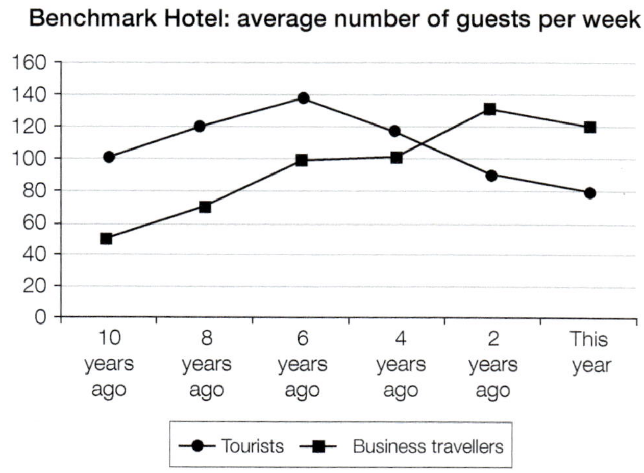

Chart 2

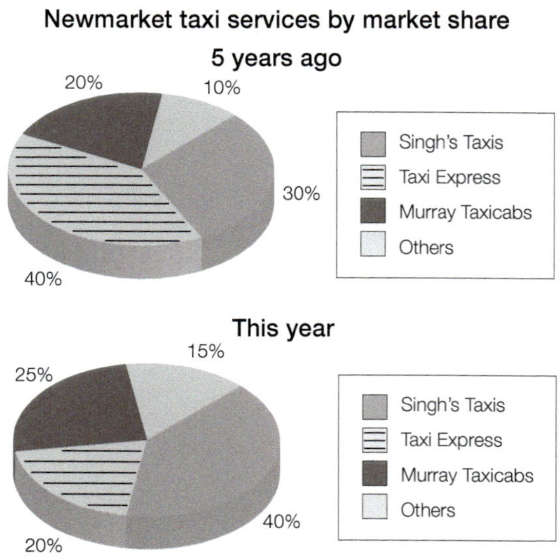

Chart 3

2 Read this sample report about Chart 1. Complete the report using the words and phrases in the box.

a breakdown in contrast in other words
in the last two years in total since then
ten years ago the following eight years

The report gives **1** .... of guest numbers per week at the Benchmark Hotel over the last ten years. **2** .... , the Benchmark Hotel received an average of 50 business travellers as guests each week. This number rose steadily over **3** .... to reach 130 per week two years ago. **4** .... , numbers have decreased slightly, and this year, the average has been 120 guests per week.

5 .... , ten years ago Benchmark Hotel received on average 100 tourists per week, **6** .... twice as many tourists as business travellers. This number also rose steadily until six years ago, when it reached 140 guests per week. **7** .... , the number has declined, and this year the hotel receives just 80 tourists per week, and fewer guests **8** .... than two years ago, when it received in all 220 guests each week.

3 Read this report based on Chart 2 and put the verbs in brackets into the correct tenses.

This report **1** .... (*summarise*) the changes in market share for the principal taxi companies in Newmarket during the last five years. Five years ago, the dominant company **2** .... (*be*) Taxi Express, who **3** .... (*have*) 40 per cent of the market, whereas this year, they **4** .... (*reduce*) to just 20 per cent of the market, and their dominating position **5** .... (*take*) by Singh's Taxis, who **6** .... (*increase*) over five years from a 30-per-cent to a 40-per-cent market share.

The other major player is Murray Taxicabs, who five years ago **7** .... (*have*) 20 per cent of the market and this year **8** .... (*raise*) their share to 25 per cent. There **9** .... (*be*) a number of other taxi companies whose market share (**10**) .... (*rise*) from 10 to 15 per cent over the same period.

4 Study the two reports again and highlight

1 useful linking phrases, e.g. *In contrast*
2 useful time phrases, e.g. *over the last five years*

5 Write your own report about Chart 3. Use the reports in Exercises 2 and 3 as models.

To try a real exam task, see below.

Writing Paper Part 1: Exam practice

Question 1

- The bar chart below shows a company's gross income from domestic sales, gross income from export sales and fixed costs.
- Using the information from the chart, write a short report comparing the two sets of income and fixed costs.
- Write **120–140** words in the space provided.

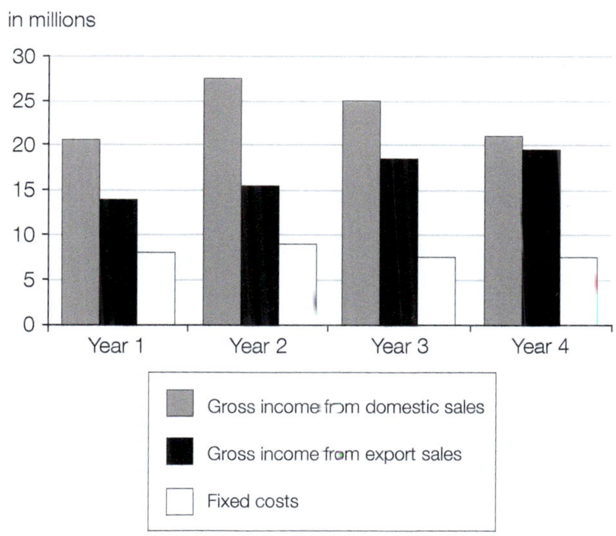

Writing Paper Part 2: Exam skills

In Part 2, you are given a choice of:

- a proposal
- a report, or
- a letter.
- Length: 200–250 words
- Time: 45 minutes (if you have spent 25 minutes on Part 1)
- Marks: You are given marks out of 20 for this part. The writing paper carries a total of 30 marks.

You practised writing:

- a proposal in Unit 7 (page 39)
- a report in Unit 11 (page 57) and in Unit 19 (page 93)
- a letter in Unit 15 (page 75) and Unit 23 (page 111).

This part of the exam tests:

- your ability to do a longer writing task, including planning and organising your writing in a logical and coherent manner
- whether you can use the correct format and appropriate register for the type of task (correspondence, report or proposal) and the type of reader.
- your range of grammar and vocabulary.

- If you decide to write a report, you will probably have to **describe** and **summarise information**.
- If you decide to write a proposal, you may have to **describe**, **summarise**, **recommend** a course of action and **persuade** the reader.
- If you write a letter, you may have to carry out a variety of functions such as **complaining**, **informing**, **enquiring**, **apologising**, etc.

Report or proposal?

The format and style of reports and proposals is very similar. However:

- a report concentrates on information which you have gathered and may give recommendations for further action
- a proposal makes suggestions for possible courses of action to take in the future.

Who is the reader?

It is really important to identify in the question who you are writing to or for. Is it your manager, the board of directors, a customer, or your colleagues? This will decide the register and tone of your writing.

When you are writing, a good technique is to imagine that you are playing a role and to imagine the actual manager or customer who you are writing for. This will make the exercise feel more authentic, and you will forget that the real reader is the person marking your exam!

Suggested exam technique

1 Read all three questions and choose the one you think you can do best. Ask yourself:
- Do I know enough about the topic?
- Have I got a good range of vocabulary for this task?
- Can I write in an appropriate style?

2 Read the instructions, carefully underlining key information:
- What type of task is it (letter, report, etc.)?
- Who is the reader (a customer, your managing director, etc.)? This will decide the register.

3 Write a plan. Make sure your plan covers **all the points required in the question**. Organise your plan in a logical way.

4 Write your answer from your plan using
- **the correct format**
- an appropriate register

5 Use linking words and phrases to connect your ideas (e.g. *however, although, also, as a consequence, as a result*, etc.).

6 Check your answer for mistakes.

Exercises

1 Read this question and answer the questions which follow.

You have recently returned from a two-day training course which you were sent on by your company. Your human resources manager has asked you to write a report, evaluating how useful the course has been.
Write the report including the following information:

- what the course consisted of
- how useful the course was for you
- how your training will benefit the company
- advice for colleagues on how to benefit from courses like these.

Write 200–250 words.

1 Who will read this report: only the human resources manager or other people as well?
2 What register would be most appropriate in this case: formal, neutral or colloquial?
3 Before you start writing, what details will you have to invent?
4 What would be suitable section headings for your report?

2 **Work alone and write a brief plan for this report. When you have finished, share your ideas with a partner. Add any of your partner's ideas which you think are useful to your own plan.**

Planning before writing

When you do the exam, you may well see people who start writing their answers as soon as they sit down. This is a mistake. It is much better to take your time to:

- analyse the question
- write a clear, logically structured plan
- think about your answer
- write your answer following your plan.

By doing this, you are dividing the task into different activities. First, you are thinking about and planning the content of your report. Then, when you start writing, you only have to concentrate on *how* to express your ideas, i.e. the language you need.

3 **This answer to the question contains a wrong word in most lines. However, some lines are correct. Read the report and correct the mistakes by crossing out the wrong word and writing the correct word. If a line is correct, write *correct*.**

Report on time-management course	
Introduction	
~~Like~~ a junior sales manager, I was sent on a time management course at the local	1 ...As...
Chamber of Commerce by my department two week's ago.	2 ....
The course	
The course consisted in a series of workshops and practical exercises designed to	3 ....
improving the trainees' time management skills. During the course, we analysed	4 ....
how we spend our time before learn techniques for reducing the amount of time	5 ....
which is wasted. This should result in us being more efficient and also reduce	6 ....
work-related stress. We were also showing how to employ our time better when	7 ....
no working as a way of improving our work–life balance.	8 ....
The course had benefited me by allowing me to spend my working time more	9 ....
profitably and consequently more enjoyable as I have learnt techniques which	10 ....
reduce time-related pressures.	11 ....
Benefits for the company	
Apart of the obvious advantages for the company in having a more efficient	12 ....
worker, one of the conditions for me going on the course were to cascade my	13 ....
learning experience to my colleagues. This should result in clear benefits for the	14 ....
whole department.	15 ....
Conclusion and recommendations	
I think short courses like this are some really useful break from work routine. They	16 ....
allow you to think of how you work while at the same time giving you the chance	17 ....
to exchange experiences with employees from other companies. To obtain	18 ....
maximum benefit from them, trainees should be ready for talk about their	19 ....
experiences and mistakes, and be prepared to try new working techniques.	20 ....

Checking for mistakes

When you get back writing tasks you have done for homework, analyse your mistakes. If you make the same mistake more than once, record it in a section of your notebook called 'My Favourite Mistakes'. The next time you do homework, when you have finished, check for those 'favourite' mistakes.

When you go to the exam, you will be very aware what your typical mistakes are and you will be able to avoid them.

To try a real exam task, go to page 148.

Writing Paper Part 2: Exam practice

Write an answer to **one** of the questions **2–4** in this part. Write your answer in **200–250** words.

Question 2

- Your company recently made changes to its delivery systems. Your manager has asked you to write a report on the success of these changes.
- Write a **report**, including the following information:
  - what changes were made to the delivery systems
  - how the success of the changes was monitored
  - whether the changes have led to a more effective delivery system or not.

Question 3

- Your department has been trying to improve the effectiveness of the presentations given by staff. You have been asked to arrange training sessions with an external consultant for some of the staff in the department.
- Write a **letter** to the consultant, including the following information:
  - the problems staff have with giving presentations
  - which grade of staff you propose to put forward for the training and why
  - what type of training the staff require.

Question 4

- Your company is considering developing a new product. You have been asked to write a proposal to your manager assessing the desirability of developing this product.
- Write your **proposal** to your manager:
  - commenting on which markets the new product would appeal to and why
  - explaining the problems likely to be encountered
  - suggesting how these problems could be resolved.

Sample answers are given on page 169.

Speaking Test Part 1: Exam skills

The Speaking Test lasts 14 minutes and you do it in pairs, or sometimes in groups of three. You are assessed by two people: the interviewer and another examiner who doesn't speak (except to say hello).

In the test, you are given marks for:

- **grammar and vocabulary**
- **discourse management** (your ability to speak knowledgeably and logically about the subject and for the right length of time)
- **pronunciation**
- **interactive communication** (your ability to share and participate in a conversation with the other candidate and with the interviewer).

Part 1 consists of:

- one general question, in which the interviewer asks you about
  - where you are from.
  - your job or your studies.
  - why you are studying English, etc.
- one general question to each candidate about some aspect of business.

This part of the test lasts about three minutes.

This part of the exam tests your ability to:

- talk about yourself
- express opinions, agree and disagree.

Suggested exam technique

1 Make sure, before you go into the Speaking Test, that you can:
   - talk about yourself
   - describe what your job or your studies consist of, your duties and responsibilities
   - describe your company's activities
   - talk about your ambitions/hopes for the future.

2 When you go into the interview, speak clearly so you can be heard.

3 Don't answer the questions with one or two words – answer with one or two sentences.

4 When you answer a question, give a reason for your answer or an example.

Some extra advice

- Talk to the interviewer and also, when appropriate, to the other candidate.
- If you don't understand a question, ask the interviewer to repeat it.
- If you notice you've made a mistake, correct yourself.

Exercises

1 Work in pairs. Take turns to ask and answer these questions, which are similar to the first question you will be asked.

1 Can you tell me a little bit about you?
2 What does your job / do your studies involve?
3 What aspects of your job/studies do you enjoy?
4 Is there anything about your job/studies which you don't like?
5 How do you see your career developing in the future?
6 Why have you been studying business English?
7 If you were completely free to choose, who would you like to work for?

2 When you have finished, discuss how you could improve your answers.

Examples, reasons and extra information

- **Giving examples**
  If you are asked *What do you most enjoy about your job?*, you can say *I most enjoy the team work. We have a very good working atmosphere in my company. For example, when I've got a work problem, I can always ask my team leader for help, and she's usually ready to give it.*
- **Giving reasons**
  If you are asked *Is this a good area to work in?*, you can answer *Yes, it's quite good because there is plenty of industry and also there are plenty of facilities for enjoying oneself in one's free time.*
- **Extra information**
  If you are asked *Where do you come from?*, you can answer *I come from Fribourg* or you can give extra information, such as *I come from Fribourg. It's a town in the western agricultural part of Switzerland, not far from Berne.*

3 Work in pairs. Take turns to ask your partners these questions which are similar to the second question you will be asked.

1 How do you think business has changed in your country in the last few years?
2 What things should someone study if they are thinking of a career in business in your country?
3 What do you think will be good professions to work in in the future?
4 Do you think there are more or fewer opportunities in business nowadays? Why? / Why not?
5 What are the qualities of a good business person?

Speaking Test Part 2: Exam skills

In Part 2:

- you are given a page with three questions printed on it. Each question begins with the area of business which the question is directed at, e.g. finance, marketing, human resources
- you are asked to choose one of the three questions
- you have one minute to prepare your answer
- you must speak for one minute to answer the question
- your partner must listen and ask you a question when you have finished
- the interviewer will also ask you a question at the end.

This part of the exam tests your ability to:

- speak for a longer period of time, as you might have to do when giving a presentation or speaking at a business meeting
- communicate a series of ideas clearly
- speak about an area of business and demonstrate your knowledge of business issues and business vocabulary
- structure your speech and connect your ideas.

You practised similar skills in Unit 6 (page 33) and Unit 24 (page 113).

Interview nerves

It is natural to feel a little nervous about this part of the interview. Overcome nerves by telling yourself:

- you have something interesting and important to say
- the people in the room want you to do well
- they would be equally nervous if they had to give a talk in your language!

Above all, **keep speaking**. If you dry up, take a breath and start again.

How much can I say?

Radio reporters, when they are writing their pieces, expect to speak at a speed of three words per second. You should expect to speak rather more slowly, so in one minute you will probably manage little more than 120 words. This will give you an idea of how much you should limit your answer; if you had five minutes to prepare, you would have too much to say in the time.

Suggested exam technique

A You have **one minute** to prepare. Use it to:
  1 choose the question you think is easiest:
    - Which do you know most about?
    - Which do you have the best range of vocabulary for?
  2 think of three main ideas you want to express, or three main points you wish to make. Expand these by adding reasons and giving examples. If you want, give examples from your personal experience.
  3 make brief notes while you are thinking
  4 note down key business vocabulary you want to use.

B If you can, **use your own experience** to answer the question. If you haven't worked in business yet, don't worry: give your ideas just the same.

C When speaking:
  1 refer to your notes, but **look at the interviewer** and your partner
  2 introduce your talk by saying what question you have chosen
  3 sequence your talk by saying *firstly*, *secondly*, *finally*
  4 signpost your talk with phrases like *this is because*, *for example* and *as a result of this*
  5 watch the time and try to finish your talk with a brief concluding sentence at the end of the minute.

D When listening to your partner:
  1 think of a question you would like to ask about the talk
  2 think about what you agree and disagree with in the talk.

Exercises

1 a Work in pairs. Study topic 1 below and take two or three minutes to discuss how you could answer it. Take notes as you talk.

b Change partners and give your talk.

c When each of you has given your talk, give feedback on what you did well and what you could improve.

d Do the same for topics 2 and 3.

1 **Human resources:** How to approach internal recruitment
2 **Finance:** The importance of making accurate sales forecasts
3 **Management:** Managing change in a large organisation

2 **When you are giving a talk, it's important for your audience (the two examiners and the other candidate) to know what you are doing at each moment – making a new point, giving an example, concluding, etc.**

Complete the talk below using the words or phrases from the box.

a third aspect of this anyway but also because finally and in conclusion for example I think first that it also includes not just because the main point I'd like to make is about what I mean is

My talk is about procedures for internal recruitment. This is an essential area of human resources, **1** .... it has implications for the efficiency of the company, **2** .... of the effect it can have on inter-staff relations. So **3** .... transparency. **4** .... that the process must be fair and seen by all staff involved to be fair. How can this be achieved? **5** .... there must be a clear procedure for internal recruitment which has been agreed between management and staff representatives. This procedure must, **6** .... , include internal advertising of all posts and allowing all suitably qualified staff to apply. **7** .... a regular system of staff appraisal, which is also open and transparent. Staff know how they have been appraised and know what comments are on their personal files. They also have a right to appeal if they feel that any aspect of their appraisal has been unfair. **8** .... transparency is the composition of recruitment boards, and I say 'boards' because really internal recruitment is too sensitive to be the responsibility of one person. **9** .... , these boards should really be made up of the director or manager of the department which has the vacant post, someone from the Human Resources department, and also, though this for many managers may sound rather controversial, an elected staff representative as well. **10** .... , I'd like to say that I think Human Resources should circulate the reasons for choosing the person they finally choose, as this makes the process as transparent as possible, and makes it clear to staff what criteria were used.

8 **3** **Check your answer by listening to Frances, a personnel officer with a large company, giving a talk at a business seminar.**

4 **In her talk, Frances did the following things. Read what she said in Exercise 2 again and find the phrases which identify them.**

1 She introduced her talk.
2 She made three main points.
3 She gave an example.
4 She explained what she meant using other words.
5 She concluded her talk.
6 She used business vocabulary.

To try a real exam task, see below.

Speaking Test Part 2: Exam practice

Task card 1

A: Customer Service: the importance of getting customer feedback

B: Financial Management: how to decide on a budget for training

C: Sales: how to monitor the performance of sales staff

Task card 2

A: Recruitment: the importance of recruiting from a variety of sources

B: Purchasing: how to select a suitable supplier

C: Advertising: how to identify the best advertising methods for a product

Speaking Test Part 3: Exam skills

In Part 3:

- you are given a card with a topic to discuss in pairs
- you have 30 seconds to read the card
- you must discuss the topic for three minutes and try to reach a decision

Afterwards, the interviewer will broaden the discussion by asking both of you further questions about the same topic. This part of the exam tests your ability to:

- express opinions
- agree, disagree, compare and contrast ideas and to reach a decision
- find out your partner's opinions and react to them – in other words, your ability to collaborate in a work-type discussion.

You practised similar skills in Unit 13 (page 66).

Taking turns to speak

In this part of the Speaking Test, it's important not to monopolise the conversation. When you have said something, ask your partner what he/she thinks. Say things like: *Do you agree? What do you think? How about you?*

If your partner is speaking too much, interrupt politely by saying things like:

Yes, but … , *Possibly …* (if you disagree) or *Yes, and …* , *Yes, and another thing …* (if you agree).

Suggested exam technique

1 You are given 30 seconds to read the card before you start discussing. Use the time to:
   - study the situation (underline the key words while you are doing this)
   - make sure you know what you must discuss.
2 Start by making a suggestion, and then asking your partner what he/she thinks.
3 When your partner suggests an idea, say if you agree or disagree and give a reason. Give a suggestion of your own.
4 Make sure you decide on both points in the three minutes. If you think you have spent too long on the first point, take control of the discussion by saying *What about the second point? What do you think about …?*
5 Try to discuss the topic as if it was a real work situation in your company. Express your own ideas and opinions.

Exercises

1 Work in groups of three. One student should take the role of interviewer. The other two students should practise as candidates for the exam. The interviewer should:

- give the candidates their task (see below)
- listen and assess their performance (see the checklist at the end of the exercises)
- ask the candidates the questions which follow the task
- give feedback to the candidates when they have finished.

Task
Staff disputes

Recently there has been some bad feeling inside your company caused by disputes between members of staff and management. You have been asked to suggest ways in which staff disputes can be resolved without causing bad feeling.

Discuss together and decide:

- what aspects of staff disputes give rise to bad feeling
- what mechanisms can be introduced to deal with these disputes.

Interviewer's questions to follow the task

1 Why is it important to keep staff happy?
2 How can managers enforce staff discipline?
3 How important is good timekeeping in business?
4 Do you think companies should have dress codes?
5 Do you think that a formal or an informal atmosphere is more appropriate in an office environment?

2 Continue to work in groups of three, but this time a different student should take the role of interviewer.

Task
Responding to a competitor

One of your main competitors has started selling a similar product to one of yours at a lower price. Your manager has asked you to give advice on how to respond to this challenge.

Discuss together and decide:

- what the dangers are of entering a price war
- what other ways there are of responding to the challenge.

Interviewer's questions to follow the task

1 To what extent do you think the price of a product indicates its quality?
2 What can companies do to encourage brand loyalty amongst their customers?
3 How should you decide the price for a product or service?
4 How can a company keep track of what the competition is doing?
5 Do you think companies should be product-led or marketing-led? Why?

3 **Finally, the third student should take the role of interviewer.**

Task
Managing change

The company you work for is planning to introduce new technology systems to make the company more productive. This will mean major changes in the way staff work. The managing director has asked you to recommend ways of preparing the staff for these changes.

Discuss together and decide:

- how staff should be prepared for change
- what incentives they should be offered to facilitate the changes.

Interviewer's questions to follow the task

1 Why are workers sometimes unwilling to accept changes in working practices?
2 What do you imagine the office of the future will be like?
3 What are the advantages for a company of allowing its office staff to work from home?
4 And what are the disadvantages?
5 In the last 20 years, how have new technologies changed the way people in offices work?

To try a real exam task see below.

Speaking Test Part 3: Exam practice

Improving Public Relations

Your company is looking at ways of improving its public relations. You have been asked for your views on this.
Discuss and decide together:

- why good public relations are important (to a company)
- what good public relations involve.

Answer keys

UNIT 1
Corporate culture

Getting started

1 1 b 2 g 3 e 4 d 5 f 6 c 7 a
2 1 mentor 2 dress code 3 goals 4 autocratic 5 bonuses 6 do things by the book 7 vision 8 entrepreneurial

Aspects of corporate culture

Listening

1 1 g 2 j 3 a 4 i 5 d 6 e 7 c 8 b 9 f 10 h
2 Candela: 5 Henry: 4 Sonia: 7 Omar: 3

Vocabulary

1 out 2 through 3 up with 4 to 5 turn 6 getting 7 down

Creating a corporate culture

Reading

1 1 The board of directors
2 It can affect ethics, risk-taking and bottom-line performance.
3 Board members often lack an understanding of corporate culture.
3 1 G 2 F 3 D 4 C 5 A 6 E

Vocabulary

1 b 2 g 3 c 4 a 5 d 6 f 7 e

Grammar workshop: defining and non-defining relative clauses

1 How should a director think about the "corporate culture" of the company on **whose** board he or she serves?
2 Consult a management text on organizational culture and you'll find a chapter or more of definition **which/that** boils down to something like "a pattern of shared basic assumptions."
3 Every organization has a culture **which/that** manifests itself in everything from entrepreneurship to risk-taking all the way down to the dress code.
4 An understanding of corporate culture is one of the main things missing on boards, but they really need it if they're going to monitor **what**'s going on inside the corporation.
5 Nucor's culture, **which** he describes as "extraordinarily powerful, effective, and unique," can be traced back to the values and vision of its legendary founder, F. Kenneth Iverson.

UNIT 2
Leaders and managers

Getting started

1 1 h 2 f 3 b 4 c 5 e 6 g 7 a 8 d

Great leaders and great managers

Reading

3 1 D *... says his goal is to turn Virgin into 'the most respected brand in the world'.* (paragraph 1)
2 B *'I think being a high-profile person has its advantages,' he says. 'Advertising costs enormous amounts of money these days. I just announced in India that I was setting up a domestic airline, and we ended up getting on the front pages of the newspaper.'* (paragraph 2)
3 C *I have to be willing to step back. The company must be set up so it can continue without me.* (paragraph 4)
4 D *For the people who work for you or with you, you must lavish praise on them at all times* (paragraph 5)
5 A *Employees often leave companies, he reasons, because they are frustrated by the fact that their ideas fall on deaf ears.* (paragraph 6)
6 B *... then give chief executives a stake in the company* (paragraph 7)

Vocabulary 1

1 founder 2 venture 3 underlying 4 flamboyant 5 from scratch 6 lavish praise on 7 slipped up / made a mess of something 8 firing 9 immersed 10 the ins and outs 11 stake

Listening

1 vision 2 implementation 3 hands on 4 experienced, good people 5 opportunity to develop

Grammar workshop: *as* or *like*?

1 b 2 a (like) 3 c 4 a (as well as) 5 d (as ... as)

Vocabulary 2

1 g 2 d 3 a 4 c 5 b 6 e 7 f

Managing staff

Listening

2 1 directional strategy 2 (responsibility and) ownership 3 superficial level 4 opportunities 5 (kind of) mentor

UNIT 3
Internal communications

Getting started

2 Suggested answers
1 memo
2 memo or email
3 email or suggestion box
4 interview
5 memo or informal chat
6 meeting
7 note

Internal messages

Reading

1 1 C 2 B 3 A 4 C 5 A 6 D 7 B 8 B
2 1 D 2 B, C 3 B, C, D 4 A, B 5 C 6 C 7 D

Writing

1 Suggested answers
1 Dear Max,
Apologies for my lack of punctuality recently. This has unfortunately been due to roadworks on the way in to work, which are making journey times rather unpredictable at the moment and, although I'm leaving home earlier, sometimes I'm delayed in traffic jams for as much as 40 mins.
Can I suggest that we start team meetings half an hour later from now on? This should ensure that no one is kept waiting.
Best wishes,
Angela
2 Hi Mohammed,
Thanks for this summary of our meeting. Just a brief note to say that there are a couple of things which I think we agreed slightly differently:
- Staff will have Fri p.m. free from 2 p.m. onwards.
- We agreed to one more part-time post to provide extra cover at peak times and on Saturday mornings.

Do call me if you'd like to discuss this further.
Best wishes,
Jenny

3 Janice – envelopes as requested – haven't posted letters 'cos I've got an urgent meeting. Phil fixed yr printer – it was unplugged! Cheers – Carl

4 Dear Melanie,
I would be interested in attending the coffee morning on Thursday for the delegation from the Haneul Corporation. This is because I am hoping in the future to form part of our sales team in East Asia. Although I am not a member of the management team, I wonder if it would be possible for me to do so.
Yours,

Vocabulary

1 1 Best wishes 2 minutes 3 please 4 could 5 your (can also be *year*, but not here) 6 as soon as possible 7 Personal Assistant 8 Chief Executive Officer

2 1 reference 2 Further 3 Good; input 4 know 5 note 6 answer 7 advance 8 details 9 hearing

Grammar workshop: future simple or future continuous?

1 Future simple: will help (A), will advertise (B), will … know (D), will all make (D), will include (D)
Future continuous: will be visiting (D), shall also be showing (D), will be meeting (D)

2 1 d 2 b/c 3 c/b 4 a

3 1 d will be visiting, shall also be showing, will be meeting
2 b will advertise, will include
3 c will help, will all make
4 a will … know

Advice for communicating with colleagues

Listening

1 Larry: **G** Marina: **D** or **H** Magdi: **A** Thérèse: **B**

Vocabulary

1 overdo 2 knock off 3 barging into 4 query 5 courtesy 6 overworked

Writing

2 Suggested answers

Task A

To: Customer Services Department
From: Customer Services Manager
Subject: Change to customer complaints procedure

Dear colleagues
Following a couple of incidents last month where customer-service staff gave inappropriate replies to customer complaints, I have decided to change the procedure for handling such complaints. In future, the procedure will be as follows:

1 Staff will continue to reply to written complaints in writing, but all replies must be signed by me personally. This is to ensure that answers to customer complaints and suggestions are handled in the same way and written in the same style. As you know, model letters are available on file for you to use when drafting your reply.
2 Spoken complaints, either when talking directly to customers or by telephone, will be dealt with according to existing procedures.

Thank you for your co-operation in this matter. Please let me know if you have any further suggestions for improvements in procedures.

GC

To: Giovanni Castelli
From: Franz Craven
Subject: Change to customer complaints procedure

Dear Giovanni
With reference to your memo about changes to the customer complaints procedure, could I just point out that many staff will probably find these changes demotivating, as it appears we cannot be trusted to handle complaints responsibly. I would also like to point out that the incidents in question were the fault of one temporary member of staff who is now no longer with us and therefore the change is not necessary.
May I suggest instead that all written complaints are handled by permanent members of the customer-service team, rather than temporary workers?

Best wishes
Franz

Task B

To: Nagwa Moulid
From: Kamal Salim
Subject: Post of Human Resources Manager (Recruitment)

Dear Nagwa
As you may know, the HR Department is advertising internally for a Human Resources Manager responsible for recruitment. Although I'm happy working in this department, I'd like to apply for this post, as it represents an opportunity for promotion within the company and is also the type of challenging administrative post which I think I'm now ready for.
The application form states that applications should be accompanied by recommendations from the applicant's line manager, and I'd be very grateful if you could do this for me.

Many thanks
Kamal

To: Kamal Salim
From: Nagwa Moulid
Subject: Re: Post of Human Resources Manager (Recruitment)

Dear Kamal
Thank you for this. I regret to say, however, that I don't consider you ready for the post you mention, as you've only been in your present post for six months. I believe, both for your own benefit and for the benefit of the department, it would be better if you stayed with us and built up your experience and competencies for at least another six months, after which time we could review the situation.
I would be very happy to discuss this with you when I return next week. I'm sorry to give you this disappointing news and would like to add that I consider your work to be satisfactory and that you are a valuable member of our team.

Best wishes
Nagwa

Task C

Contract with Haneul Corporation

Following the very successful visit of the delegation from the Haneul Corporation last week, I'm delighted to announce that they have signed a contract with us for the purchase of 40 of our SN printing machines for a total price of €72 million, including installation and after-sales service. This is excellent news for the company, as it represents a major breakthrough for our marketing effort in East Asia. It will also allow us to expand our production facilities here at home, as we had hoped.

I would like to thank all of you for the part you played in landing this contract, both those who contributed directly to the marketing effort and negotiations with Haneul, and those of you who, through the high quality of your work, have made us the supplier of choice for Haneul.

On Friday lunchtime, we will be holding a brief celebration of this good news in the Directors' Boardroom. You are all most welcome to join us there.

Manfred Schüller
CEO

Dear Manfred,
Just a brief note to congratulate you on this important new contract. It really is splendid news! I'll be delighted to attend the celebration.

See you then,
Sofia

UNIT 4
Chairing meetings

Advice for chairs

Reading

3 1 B 2 C 3 D 4 B 5 A 6 B 7 A 8 D 9 A 10 D 11 B 12 D

Key phrases for chairs

Listening

1 1 D 2 A 3 H 4 C 5 G

2 1 get 2 copy 3 minutes 4 purpose 5 views 6 sum 7 have 8 to 9 what 10 about 11 break 12 look 13 summary 14 other

4 Starting and managing a meeting: 1, 2, 3, 4, 10, 11, 12, 14
Asking for other opinions: 5, 7
Keeping the meeting focused: 8
Summarising: 6, 9, 13

Holding meetings

Vocabulary

1 1 h 2 a 3 g 4 b 5 c 6 f 7 e 8 d

Summarising action points

Reading

1 to 2 also 3 more 4 were 5 *correct* 6 of 7 you 8 time 9 *correct* 10 at 11 intending 12 *correct* 13 down 14 made 15 up 16 for

GRAMMAR WORKSHOP 1

Defining and non-defining relative clauses

1 1 which 2 whose 3 –/that/which 4 which 5 –/that/which 6 who/whom 7 who/that 8 who 9 when 10 –/that/who/whom

2
1 Thank you for circulating the report (which/that) you wrote.
2 The head of the department where I work would like to discuss it with you.
3 She would like several of the marketing people whose input you obtained to be present at the meeting.
4 Could you suggest a time when it would be convenient for us to meet?
5 Please pass my congratulations to Andy Drake, who did the graphics.
6 The report contained a number of statistics (which/that) I thought were surprising.
7 I had an interesting conversation with Maria Kalitza, whose comments you included in the conclusion.

Some meanings of *as* and *like*

1 as (a) 2 as (b) 3 as (a) 4 like (h) 5 as (g) 6 as (b) 7 like (h) 8 as (f) 9 like (i) 10 as (c) 11 as (d)

Future simple or future continuous?

1 will be giving 2 she'll make 3 will be producing 4 we'll be discussing

UNIT 5
Customer relationships

Getting started

Suggested answers

1
a loyalty, information about future needs
b after-sales service, information about product updates
c cost savings, personalised treatment

2 Other activities can include: interactive websites, after-sales services, call centres and helpdesks, regular updates on products by direct mail or email, loyalty cards, discounts for existing customers, clubs and competitions

Problems with customer relations

Reading

3
1 B (the whole paragraph)
2 C *... and that gap is the next big business opportunity.*
3 A *When firms cut costs, ... they put pressure on frontline staff who handle complaints, cutting the time each call-centre operative is allowed to spend on a pacifying call*
4 D *The difficulty begins with companies promising customers support that they cannot deliver. Electronic networks mean that firms now know more about their customers than ever before, so they believe that they can treat customers as individuals.*
5 D *... because it knows that retaining existing customers costs far less than recruiting new ones.*
6 B *That depends on whether consumers are willing to pay for support.*

Vocabulary

1 helpdesk 2 shipped 3 reliability 4 handle 5 retaining 6 outsourcing 7 redundant

Customer Relationship Management (CRM)

Listening

2 1 profitability 2 (their) competitors 3 information systems
4 (marketing) budget 5 sales process
6 loyalty (and) satisfaction 7 (the) Internet

Reading

3 1 E *Such an organisational structure makes it difficult to comprehend the total value of a customer and therefore can't capture important opportunities such as cross-selling.*
2 A *While providing customer service, clever companies are also gathering data on their customers' buying habits and needs*
3 D (the whole extract)
4 B *It simply can't be the 'project of the month'.*
5 A *… businesses can transform themselves into the proverbial friendly general store – to provide the same levels of customer service that were typical decades ago.*
6 A *… with the ultimate aim of turning consumers into customers for life.*
7 C *The customer is more interested in service than the technology that delivers it.*
8 D *While investors implicitly value product-development and R&D expenditures, considering them assets that are potentially useful over a long period of time, they undervalue marketing and customer-acquisition costs.*

UNIT 6
Competitive advantage

Getting started

1 1 e 2 g 3 a 4 d 5 b 6 c 7 f

Submitting tenders

Listening

1 1 d 2 e 3 g 4 h 5 c 6 a 7 b 8 f
3 1 sufficient quality 2 value (for money) 3 documents
4 past projects

Reading

1 1 By looking at recent contracts and comparing revenues with costs, and by matching tenders to business objectives.
2 By being members of relevant professional bodies, monitoring the trade press, attending networking events and using an online tracking tool for public contracts.
3 People with suitable skills, who have not too great a workload.
4 They hold meetings at key stages and map critical paths.
5 They study budget briefs and compare their prices with other similar agencies.
2 1 set 2 as 3 so 4 being 5 At 6 if 7 their 8 what 9 on
10 which 11 each
3 1 e 2 g 3 h 4 c 5 d 6 a 7 f 8 b

Winning contracts

Listening

2 1 C 2 B 3 A 4 C 5 B 6 A

Vocabulary 1

1 1 d 2 f 3 a 4 b 5 g 6 e 7 h 8 c
2 1 go for 2 teamed up with; came out with 3 go about
4 work out; comes to 5 bid for 6 Putting together

Grammar workshop: speaking hypothetically

1 1 *We'd expect, we would hope*
2 To say this is an imaginary rather than an actual situation.
3 Present simple and present continuous.
4 None really; the time is indefinite.
2 1 don't land 2 doesn't happen/hasn't happened 3 have
4 would approach
5 'd ask 6 is 7 'd hope 8 would give 9 ('d) manage
10 relies 11 ('d) do

Vocabulary 2

1 assessing; submitting 2 devote 3 compete 4 cover; go
5 itemise; establish

UNIT 7
A proposal

Extending the product range

Listening

1 1 Board of Directors 2 range of software 3 (our) existing clients
4 types of product 5 resources 6 extra costs
7 next board meeting

Reading

1 Yes, he has.
2 1 C 2 D 3 C 4 A 5 D 6 B 7 B 8 D 9 C 10 D
3 1 It has a title, and it's divided into sections with section headings.
2 Yes.
3 Future activity.
4 Formal.

Vocabulary

1 1 a 2 b 3 a 4 c 5 f 6 g 7 d 8 c 9 e
2 1 Since 2 While 3 in turn 4 at the same time
5 Therefore; in turn 6 in response to 7 apart from
8 in connection with 9 Furthermore
3 1 existing 2 identify 3 retail outlets 4 VAT returns 5 payroll
6 updates 7 generate 8 envisage/foresee

Grammar workshop 1: compound nouns

1 1 product range 2 accounting software 3 small retail outlets
4 existing products 5 client satisfaction 6 market research
7 recruitment requirements 8 marketing costs
2 1 customer service(s) manager 2 suggestion(s) box 3 holiday pay 4 resource management 5 job satisfaction 6 candidate selection process 7 client response 8 complaints procedure

Grammar workshop 2: the passive

1 The market research, which **was carried out** in Liverpool between May and September, revealed that **the price could be raised** by 50% with only a 5% loss of market share.
2 **Twenty-seven candidates have been interviewed** for the job, but **none of them are considered** to be suitable.
3 **Your order was received** the day before yesterday, and **the goods have just been dispatched**, so **they should be delivered** within the next 24 hours.
4 **No more goods will be supplied** (to you) until **the outstanding invoice has been paid**.

Writing a proposal

Reading

1 to 2 take 3 had/received 4 if 5 which/that 6 In 7 done
8 out 9 soon 10 advance

UNIT 8
Presenting at meetings

The Chinese ice-cream market

Listening

2 1 market 2 (market) growth rate 3 market share 4 annual purchase / consumption 5 production facilities 6 transportation costs 7 regional markets / local tastes 8 (fierce) price war

3 1 23 billion yuan (2.3 billion euros) 2 foreign companies (30%) 3 national companies (27%) 4 others (43%) 5 market growth (rate)

4 1 True It is, however, very informal and fairly brief.
2 False She uses contractions, informal phrasal verbs (e.g. *get in*) and adverbs (e.g. *pretty*) and asides (e.g. *I'm not sure I've got the right pronunciation there*).
3 False See above.
4 True She says *you can see that, as Chinese incomes rise, ice-cream consumption is a pretty hot prospect.*
5 True She says how many points she is going to make and uses markers (e.g. *firstly*; *Now, my second point*; *And now my third and final point*) to indicate where she is in her talk.
6 True She says *That, I think, answers the first part of your question as far as I can; as to the second, …*

Grammar workshop: embedded questions

1 I'd just like to know what the total sales for the Chinese market are.
2 Can you tell me how Chinese companies are reacting to this competition from abroad and also how these competitors are going about increasing their market share?
3 I wonder what sort of price you think we could sell our products at.
4 How do you think we would position them?

GRAMMAR WORKSHOP 2

Speaking hypothetically

1 1 advertised; would/'d find 2 hadn't/had not managed; 'd/would have gone 3 had; would … be 4 had/'d stayed; would/'d have known 5 were/was; wouldn't/would not mind; had /'d realised; would/'d have left 6 had/'d put; would/'d have landed 7 taught; would be 8 had/'d ordered 9 had not/hadn't won; would/'d probably be 10 did not/didn't have; would not/wouldn't have sold

2 1 'd/would first have 2 would also need 3 had budgeted 4 wouldn't/would not have bought 5 (would) look 6 (would) even assess 7 would/might/may/could cause 8 wouldn't/would not want

Compound nouns

1 an accounting procedure 2 a car manufacturer 3 a negotiating session 4 a rival firm 5 the finance director 6 a price list 7 a market research survey / a market-research survey 8 (job) application forms 9 a motorcycle delivery service 10 a typing error

Embedded questions

1 1 I wonder when the new factory site will become operational.
2 Do you have any idea how long the construction work is expected to take?
3 Could you please tell me why the goods couldn't have been delivered on time?
4 Several people have asked me if we have to send the invoice with the goods.
5 Tell me what time you finally finished writing the report.
6 I'd be grateful if you could tell me when we must have the work completed by.
7 I'd like to know if they brought the samples with them.
8 I'd appreciate it if you could answer a few questions for me.

UNIT 9
Advertising and customers

Getting started

1 1 building 2 awareness 3 launch 4 boost 5 market 6 customer

The effectiveness of advertising

Vocabulary

1 1 banner (a) 2 classified (e) 3 street (d) 4 point-of-sale (c) 5 endorsement (b)

Reading

2 The writer believes advertising is becoming less effective because there are more types of media and consumers are becoming more sceptical.

3 1 A 2 C 3 B 4 A 5 B 6 D 7 D 8 B 9 C 10 D 11 A 12 B 13 C 14 B 15 A

Grammar workshop: adverbs

1 still, actually 2 actually 3 particularly, increasingly, highly 4 as never before 5 For instance, Hence 6 constantly 7 literally 8 within a minute

Listening

2 1 (the) most cost-effective / (possibly) the best 2 point of purchase 3 budget 4 mood 5 cosmetic brand 6 throughout the day

Measuring the effectiveness of advertising

Reading

2 Suggested answers
1 There is no reliable correlation between the amount of money spent on advertising and how this affects consumers' decisions to buy. Advertising campaigns are not carried out with just one advert in one medium, but as part of a larger marketing campaign, so even if sales increase, it is usually not possible to know which part of the combination has been more effective and which less effective.
2 Because it is a cost, and costs have to be justified. If you can measure the effectiveness of advertising, you can make informed decisions for future publicity.
3 Only approximately, by using market research, i.e. asking samples of customers and target audiences, by monitoring changes in sales figures coinciding with advertising campaigns.

3 1 A *… developed to detect inaudible codes placed in radio and TV commercials, as well as other forms of electronic media ranging from the cinema to background music in places like supermarkets.*
2 E *Two-thirds of consumers feel 'constantly bombarded' with too much advertising*
3 D *advertisers will also be able to limit the number of times an ad is shown to an individual in order to avoid irritating him.*
4 B *it has always been difficult to put it all together to establish a link between exposure to ads and buying behaviour. This is what Apollo is designed to achieve.*
5 E *People are increasingly able to filter out ads.*
6 A *To measure their exposure to electronic media, they will carry an Arbitron device*
7 C *The response to the ads increased significantly*
8 C *Individuals using the websites remain anonymous*

Vocabulary

1 households 2 exposure to 3 inaudible 4 scanners 5 barcodes
6 (electronic) tracers/cookies 7 tracked 8 filter out / block
9 subjected to 10 bombarded (with)

UNIT 10
Advertising and the Internet

Internet sales
Listening

	Product/Service	Why used Internet
Bruce	3	a
Tanya	1	b
Paddy	7	e
Petra	2	f
Salim	4	d

Reading

1 1 c 2 g 3 a 4 f 5 e 6 d 7 b
2 1 H 2 E 3 G 4 F 5 C 6 A 7 B

Vocabulary

1 d 2 c 3 a 4 g 5 h 6 f 7 b 8 e

Grammar workshop: *although, however, despite,* etc.

1 1 although, while 2 despite, in spite of 3 however, in contrast
4 while 5 in contrast

2
1. While few people buy cars on the Internet, many people research them there.
2. Although people study new cars on the Internet, they go to showrooms to buy them.
3. It's difficult to measure advertising's effectiveness. However, few companies believe they can do without it.
4. Despite employing a consultancy, they couldn't improve their company's image.
5. Many dotcom companies have been struggling. In contrast, eBay has been growing by 40% a year.
6. In spite of (having) a / the / their large advertising budget, they kept their product prices low.

Advertisers and the Internet
Writing

2 1 between 2 each 3 their 4 even/far/much 5 with 6 spend
3 Suggested answer
As the chart shows, there is a disparity between the quantity US advertisers spend on advertising in each of the main media and US consumers' use of the media.
While advertisers spend 38% of their budget on television advertising, US households nowadays spend only 32% of their time watching television. The difference between advertising spending and consumption of newspapers is even more accentuated with advertising taking up 36% of the budget, although people spend an average of just 9% of their time reading them. Magazines reflect a smaller disparity with spending of 8% by advertisers whereas consumers spend only 6% of their time reading them.
In contrast, advertisers tend to spend less on radio advertising (14%) in relation to audience (19%). The most surprising difference of all, however, is between the time people spend using the Internet (34% of their media consumption) compared with advertising spending on the Internet, which comes to just 4% of the total advertising budget.

Listening

1 A 2 C 3 B 4 B 5 C

UNIT 11
Sales reports

Evolving sales
Listening

1 retail sales (f) 2 e-sales (c) 3 mail order (b) 4 telephone sales (a)

Vocabulary

1 1 decrease 2 decrease 3 increase 4 increase 5 decrease
6 decrease

Reading

1 1 ~~had~~ have 2 ~~of~~ from 3 ~~hat~~ than 4 ~~too~~ to 5 ~~In~~ On 6 ✔
7 ~~had~~ have
2 increase: expand, take off
decrease: fall, halve, dwindle

Grammar workshop: present perfect simple or continuous?

1 1 present perfect continuous 2 present perfect simple
2 1 has been manufacturing 2 has risen 3 She's been working
4 have gone

Writing

2 Suggested answer
Software Solutions: software sales by category
Over the last ten years, sales of our five main categories of software have undergone quite important changes. Ten years ago, our main product was accounting software, which constituted 55% of our total sales. This category has more than halved to just 20% nowadays. The other line which has not performed so successfully is stock-control software, whose sales have shrunk from 20% of the total to just 12%.
On the other hand, other categories have been remarkably successful. Our CRM software has soared from just 5% of the total to 27% at present. Similarly, our payroll software has trebled its sales, rising from 5% to 15%, while our shipment tracking packages have taken off and now account for 25% of sales where ten years ago they stood at just 15% of the total.

Report on a sales event
Reading

2
a Successful (orders and sales exceed investment in the event, attendees have asked for it to be repeated).
b Outcomes: immediate orders of £1.6m and £2.2m in sales in the future.
Reactions: need for EU payroll and accounting software, lack of interest in the CRM software, more informal presentations from clients, next event in a central European location.

3 1 B 2 A 3 D 4 C 5 C 6 A 7 D 8 C 9 B 10 C

UNIT 12
The sales pitch

Cold-calling

Listening

1 1 Property-management companies generally let or lease or rent out properties on behalf of their owners. They find people or companies who want to rent the properties, they supervise the contract and also make sure that the people renting the property (or the owners, if it is their responsibility) maintain it in good condition.

2 1 physically threatened 2 visiting properties 3 (large) mobile-phone 4 (call) the police 5 (the) office 6 locate (the) 7 reception desk

3 1 False 2 False 3 True 4 False 5 True

5 1 e 2 a 3 c 4 b 5 d

Providing services to large companies

Speaking

1 He wants to service and repair their employees' cars by collecting them and returning them while the employees are at work.

2 He wants suggestions about how to get a chance to make his sales pitch to the companies' human resources departments.

Reading

2 1 C *One way we solicit referrals is by identifying the decision-makers in a big company and then determining if we know someone who knows them. We then educate the person that we know about the things we can offer that the big company couldn't find somewhere else.*

2 B *they tend to focus on the things that could go wrong*

3 B *Can you track down the owners of those local businesses and gain insight into the relationship structure and the decision process that got them on board?*

4 A *you'll be trying to crack a bigger bureaucracy*

Vocabulary

1 g 2 d 3 a 4 f 5 c 6 b 7 e 8 h

Making a sales pitch

Listening

1 24 / twenty-four 2 (are) specially trained 3 press a button 4 give (them) advice 5 the (potential) problem 6 a few metres 7 contact number 8 five or ten / 5–10 9 leasing (the) equipment 10 (fixed) monthly charge

Grammar workshop: cleft sentences

1 1 b 2 a 3 a 4 b

2 1 b 2 a 3 a 4 b

3 1 What we do is deliver the pizzas to your home.

2 All you have to do is provide the venue.

3 It's the paperwork (that) we find too time-consuming.

4 The last thing you should do is settle the invoice before you've received the goods.

GRAMMAR WORKSHOP 3

Position of adverbs

Suggested answers

(The second and third alternative answers, where given, are possible, but perhaps not used so frequently.)

1 The advertising campaign which we carried out in major European newspapers last month has proved a great success.
The advertising campaign in major European newspapers which we carried out last month has proved a great success.

2 Interestingly, brand awareness rose by 5% in the first three months.
Interestingly, in the first three months, brand awareness rose by 5%.

3 In my opinion, this is due to our having targeted our audience very carefully before we started.
This, in my opinion, is due to our having very carefully targeted our audience before we started.
This is due, in my opinion, to our having targeted our audience very carefully before we started.

4 Consequently, we have already managed to meet our sales targets for several lines.
Consequently, we have managed to meet our sales targets for several lines already.

5 For example, sales of our most popular brands have risen spectacularly since we began advertising.
Sales of our most popular brands, for example, have risen spectacularly since we began advertising.
Since we began advertising, sales of our most popular brands, for example, have risen spectacularly.

6 Unfortunately, however, our top-of-the-range brands have not performed so impressively.
However, unfortunately, our top-of-the-range brands have not performed so impressively.
Unfortunately, our top-of-the-range brands have not performed so impressively, however.
However, our top-of-the-range brands have unfortunately not performed so impressively.

7 Sales of these have stayed at the same level, or even dropped slightly.

8 As a result, I think we should meet soon to discuss this.
As a result, I think we should meet to discuss this soon.

9 We need to find a solution urgently, although it shouldn't prove especially difficult.
We urgently need to find a solution, although it shouldn't prove especially difficult.

10 Could you call me later today on my mobile?
Could you call me on my mobile later today?

Present perfect simple and continuous

1 has just decided 2 I've been trying 3 he's worked 4 he's made 5 Have you always occupied 6 haven't sent; have you been doing 7 I've been working 8 I've phoned 9 have been getting

Cleft sentences

1 What had a positive effect on sales was the CRM system.
2 What they did was outsource their production to Indonesia.
3 What they sold was/were paper products.
4 It's the time (which/that) it takes which/that is the problem.
5 It's Internet fraud which/that is our biggest problem.
6 All he does is complain.
7 All this shop sells is paint.
8 The last thing I want is your advice.

UNIT 13
Forecasts and results

Forecasting sales

Listening

1/2

	Contribution	Reason for inaccuracy
Olivia	(2) predictions about interest rates	(a) There was a shift in fashion.
Jaime	(6) the success of competitors' products	(f) Our publicity was more effective than we expected.
Gary	(4) intuition	(b) We were affected by a press report.
Sylvie	(8) the marketing budget	(c) There was an unexpected disaster.
Nesreen	(3) reports from sales teams	(h) We experienced a shortage of qualified staff.

Vocabulary 1

1 c 2 g 3 d 4 e 5 b 6 a 7 f

Reading

2 1 *It's emotionally difficult for people to do negative scenarios.* (paragraph 1)
2 *it is useful to bring together people from various departments who think about the future in different ways.* (paragraph 3)
3 *"We compare the machine forecasts to the human forecasts every month … The numbers have got to be in sync with each other." If they're not, Wise wants to know why. But when in doubt, he says the human forecast … wins.* (paragraph 4)
4 *Ertel prods them instead to look for ways they can take advantage of competitors' inactivity or retrenchments. The goal isn't to predict what's ahead precisely but to imagine both positive and negative outcomes, understand what might prompt them and consider how you might handle each one.* (paragraph 5)

3 1 H 2 F 3 C 4 E 5 D 6 B 7 G

Vocabulary 2

1 go bust 2 stock price 3 earnings shortfalls 4 layoffs 5 in sync 6 cross-section 7 discontinuities 8 resilient 9 prods 10 retrenchments

Grammar workshop: conditional sentences

1 1 e 2 c 3 a 4 b 5 d

2 1 a, c and e refer to present/future time; b and d refer to past time.
2 *If* + past perfect, *would/could have* + past participle
3 *If* + present, future simple/continuous; *If* + past, *would/could* + base form (simple or continuous)

Reporting results

Vocabulary

1 1 loss 2 turnover 3 pre-tax profits 4 dividends 5 profit and loss for the period 6 equity 7 debtors 8 equipment 9 liabilities

2 1 premises 2 depreciation 3 overdraft 4 retained earnings 5 assets 6 stock 7 goodwill

Talking point

Suggested answers

1 **The share price** – especially in relation to the value of the company. A low share price may lay the company open to a takeover bid.
How much profit has been made and what the company can afford, especially in relation to the company's other expenditures.
Shareholders' expectations

2 They can spend money before it registers as profits, for example by reinvesting it in company operations, or by spending it on things which are tax deductible such as charities.

3 Goodwill includes the good reputation of the company, the reputation of its brands and its brand names and brand equity, and the value of its customer relations.

UNIT 14
Financing the arts

The theatre business

Listening

1 1 d 2 c 3 a 4 e 5 b 6 f

2 1 B 2 A 3 B 4 B 5 A 6 C 7 A

Vocabulary

1 1 f 2 b 3 h 4 e 5 c 6 d 7 g 8 a

2 1 break down 2 running costs 3 backers; put up 4 break even 5 sue

Sponsoring the arts

Grammar workshop: infinitive and verb + *-ing*

1 1 Because it represents a low-cost opportunity to enhance the company's image both locally and nationally; sponsorship can be offset against tax.
2 It would involve investing £10,000; in return, the company would have its name and logo on all publicity material and theatre programmes, and the logo would appear in the theatre.

2 1 sponsoring 2 to examine 3 doing 4 promoting 5 to give 6 backing 7 Sponsoring 8 hiring 9 to receive 10 To cover 11 to include 12 to be agreed 13 to fund 14 to enhance 15 to offset

3 1 (to) sponsoring (1), (of) doing, (to) promoting, (by) backing
2 Sponsoring (7)
3 include hiring
4 tend to give, expect to receive, undertake to include, agree to fund
5 to examine, To cover
6 opportunity to enhance
7 to be agreed

Listening

1 B 2 C 3 B 4 A 5 C 6 A 7 A 8 A

UNIT 15
Late payers

Late payers and small businesses

Vocabulary

1 h 2 j 3 e 4 k 5 a 6 g 7 i 8 d 9 b 10 f 11 c

Reading

3 1 Lack of cash (because you are a victim of late payment / falling order book / overtrading due to rapid growth) or poor financial management.
2 Cashflow problems, unauthorised overdrafts and high bank charges, time-consuming and stressful.
3 Businesses which are victims of late payment may refuse to do business, may only accept cash in advance, will not trust late payers in future.
4 Check credit worthiness, set credit limits, automate bookkeeping and monitor payments of invoices, keep your bank informed, have procedures for recovering debts.

4 1 constraints 2 unauthorised 3 punitive (bank) charges 4 undue 5 upfront 6 overdue 7 sound 8 root causes

Letter to a late payer

Listening 1

1 1 two (major) customers 2 cash-flow/cashflow difficulties 3 (our) overdraft 4 credit limit 5 (a) registered letter 6 11 days

Grammar workshop: complex sentences

1 1 According to 2 However 3 which 4 As 5 As a consequence 6 not only 7 but also 8 since 9 with whom 10 and that

2 1 The bank which normally handles our transactions has agreed to extend our overdraft for another month.
2 I regret to inform you that not only do we keep a list of late payers, but also we share this information with other suppliers. / … but we also share this information with other suppliers.
3 We may have to put this matter in the hands of our lawyer, which we would regret having to do.
4 As I informed you in my previous letter, we shall not be supplying you with any further goods.
5 According to my accountant, we should set a credit limit of £5,000.

Vocabulary

1 in a position 2 deeply regret 3 unpleasantness 4 mutually profitable 5 further 6 settle your account with 7 assured 8 prompt 9 indicated 10 shortly 11 outstanding 12 awaiting

Listening 2

1 cash flow / cashflow 2 pay promptly 3 no good reason 4 (finance) team 5 (very) legitimate reasons 6 satisfied with

Writing

1 1 paragraph 1 2 paragraph 2 3 paragraph 2 4 paragraph 3 5 paragraph 3 6 paragraph 3 7 paragraph 4

UNIT 16
Negotiating a lease

Hard bargaining

Listening

	Type of negotiation	Problem
Vasili	C	J
Melinda	G	O
Glenn	D	L/P
Carla	H	I
Naomi	B	M

Vocabulary

1 a 2 h 3 b 4 c 5 g 6 d 7 f 8 e

Leasing office space

Reading

3 1 impact 2 meets 3 mind 4 stock 5 term 6 lock 7 interruption 8 come 9 restrictions 10 comes 11 unlimited 12 leverage

Listening

1 (an) (upfront) deposit 2 (commercial) activity 3 (the) inflation (rate) 4 alterations or repairs 5 renewable 6 (staff) parking space(s)

Grammar workshop: conditional sentences: alternatives to *if*

1 1 Supposing 2 unless 3 as long as 4 provided 5 on condition that

2 Suggested answers
1 Will we be able to undercut them?
2 Imagine that you were suddenly made redundant.
3 … you pay the additional premium.
4 We'll reduce the rent by 5% …
5 … you achieve all your performance targets.

Role-play

1 f, l; 2 c, e; 3 b, h, j; 4 a, m, n; 5 d, k; 6 o; 7 g, i

GRAMMAR WORKSHOP 4

Conditional sentences

1 launch; will almost certainly lose 2 went (were to go) / go; would be / will be 3 hadn't run; might have met 4 increases; will rise *or* increased; would rise 5 had been; could have made 6 could; would be

Infinitive and verb + *-ing*

1 Going; taking 2 to continue; going 3 to spot; running 4 To discourage; going; to close 5 to know; visiting 6 to hold; completing

Complex sentences

Suggested answers
1 We experienced a shortfall in earnings last year as a result of losing one of our most important customers, who started buying from our principal competitor.

2 I'm writing to thank you because the goods you dispatched to us last week arrived at our warehouse in record time, which means that our production is now ahead of schedule.
3 Martin Peters, whose appraisal, you may remember, was not very satisfactory, has decided to leave the company, so we will have to start recruiting a replacement as soon as we can.
4 While travelling home last night, I came up with a brilliant solution to our staffing problems, which I'm going to put in an informal proposal to be circulated among senior managers.
5 Unless Tasker Ltd offers its employees more attractive financial incentives, they will never manage to reach the productivity agreement which would put them ahead of the competition.
6 There's a shortage of skilled workers in the chemical industry due to insufficient numbers of young people studying science subjects at school.
7 Redland Electronics have announced record profits for the fourth year running as a result of their partnership with Kawasaki Electronics of Japan.

UNIT 17
Workplace atmosphere

Motivating employees

Reading

1 David Sirota would probably agree with 3, 5 and 6. He would probably disagree with 1, 2 and 4.

2 1 C *firms where employee morale is high tend to outperform competitors.*
2 D *they retrain workers*
3 B *The team could look at quality and at what kind of maintenance and support were needed, and it could decide how to rotate workers.*
4 A *Research has verified a system such as 'gain sharing', in which a group of workers judges its performance over time.*
5 C *Then there is transactional … The attitude is, 'We paid you, now we are even …' That's where most companies have gone today.*

Grammar workshop: reference devices

1 1 *This* and *it* both refer to *camaraderie*.
2 *they* refers to *some companies*.

2 for which (line 10) = the organisation
it (line 10) = your job
This (line 11) = camaraderie
it('s) (line 11) = camaraderie
do (line 16) = laying off people
they (line 18) = some companies
that (line 25) = having groups of employees build an entire car
it (line 29) = the team
this approach (line 30) = Toyota said … rotate workers
thus (line 31) = as opposed to the usual top-down management
this kind (line 35) = recognition, appreciative of good work
such (line 42) = a reward
That result (line 46) = greater efficiency
This (line 47) = The result should be shared with workers
the first one (line 50) = form of management
Then there is (line 51) = form of management
That's where (line 55) = the transactional form of management
The fourth (line 57) = form of management
It (line 58) = the partnership organisation
that way (line 59) = because I paid you, now we're even.

3 1 for which 2 This, that 3 do 4 that
5 this approach 6 such 7 the first one, Then there is, The fourth
8 it, they

Stress in the workplace

Reading

2 1 the former 2 the same / this 3 the following 4 They
5 this / the same 6 themselves

3 1 trends 2 pronounced 3 underwent 4 slight
5 an all-time low 6 peaking

Listening

1 Suggested answers
Causes of stress: perception of lack of control over one's life, harder work, close supervision, changing jobs, faster lifestyles, more intensive work, less social cohesion at work, work more invasive of non-working time, more time to worry about work, work more central to our lives and fashionable to complain about

2 1 B 2 A 3 B 4 C 5 E 6 A 7 C 8 B

Writing

3 Suggested answer
This report summarises the findings of a survey of managers conducted to investigate the effects of stress on organisations
The main effect of stress is an increase in absenteeism, which 76% of managers reported. This is reflected in the figures for increased costs due to absenteeism in small companies, which have risen in companies with fewer than 100 employees from €250 to €320 per employee over the last five years, while in companies of between 100 and 249, these costs have increased from €310 to €510 per employee.
Stress also leads to decreased productivity (reported by 71% of managers), poor judgement and poor-quality products (54% each) and lower standards of customer care (41%). Managers also complain that staff leave the company more frequently, are less creative and have a higher rate of accidents.
In conclusion, stress-related problems are a major cost for organisations.

UNIT 18
The workforce of the future

Getting started

1 f 2 i 3 d 4 h 5 c 6 g 7 j 8 e 9 a 10 b

The millennium generation

Reading

2 1 E *hungry for quick results*
2 C *more young people have been striking out on their own.*
3 A *They have less baggage and can therefore afford to take risks.*
4 C *capital for the taking*
5 B *They define themselves by their skills*
6 D *You can always go back to college*
7 E *intolerant of technophobes*
8 E *most will freelance*

Vocabulary

1 less baggage 2 frenetic 3 obsolete 4 pervasive 5 places a premium on 6 roam 7 booming 8 striking out on (their) own

Job sharing

Talking point

1 1 f 2 e 3 c 4 a 5 b 6 d

Listening

1 career continuity / (flexibility) 2 family responsibilities 3 rejoin (the) workforce 4 go for promotion 5 less training 6 overtime 7 more productive / work harder 8 staff turnover 9 Sickness absences 10 job functions 11 communication (problems) 12 more experienced partner

How people feel about their jobs

Listening

1

	Views of the present	Hopes for the future
Lechsinska	D	G
Ganesh	E	J
Francesca	F	I
Darron	C	L
Irenke	B	H

Vocabulary

1 1 apart 2 going 3 stuck 4 go 5 run 6 dire 7 taken 8 good; cut

UNIT 19
Productivity

Productivity at Magro Toys

Reading

2 1 ✔ 2 of 3 were 4 yet 5 the 6 ✔ 7 in 8 had 9 ✔ 10 ✔ 11 an 12 which 13 ✔ 14 ✔ 15 up 16 it 17 ✔ 18 on 19 are 20 the 21 ✔ 22 forming 23 ✔ 24 companies 25 be 26 ✔

3
1 were achieved, have not been maintained, was decided, was carried out, should not be allowed
2 the automation of our Villena plant, the implementation of this decision, a reduction of payroll costs, increase in turnover, increase in sales

Grammar workshop: expressing causes and results

1 The introduction of a new computer system <u>led to</u> an initial decrease in productivity. However, <u>as a consequence of</u> an intensive staff training programme, productivity soon rose to record levels.

2 resulted in, gave rise to, resulting from, one consequence of … has been …, this in turn has meant that …, due to

3 1 b 2 a 3 e 4 f 5 c 6 d

4 Suggested answers
1 Higher interest rates have resulted in cashflow problems.
2 Our incentive scheme for sales staff has given rise to a 50% increase in sales.
3 One consequence of doing market research has been that our products are even more suited to our customers.
4 New environmental regulations have meant that we have had to reduce pollution from our plants.
5 Due to the installation of new machines in the factory, we have managed to increase shop-floor productivity.
6 As a consequence of our staff training programme, our employees are making more efficient use of the computer systems.

Productivity concerns

Vocabulary

1 f 2 g 3 h 4 a 5 e 6 c 7 b 8 i 9 d 10 j

Listening

1 C 2 B 3 B 4 A 5 C 6 A 7 A 8 C

UNIT 20
Staff negotiations

Travelsafe Insurance

Listening

2

	Complaint	Demand
Wendy	H	I
Demitri	A	J
Naline	F	P
Claudio	C	K
Toya	B	M

Vocabulary

1 b 2 c 3 a 4 g 5 e 6 h 7 d 8 f

Grammar workshop: variations on conditional sentences 1

1 a, c, d, e
2 b
3 *in the event of, provided* (other possibilities: *providing, suppose, supposing, imagine, as long as, unless, on condition that*)
4 a
5 b
6 e

Reading

2 1 part 2 view 3 This 4 by 5 above/earlier 6 in 7 for 8 more/details 9 during/at/in 10 have/make/offer

Grammar workshop: variations on conditional sentences 2

1 1 c 2 h 3 b 4 f 5 a 6 g 7 d 8 e

3 Suggested answers
1 … not been given promotion.
2 … I'm given more responsibility.
3 … the amount of work he has to get through.
4 … a factory closure.
5 … I have a chance to put my training into practice.
6 … he's given a pay rise.

Horse-trading at Travelsafe Insurance

Listening

1 20% / twenty per cent 2 financial incentives 3 salary increase 4 one-off payment 5 paid leave 6 legal entitlement 7 outplacement service

Role-play

2 **A:** 1, 2, 12 **B:** 10, 11, 13 **C:** 3, 5, 6 **D:** 4, 8, 9, 14 **E:** 7, 15

GRAMMAR WORKSHOP 5

Reference devices

1 does 2 one; It/Another 3 done so 4 thus 5 One; the other; The former; The latter 6 This/It 7 This/It

Modal verbs to express degrees of certainty

1 can't have been cancelled
2 should/must have arrived
3 may/might/could be
4 can't be losing
5 must be holding
6 must have dialled
7 might not / may not / can't have had
8 should find / must have found

Variations on conditionals

1 If it weren't for the view, these offices would be perfect.
2 If it weren't for the transport costs, I'd place an order.
3 If the staff were to (go on) strike, the company would go bankrupt.
4 Had management been ready to negotiate seriously, there would have been no problem.
5 In the event of an interruption in/to/of our supply chain / In the event of our supply chain being interrupted, we'll need to be able to source alternative parts quickly.
6 Providing you pay me overtime, I'll do the extra work on Saturday morning.
7 As long as we replace the part, the customer has promised not to complain / the customer won't complain.
8 Supposing they raised the price, how would you react?

UNIT 21

Corporate ethics

Corporate Social Responsibility (CSR)

Reading

1 1 Large companies must be socially responsible, not just profitable.
2 Examples of how to be socially responsible.
3 Corporations should recognise their obligations to society, either voluntarily through CSR or through government legislation.
4 How everyday business activities can be made to appear to give a social benefit.
5 Seemingly worthy actions can have an unseen detrimental effect.
6 Maybe it would be better if businesses concentrated on making profits and left governments to help other countries.

3 1 H 2 F 3 C 4 G 5 A 6 E 7 B

Vocabulary 1

1 f 2 a 3 h 4 d 5 e 6 c 7 g 8 b

Vocabulary 2

1 1 at least 2 merely 3 supposedly 4 all the while 5 thus 6 all things considered 7 simply put 8 unfortunately

2 1 Simply put 2 all the while / unfortunately 3 Unfortunately 4 all things considered 5 supposedly; merely 6 At least 7 thus

Fair trade

Listening

2 1 B 2 A 3 B 4 A 5 C

Grammar workshop: articles

1 a 2 – 3 a 4 the 5 the 6 – 7 the 8 a 9 – 10 the 11 – 12 – 13 the 14 the/– 15 – 16 – 17 a 18 –

UNIT 22

Expanding abroad

Wolseley's strategy

Reading

1 1 Wolseley expands organically, i.e. by opening new branches, and through acquisitions.
2 They achieve this through:
- continuous improvement
- using their international position both to sell and to purchase
- providing customers with an increased choice of products, etc.
- attracting the best employees.

2 1 B 2 B 3 D 4 D 5 C 6 A 7 C 8 D 9 C 10 A 11 D 12 B

Vocabulary

1 acquisitions 2 sustained 3 complacent 4 leveraging 5 a diverse footprint 6 synergies

Listening

1 with experience 2 joint ventures 3 manufacturing 4 growth potential 5 expertise 6 outlets / financial performance 7 financial performance / outlets 8 realise cash 9 lower purchasing prices / experience and expertise 10 their own markets

Wolseley's Chief Executive

Reading

3 1 G 2 C 3 A 4 E 5 F 6 B

Vocabulary

1 surged 2 FTSE 100 3 topped 4 hard-driving 5 briefings 6 clutch 7 pay off 8 broaden our customer base

Supervising overseas subsidiaries

Listening

2 1 discuss (the) objectives 2 (the) financial performance 3 senior management 4 annual conferences 5 (European) graduate programme 6 mid-management level 7 own branch network 8 awareness 9 (many) retailers 10 economies of scale 11 service

Vocabulary

1 Order from most frequent to least frequent: every half hour, hourly, daily, twice weekly, fortnightly, monthly, every two months, quarterly, biannual(ly), annual(ly)

2 1 twice-weekly 2 annual 3 every half hour 4 quarterly 5 fortnightly

UNIT 23

An overseas partnership

Finding an overseas partner

Listening

1 1 same (basic) letter 2 formal style 3 (some) sales figures 4 production capacity 5 joint-venture partner 6 Asian tour 7 provide (a) translation

Reading

1 1 other 2 As 3 capable 4 its 5 over/under 6 Due/Owing/Thanks 7 in 8 with 9 or 10 which/that 11 for 12 will 13 view 14 let 15 most

Grammar workshop: complex sentences

1 1 based in 2 As you may have read in the trade press 3 in its original form 4 Due/Owing/Thanks to our excellent sales projections 5 are now also in a position to begin 6 with that objective in mind 7 in the pipeline 8 with a view to

2
1 We are a large chemical company based in Bahrain.
2 As you may have heard on the news, we are thinking of moving our offices to Abu Dhabi.
3 In its original form, this book sold very successfully in the USA and Canada.
4 We are launching an updated version of this product due to some technological innovations. / Due to some technological innovations, we are launching an updated version of this product.
5 Our training budget has been approved, so we are now in a position to run the course.
6 We are hoping to increase our sales in India, and, with that (objective) in mind, we are launching a multi-million-rupee advertising campaign.
7 We have various new products in the pipeline at the moment.
8 We shall be launching a new publicity campaign with a view to increasing our share of the North American market.

Going into new markets

Listening

1
1
A global ambitions, move upmarket
B cut costs, move a lot of product
C affluence, spending power
D undercut the competition, wage a price war
E go into a whole new area, spread risks
F an approach, write to accept
G keep to targets, meet targets
H an opening, a gap in the market

2 Suggested answers
I cut-throat, fierce rivalry
J language problems, hard to get our ideas across
K problems finding top-quality employees, good staff
L change the way we work, accept their way of doing things
M adapt appearance, change the packet
N invest heavily, spend a lot of money
O new publicity, new promotional material
P seek a local partner, get assistance

2

Speaker	Reason	Problem
1	A	N
2	H	M
3	E	I
4	B	J
5	D	O

Grammar workshop: tenses in future time clauses

1 1 have got / 've got / (get) 2 gets 3 sends / has sent 4 're selling / (sell)

Replying to Magiczne Lustra's approach

Reading

1 1 b 2 g 3 e 4 c 5 f 6 h 7 i 8 d

2 1 ~~that~~ which 2 ~~for~~ in 3 ~~Like~~ As 4 ✔ 5 ~~too~~ also 6 ~~For~~ In 7 ✔ 8 ~~pieces~~ parts 9 ~~are~~ were 10 ~~about~~ of 11 ~~could~~ would 12 ~~seeing~~ see 13 ✔ 14 ~~a~~ an 15 ~~possible~~ possibility 16 ✔ 17 ~~absence~~ absent 18 ~~Although~~ However 19 ~~do~~ make 20 ✔ 21 ~~visiting~~ visit

UNIT 24

A planning conference

Making presentations to colleagues

Listening

1 1 good marketing activities 2 critical media coverage 3 customer expectations 4 cost-cutting exercises 5 polluting the environment 6 exploit (their) workers 7 marketing led 8 prime objective

2 1 True 2 False 3 True 4 True 5 True 6 True 7 False 8 True

3
1 I'm going to talk to you, briefly, about …
2 By way of introduction, I should say that …
3 I think there are three main points in …
4 First, …
5 My third point concerns …
6 In conclusion, …

Grammar workshop: concession

1 Even if a brand has a good reputation, it can be ruined overnight by critical media coverage.
2 Although there may be pressures from shareholders, the customer comes first in any business.
3 Despite your finance department wanting to implement cost-cutting exercises, brand quality should never be compromised.
4 People will just stop buying them, however many millions you spend on advertising.
5 No matter what you do in whatever area of corporate activity, you should first consider whether this could affect the health of the brand.

Risk management

Reading

2
1 B *managers now have to be prepared for a range of risks that were unthinkable not long ago.*
2 E *the misdeeds of one company can tarnish all its competitors as well.*
3 D *If a company suffers a blow to its reputation, it can collapse with astonishing speed … Even if a company survives damage to its reputation, the loss of business can be devastating.*
4 B *identify your risks. Be prepared for each of them individually*
5 C *companies spent millions … to guard against the Y2K bug … Managing risks can seem a waste of time and money*
6 A *Yet risk is trickier to handle than mergers or product launches.*
7 E *the government, the public and the media, and, increasingly, the Internet, which has greatly improved transparency. Corporate secrets are becoming ever harder to keep.*
8 E *As they rely more on outsourcing, they may be held responsible for the sins of their subcontractors.*

Listening

1 Increased risks from: natural disasters, international nature of business,
Reduced risks because of: insurance, limited-liability companies, government regulations, computer projections

2 1 B 2 B 3 A 4 C 5 C

GRAMMAR WORKSHOP 6

Articles

1 the 2 a 3 the 4 the 5 the 6 – 7 a 8 the 9 – 10 a 11 – 12 the 13 – 14 a 15 the 16 the 17 the 18 a / the 19 a 20 –

Future time clauses

1 1 finish / have finished 2 am working 3 is completed / has been completed 4 are visiting 5 speak / have spoken

2 Suggested answers
1 … I am paid more for it.
2 … I have perfected my pronunciation.
3 … I retire.
4 … they are retooling the factory, I'll take my annual holiday.

Concession

1 Profits are up, though productivity is down.
2 We won't be able to meet the deadline however hard we work. / However hard we work, we won't be able to meet the deadline.
3 No matter how high a salary you pay him, / No matter how much you pay him, he won't work harder.
4 Despite his good keynote speech / Despite his making a good keynote speech / Despite his having made a good keynote speech, the shareholders voted him off the board.
5 Even though interest rates are falling, consumer demand is not increasing. / Consumer demand is not increasing, even though interest rates are falling.
6 Whatever he asks (you), don't reveal our commercial plans.
7 In spite of our excellent psychometric tests / In spite of our running excellent psychometric tests, we never manage to recruit the ideal candidate.
8 However small our budget (is), the project will go ahead. / The project will go ahead, however small our budget (is).
9 Despite our model winning an innovation award / Despite the innovation award (which was) won by our model, sales never really took off. / Despite winning an innovation award, sales of our model never really took off.

EXAM SKILLS AND EXAM PRACTICE

Reading Part 1: Exam skills

1 1 Business schools are partly responsible for management's failure to evolve.
2 Completing a business course is not so problematic as obtaining a place on the course.
3 During their courses, students' attitudes generally change in unintended ways.
4 Many business students are ill-equipped to take advantage of their courses.
5 Many courses do not teach the skills required for running businesses.
6 Students do not appear to benefit financially from obtaining business qualifications.

3 1 C *Rakesh Khurana, of Harvard Business School, is writing a book on why management has failed to develop as a profession.*
2 A *Of course, business schools may be important mainly as a screening mechanism – their basic skill may be choosing students, not teaching them. Once in, and the vast bill paid, few are ever thrown out for failing their exams.*
3 C *In 2002, the Aspen Institute surveyed 2,000 MBA students and found that their values altered during the course.*
4 B *Their students are often too young and inexperienced to learn skills …*
5 B *Conventional MBA programmes, he complains, ignore the extent to which management is a craft, requiring zest and intuition rather than merely an ability to analyse data and invent strategies.*
6 A *little evidence that getting an MBA had much effect on a graduate's salary*

Reading Part 1: Exam practice

1 D 2 B 3 A 4 B 5 D 6 C 7 E 8 C

Reading Part 2: Exam skills

1 A But how do you measure the 'quality' of communication with workers or incentives for employees?
B For instance, under one heading a British consumer-products firm whose managers' only meaningful performance target was volume (with no mention of quality or waste) scored 1.
C So, if poor management does not pay, why does it last?
D There is little evidence, though, that competition raises standards by forcing managers to work better.
E They ascribe some of the gaps to differences in the quality of capital equipment, or in the development and installation of new technology.
F Thus, even among competing neighbours, there was huge variation in management practices.
G A further reason appears to be connected with something economists call 'management culture'.
H In fact, the system is nothing like as ruthless as it is cracked up to be.

2 1 E 2 A 3 B 4 F 5 C 6 D

Reading Part 2: Exam practice

9 C 10 F 11 A 12 G 13 E 14 B

Reading Part 3: Exam skills

1 1 paragraphs 1, 2 and 4
2 paragraphs 2, 3 and 4
3 paragraph 6

2 1 B *high turnover rates*
2 C *positive emotions from home spilled over and caused people to be more engaged with work*
3 A *Negative emotions also spilled over and caused people to be more engaged with their work*
4 B *the hardest part of their job is that they know how to help the customer, but do not have the authority to take action*
5 D *An individual who avoids risk and accepts supervision is likely to feel satisfied and comfortable in the job*

Reading Part 3: Exam practice

15 C 16 A 17 B 18 C 19 D 20 C

Reading Part 4: Exam skills

1 1 B 2 B 3 C
2 1 C 2 A 3 B 4 B 5 A 6 D
3 1 A 2 D 3 C

Reading Part 4: Exam practice

21 B 22 A 23 D 24 C 25 B 26 D 27 A 28 B 29 D 30 C

Reading Part 5: Exam skills

1 1 whose (relative pronoun) 2 despite (preposition) 3 due/owing (preposition) 4 have (auxiliary verb) 5 be (verb) 6 off/back (preposition) 7 as (preposition) 8 This (pronoun) 9 such (determiner) 10 One (pronoun)

2 1 as 2 according 3 hardly/scarcely/barely 4 despite/notwithstanding 5 on 6 the/their 7 away 8 fall/fell 9 what 10 This/That

Reading Part 5: Exam practice

31 ahead 32 in/for 33 This/That 34 part 35 back 36 themselves 37 one 38 that/which 39 During/Throughout 40 on

Reading Part 6: Exam skills

1 1 will 2 up 3 we 4 being 5 a 6 of 7 then 8 in 9 they 10 so

2 1 hardly 2 still 3 when 4 forming 5 too 6 *correct* 7 put 8 *correct* 9 for 10 been 11 a 12 once

Reading Part 6: Exam practice

41 so 42 CORRECT 43 as 44 up 45 CORRECT 46 by 47 even 48 it 49 when 50 CORRECT 51 them 52 yet

Listening Part 1: Exam skills

3 1 brand portfolios 2 specialist 3 mergers and acquisitions 4 (constantly) innovate 5 losing market share 6 move up-market 7 edge/cost-competitiveness 8 Manufacturing processes 9 (management) decisions 10 (operating) profits 11 (Rigorous) analysis 12 (continually) streamlining

Listening Part 1: Exam practice

1 sleeping partner 2 45% 3 permanent 4 whole process 5 (best) strategy 6 job fairs 7 internal candidates 8 downsizing/outplacement training 9 long-term contracts 10 private equity group 11 float 12 three sectors

Listening Part 2: Exam skills

1a Suggested answers

A key brands, running at a loss
B disappointing at first, the board, slow off the mark
C disappointing at first, not much take-up, slow off the mark
D helpline never stopped ringing, went over to the competition
E missed a deadline, slow off the mark,
F called in a maintenance crew, system crashed
G top customer, went over to the competition, the board
H key files, system crashed, vanished completely, wiped off

2b

	Problem	Cause
Speaker 1	D	P
Speaker 2	G	L
Speaker 3	C	J
Speaker 4	B	O

Listening Part 2: Exam practice

13E 14A 15F 16C 17B 18B 19E 20D 21C 22H

Listening Part 3: Exam skills

2 1 C *More to the point, though, is that managers start thinking that everything they are doing will go well and they tend to forget that they have rivals out there who might be even better than them. That's when things really start to go wrong.*

2 A *in a recent survey it was discovered that 40% of Americans thought that eventually they would end up in the top 1% of earners.*

3 B *the first price mentioned, the opening position, becomes the point of reference around which all discussions seem to revolve*

4 C *The problem really arises when managers spend too much time analysing the information for each decision. I mean some of the decisions are quite trivial*

5 A *they continue to pour money into researching and developing a no-hoper*

6 C *They just continue to live with them.*

7 B *especially if you're a serious investor, investing in a variety of markets and properties is a much safer and more reasonable decision.*

Listening Part 3: Exam practice

23 A 24 B 25 A 26 C 27 A 28 B 29 A 30 C

Writing Part 1: Exam skills

2 1 a breakdown 2 Ten years ago 3 the following eight years 4 In the last two years / (Since then) 5 In contrast 6 in other words 7 Since then 8 in total

3 1 summarises 2 was 3 had 4 have been reduced / were reduced 5 has been taken / was taken 6 have increased / increased 7 had 8 have raised / raised 9 are / were 10 has risen / increased

Suggested answer

This report gives a breakdown of annual sales figures in each division of New Age Leather Goods Ltd over the last four years. While four years ago the clothing division achieved annual sales of £5 million, these rose to £5.5 million two years ago and are expected to reach £6.5 million this year. The shoe division has been even more successful, with sales rising from £4 million four years ago to £6 million two years ago, and sales for this year forecast to reach £8.5 million.

In contrast, accessories are undergoing a slump in sales. Four years ago, they stood at £2 million, rising to £4 million two years ago, but have since fallen back, so that this year they are not expected to exceed £2.5 million.

Writing Part 1: Exam practice

Suggested answer

This report compares gross income from domestic and export sales of the company and the company's fixed costs across a period of four years.

Income from domestic sales was consistently higher than that from export sales. Domestic income rose considerably in Year 2 but since then has fallen off and in Year 4 was not much higher than at the beginning of the period. In contrast, income from export sales has shown a steady rise since Year 2 and is now at almost the same level as income from domestic sales.

Over the same period fixed costs rose in Year 2, but have fallen since then to levels below that of Year 1. They have remained at the same level in the last two years of the period. This slight reduction in fixed costs over the period is likely to mean an increased profit margin.

Writing Part 2: Exam skills

1 Suggested answers

1 Probably colleagues as well.
2 Neutral, since it's for colleagues also.
3 What the course consisted of, how useful it was, how it will benefit your company, advice for colleagues.
4 Introduction, The course, Usefulness and benefits, Conclusion and recommendations

3 1 ~~Like~~ As 2 ~~week's~~ weeks 3 ~~in~~ of 4 ~~improving~~ improve 5 ~~learn~~ learning 6 *correct* (though *reduce* could be changed to *reducing*) 7 ~~showing~~ shown 8 ~~no~~ not 9 ~~had~~ has 10 ~~enjoyable~~ enjoyably 11 *correct* 12 ~~of~~ from 13 ~~were~~ was 14 *correct* 15 *correct* 16 ~~some~~ a 17 ~~of~~ about 18 *correct* 19 ~~for~~ to 20 *correct*

Writing Part 2: Exam practice

Suggested answers

Question 2

Report

Introduction

The aim of this report is to detail changes that were made to our delivery systems and to discuss how the changes were monitored. It will also assess whether or not the changes were effective.

Changes to delivery systems

We made changes to the delivery systems in order to try and achieve a faster turnaround between ordering and delivery to the customer. A new computerised system was installed so that orders are now sent direct to the warehouse without having to be processed by the finance department first. Current staff received training in the new system and extra staff were employed to cope with the faster turnaround time.

Monitoring the changes

A control system was set up to double check that orders were received in the warehouse on time and were processed correctly. In addition, a member of staff monitored the warehouse on foot to see whether staffing was adequate and to check if any problems arose. Furthermore, customers were canvassed to get their views on the new system.

The success of the changes

Overall, the system proved effective, though there remain several teething problems to be ironed out. Staff do not always input the correct values if they are working too quickly so a control system needs to remain in place. In addition, we need to have a marking system for goods where payment is delayed to ensure these do not leave the factory before settlement. However, in general, staff and customers were satisfied with the improved service.

Question 3

Dear Mr Markin,

I am writing to you as I understand your consultancy can arrange training sessions in giving presentations. I am writing on behalf of our sales department as we feel that the presentations given by staff could be improved.

When giving presentations, staff tend to have a poor delivery method (speaking too quickly, etc.) and also fail to get across the main points that need addressing during the presentations. They also seem to handle questions from the audience very badly.

In general, most staff in the department have to give presentations at some stage but I am particularly concerned about our junior sales staff, who need to improve their presentation skills in order to achieve their sales targets. There are about eight of them who I would put forward for this training.

As we need to see substantial improvements, I would like staff to receive training over a period of several weeks. This ideally should include material to address the problems I have raised above, plus some sort of monitoring or testing system whereby staff can see any improvements they have made. This system should also make them aware of areas they still need to focus on. An off-site course would be preferable, so that staff can focus on the matter in hand.

If your consultancy is able to help us in this matter, please contact me so that we can discuss.

Yours sincerely,

Question 4

Proposal

Introduction

The purpose of this proposal is to comment on the market for our new MP3 player and to outline any problems with developing the product and suggest ways of addressing these.

Potential markets

The issue of whether to market the new MP3 player in Europe has already been discussed but there is more potential for growth if we expand our target market to include India and some of the Gulf States as well. Both these regions have a high proportion of young people who fit our customer profile. In addition, our competitors are offering players which have been on the market for a while and need upgrading. Our product would offer new features and therefore should eat into some of our competitors' market share.

Potential problems

One of the main problems we may encounter is the cost of arranging an adequate distribution system in markets where we have no presence at the moment. In addition, there may be a problem in all markets of managing repairs and after-sales service.

Suggested solutions

In order to arrange an effective distribution system it would be sensible to contact agents used by our parent company and investigate what they can offer us and at what cost. We would also need to check whether or not they were also operating for our competitors. Regarding after-sales service, I would suggest this is put to competitive tender.

Speaking Test Part 2: Exam skills

2 1 not just because 2 but also because 3 the main point I'd like to make is about 4 What I mean is 5 I think first that 6 for example 7 It also includes 8 A third aspect of this 9 Anyway 10 Finally and in conclusion

4 1 My talk is about …
2 I think first …; It also includes …; A third aspect …
3 This procedure must, for example, …
4 … and I say 'boards' because …
5 Finally and in conclusion, …
6 procedures for internal recruitment, human resources, efficiency of the company, inter-staff relations, management and staff representatives, internal advertising of all posts, staff appraisal, personal files, recruitment boards, director or manager of the department, Human Resources department, elected staff representative

Transcripts

UNIT 1

02 Listening, page 11

Omar: So, Candela, what's it like working for a large car manufacturer?

Candela: You'd be surprised, actually. You hear so much about cut-throat competition amongst managers in my type of company, but in fact, as someone starting out on the management ladder, I get a lot of back-up from senior staff. We have twice-weekly get-togethers where we talk through our difficulties and come up with ideas and solutions. It's great. I don't get the feeling that it's 'sink or swim' at all.

Omar: And you, Henry?

Henry: Well, as you'd expect working in hospital administration, there's plenty of red tape. We have to stick to the rules fairly carefully because at the end of the day, people's health's involved, and we're publicly accountable. But that doesn't mean there's no room for inventiveness. We're always looking for ways of streamlining procedures and making efficiency gains.

Omar: And saving taxpayers' money.

Henry: That's right.

Omar: Now, Sonia, what's it like working for a dotcom?

Sonia: It's not exactly a dotcom. As a matter of fact, it's more a software developer. And it really suits me, you know, I nearly always turn up at work wearing jeans and a T-shirt, which is great for a manager, and everyone talks to everyone else in a really relaxed way. There's none of that 'them-and-us' feeling between management and staff that you get in other industries. I mean, in most ways the staff are more expert than the managers! And what about you, Omar?

Omar: My company, as you know, is a consumer products company, and we're all organised in divisions, and the divisions in teams, and we're all competing against each other. Our pay is performance-related, and nobody gets the same. Getting ahead and even keeping your job depends on your performance.

Sonia: Um, and how's performance measured, Omar? Is there a yardstick?

Omar: Not really. In the end, it boils down to performance in comparison with other teams and divisions.

Henry: Sounds quite a rat race.

Omar: For me, that's business!

UNIT 2

03 Listening, page 16

I = interviewer; RB = Rachel Babington

I: What do you think makes a great leader as opposed to a great manager, because they're quite different things, aren't they?

RB: I think I've worked in a lot of places where a lot of senior people haven't really been leaders, they've been managers, and I think I'd say probably a ... a good leader has vision and can see how to develop and take things forward and is inspirational. Really, a manager, I think, is more about the implementation of that vision, and I think too many people who are in leadership roles get bogged down with the nitty-gritty management side, which is probably not what they should be doing, but I suppose it takes a strong leader and a confident one who believes in their team to take a step back, um, and I think really they should. I don't think they should be too hands-on.

I: Can you describe a bad leader to me?

RB: I think someone who ... has a team of quite experienced, good people who won't give them the space to get on and do their job and is overbearing and involved, um, and doesn't take a step back and give ... give people the responsibility to get on with their role, and I suppose who doesn't give a person room to grow and the opportunity to develop their career, because I think that happens a lot, that you just are expected to tick along and not expect anything back from your job. Whereas if you're good at it and reasonably ambitious, you want to know you're going somewhere.

UNIT 2

04 Listening, page 17

I = interviewer; RB = Rachel Babington

I: What ... How would you describe empowerment? And how can workers be empowered, do you think?

RB: I think empowerment is ... um ... giving someone the opportunity to decide the directional strategy of a job and agreeing on it, and then leaving them to get on and do it and be in the background to help them if they need it, but not to be breathing down their neck. Um, and I suppose it is that feeling of responsibility and ownership that makes people feel empowered. I think if you work with someone who really lacks confidence to give their team responsibility, it's very difficult to break out of that cycle.

I: And has managing techniques, or have managing people, changed over the last ... in the last ten years?

RB: I don't know, I'm probably a bit cynical, but I think there's a lot, certainly, that I have noticed in the organisations I've worked in, there are a lot of steps that are taken and to be seen to be empowering individuals, and so I think things ... probably at a superficial level look to have changed, but whether they really have deep down, I'm not so sure.

I: How do you think people could be managed in order to get the very best from them?

RB: I think to get the most out of them, you want them to feel empowered, that they're achieving, that they're, they're um, developing, that there are opportunities ahead of them that they can strive to work to, that they're ... um ... under a manageable amount of pressure, um, that they're getting the right kind of support. I think what a lot of people lack is a kind of mentor and someone that'll help them develop in their career, and you can become very stale if you don't have that. So I'd say that would be important to people as well.

UNIT 3

05 Listening, page 20

Trainer: So, we've seen a bit about how internal communications is quite a neglected area in business. Now I'd like to go over to you and ask you if you have any ideas how it can be improved. Larry, what about you?

Larry: Well, I guess we all have a tendency to overdo things a bit. I mean, we think we have to reply immediately to everything that comes in, and it becomes a bit of a time-waster, always sending off messages left, right and centre. I think it's probably better to have a fixed time – you know, that quiet time just after lunch or just before you knock off for the day – and deal with them then.

Trainer: Erm, well, possibly. I guess this might depend on the type of job you're doing. Er, still, that's something we can discuss in a minute. And you, Marina?

Marina: I'm very interested in the quality of the message – it says so much about the person – and if it's well written, it's a good deal easier to understand, so I'd say to people that they should avoid incomplete sentences or sentences without verbs – when writing, of course. Good English creates a good impression.

Trainer: Um, an interesting point and that's another one we can come back to. I mean, it might depend who you're writing to and what you're writing about. What's your advice, Magdi?

Magdi: Mine's a question of respect for colleagues and basic working formality. If you're busy, you can be sure that most of your colleagues are too, so they don't want you barging into their offices without warning with some minor query or being continually phoned up. Let them get on with their work and, if they're not urgent, save your queries for coffee time.

Trainer: Um, thanks, Magdi, that's partly a time-management question, isn't it? Er, now you, Thérèse?

Thérèse: I just think common courtesy is such an important part of office life – greeting people when you arrive at the office, not losing your temper or shouting at people, however overworked you may feel. You have to work with each other and you might as well make the circumstances as pleasant as possible.

Trainer: Um, I absolutely agree … um, so now let's take those points one by one and see how you all feel about them. Now, the first one was about …

UNIT 4

06 Listening, page 23

1

Chair: OK, let's get started. Has everyone got a copy of the agenda?

Other participants: Yes. / Thanks.

Chair: Great. Would anyone like to take minutes, or shall we just keep a list of action points?

Piotr: Action points would be fine, Mat.

Chair: OK, Piotr, would you like to do that, then?

Piotr: Sure, no problem.

Chair: Thanks. So, anyway, thank you all for coming. The purpose of this meeting's to discuss how we go about investigating the East European market and seeing whether our products would have an outlet there, so the first point today is who should actually go and have a look around. I, personally, am pretty tied up till the end of May, so it might be better if it were someone else. Jane, could you give us your views on this?

Jane: Sure, thanks, Mat. Um, I honestly don't think it's that urgent. I mean, it can easily wait till June, which is less than a couple of months away and then we can make sure we have enough time …

07 2

Chair: So, if I could just sum up, what you think is that even if he hasn't been on time this time, as a customer he's too valuable to lose, so we should remind him, but in a very friendly and polite way.

Woman: That's right. I mean, he really does give us a lot of business, although as you can see from the books, if something doesn't happen soon, we're going to have problems with our cashflow. I mean, we've got our invoices to pay as well.

Chair: Point taken. Let's remind him and give him another week, then.

Woman: Fine.

Chair: Anything else to be said on this, or can we move on to the next point?

08 3

Salim: … so, quite frankly, I don't think it's good enough. I mean, we agreed to have the new procedures in place by the end of the month, which is in two weeks' time, and we're going to be nowhere near that target because the people responsible for training haven't even scheduled the training yet.

Chair: Thanks very much for that, Salim. Now, can we hear what other people have to say?

Woman: Yes, it's all very well to criticise, but we've had plenty of problems, you know. In my last job, people used to just criticise. I had a boss who …

Chair: Look, that's all very interesting, but can we keep to the issue in hand? The point is, there is a risk, and it would be bad to have an accident just when we've fallen behind with our training schedule, so let's get to the reasons for it and see how we can get things back on the rails.

09 4

Chair: … so, we clearly all agree on this, so let's not waste any more time and move on to point number five, which is whether the component really meets our specifications. Any thoughts on that? Anyone? Martin?

Martin: It clearly performs to specifications. All the tests I've run so far show that. It's just that we might have difficulty fitting it into the space we thought we had for it. It might mean we have to do a little bit of redesigning.

Chair: So, in a nutshell, what you think is that it's too large.

Martin: Well, it might be, but if they can't make it smaller, then we'll have to make do with it.

Liang: But that would add to our costs. I mean, redesigning our machine at this stage has all sorts of other implications.

Martin: I know, but the alternative is to source the component elsewhere, and I don't even know if that'll be possible.

Alex: I wonder whether it'd be worth it just for one relatively minor component.

Martin: Um, we'd have to look into that.

Chair: Well, we don't have to decide on this today. Let's think about it a bit more and come back to it if necessary next week. Now, let's take a five-minute break and then start on point number six.

10 5

Chair: So we need more information on this issue. Sandra, can you look into it for the next meeting?

Sandra: Sure.

Chair: So, in summary, we've agreed about where we're going to stay and Sandra's going to investigate prices, which potential customers we're inviting and what entertainment we're going to give them, so we're just left with the question of the timing of the event. Any ideas, anyone?

Man: Um, I don't think we want to get everyone together when it's too hot, so I guess spring would be most suitable.

Woman: Yes, because if we're going to do it in January or February, really that's too soon.

Man: Yes, if it was up to me, I'd go for April.

Chair: OK. Let's come to a quick decision on this. How many people are in favour of April? Five. Anyone against? No? Well, thanks all of you for your time. I think this has been very profitable, and we'll meet again to talk about the other points on Wednesday the 4th at the same time. See you all then.

UNIT 5

11 Listening, page 30

Interviewer: Boris Shulov, we hear a lot nowadays about Customer Relationship Management, or CRM for short. Can you tell us what it is?

Boris: Er, yes, in simple terms, Customer Relationship Management is the process of integrating marketing, sales and after-sales service within a business or other organisation with the objective of ensuring that customer relationships generate maximum profitability for the company. While, in the process, maintaining and enhancing those relationships. In other words, by working on these relationships, we can produce more revenues for the company and provide a mechanism which permits companies to stand out or differentiate themselves from their competitors. What I mean by this is that nowadays, as we all know, the products companies produce are frequently almost identical – at least in the eyes of the consumer – and what gives a company a competitive edge is the difference in the quality of service it offers.

Interviewer: This is achieved largely by the use of computer technology, isn't it?

Boris: Um, that's right. At the centre of CRM are information systems; with computer technology, it's now possible to store and transmit huge amounts of data about individual customers – you know, their preferences, their free-time activities, the make-up of their families and any other details which you think are interesting or useful. And all this information can, at least theoretically, be acted upon by organisations to give their customers personalised individual treatment. Er, to give you a … rather basic example, your customer, Mrs X, buys cosmetics from you. You know from information you've gathered that she has a teenage daughter. Perhaps she'd also like to buy cosmetics for her daughter – you could interest her in a younger range of products maybe.

Interviewer: In which areas of an organisation is CRM most likely to be used?

Boris: Well, clearly in those areas which have most contact with customers. Er, to give you a few details, er, there's Marketing Automation, which allows you to concentrate your marketing efforts on your most profitable customers and manage your campaigns so that your marketing budget is spent in the most cost-efficient and profitable way. Er, you've perhaps heard of the 20–80 rule, which says that 20% of your customers generate 80% of your profits. The common-sense conclusion to be drawn from this statistic is that we should be spending a larger proportion of our marketing budget on that 20% of customers to keep them happy, to encourage them to spend more with us – and proportionately less on the remaining 80%.

Interviewer: Interesting. I've also heard of Sales Automation. Er, can you explain for all of us what that is?

Boris: Sure. Um, Sales Automation is information systems providing key back-up for the sales process, for example, products a particular customer has bought in the past, discounts they've been given, problems that have arisen when selling to that client, etc. All this makes the sales staff's task much easier. They can offer similar discounts; they're not going to make a mess by offering a far larger or far smaller one – at least, not unless it's part of an informed strategy. They know about problems which have arisen in the past and they can avoid irritating the customer by repeating them. Then there's the final area …

Interviewer: Customer Service, isn't it?

Boris: That's right.

Interviewer: Can you explain it a little, please?

Boris: Yeah, Customer Service, as a part of CRM, is being able to deal efficiently with problems and queries when they arise in such a way that they actually enhance the customer's feelings of loyalty and satisfaction. After all, the main thrust of CRM is to have loyal and satisfied customers. These are the ones who are most profitable to a company and who pass the company's reputation on by word of mouth to other potential customers.

Interviewer: The process must be very complex. How is all this data collected and transmitted with a large organisation?

Boris: The most normal way nowadays is via the Internet because this allows both employees and customers to access information and communicate with each other efficiently.

Interviewer: Very interesting. But, I wonder, do organisations manage to handle these vast amounts of data efficiently and effectively? I would have thought these systems are fraught with pitfalls.

UNIT 6

12 Listening, page 32

I = interviewer; WBH = William Brook-Hart

I: How does your company achieve the … an advantage over its competitors?

WBH: Well, I suppose the prime way you'd get an advantage is by offering, um, sufficient quality at the lowest price. And clients are always looking for the, er, lowest-price tender, and nowadays designers and consulting engineers have to compete a lot more on price than they had to maybe 30, 40 years ago, so price is certainly probably the major element. Um, but in more recent years, there's been far more recognition by clients that actually the quality dimension is also needed. If you go for the lowest price, you may not get the best value, the best value for money. Um, so now client procurement is much more directed towards getting the right match of quality and price. Um, the result of that being … is that when we're submitting tenders to clients to win work, um, we have to devote a lot of time to demonstrating the quality that we can bring to a particular project, and ways of doing that include the quality of our documents and what we say in our documents. Um, it's also, um, developing a reputation and having past projects that we can show clients and say, look, there's a fantastic quality of job we did on that one, um, why don't you employ us because we've got the track record and experience.

13 Listening, page 34

I = interviewer; WBH = William Brook-Hart

I: So how would you describe the Gifford's brand?

WBH: Er, the … the Gifford's brand, well, that's quite a tricky one. I think we're branded a lot by the, er, projects, the past projects that we've worked on, so very much in projecting what we're about, we look towards recent projects which have been particularly successful, and, um, one of those has been the Gateshead Millennium Bridge, which … for which Gifford had to enter a design competition which was, which was supervised by the Gateshead Metropolitan Council, and there were about 200 entrants. And, um, Gifford teamed up with a leading architectural practice, Wilkinson Eyre and Associates, and jointly we came out with a completely new concept for a bridge. I don't think this type of bridge has ever been constructed before … Um, this bridge had a horizontal axis so that the entire bridge rotated horizontally to lift over the river to pass, um, ships underneath. And this particular structure's got a lot of international attention since it's been built and has been quite successful in promoting an image of Gifford, er, more widely.

I: So you'd use this project as a means of, um, obtaining further contracts, possibly?

WBH: Yes, I think it's demonstrated our, er, creativity and potential for innovation and problem-solving, in a way which others couldn't do.

I: That's very good. Just tell me, how do you or Gifford's go about getting new contracts?

WBH: Well, um, I suppose one prime route is to look at advertisements, and, um, nowadays within the European Union, um, all contracts or all public works over a certain size have to be advertised in the *Journal of the European Union*. So we keep an eye on that and identify contracts which look, er, look interesting to us. Um, other routes apart from advertisements – and really a very important route – is through personal contact and, um, preferably through having done previous contracts with a client and establishing a relationship, er, and particularly if they are a private client, or a private company, er, if they like the work that you've done previously, then they may feel there's no need to advertise. They'll come back to you for future work. And, um, establishing those business relationships and friendly partner relationships with clients is … is really vital.

I: And how would you go about deciding a price for your bid when you're in competition with others?

WBH: Er, well, with great difficulty. There's … there's two, well, there's a number of ways you look at it. One is to assess what the value of the constructed works would be and assess in percentage terms what a reasonable fee for a designer would be in relation to the ultimate value, er, of the works as constructed, so that would be, er, on a percentage basis or a top-down basis. Um, the other main route would be bottom-up in terms of … you're itemising the work and all the tasks that you have to do in order to prepare and design, um, prepare the contract document, the specifications and probably also, um, supervise the construction and the works or supervise the works construction contract, um, so you'd work out all the time on a spreadsheet from the bottom up and see what it comes to.

I: How many of the contracts that you bid for do you expect to win?

WBH: We'd expect to win about one in three, one in four of straight competitive bids where … where we're competing against maybe six other similar consultants. And we would hope to achieve that rate.

I: Putting together a proposal or bid must be expensive and time consuming. How do you cover the costs of this if you don't win the contract? Or is that just absorbed into a future contract?

WBH: The only way you can absorb the cost is out of fees earned on other contracts, so all … all tenderers have to effectively either recover their costs on other contracts or go out of business. It's as simple as that.

UNIT 7

14 Listening, page 36

Naseem: Naseem Bakhtiar.

Devika: Hi, Naseem. Devika here.

Naseem: Hi, Devika. What's up?

Devika: I think it's time to get that proposal together for the board of directors. You know, we were talking around the subject last month when we were having our round-up of points arising from the sales conference – at least, it was one of the things that we were talking about.

Naseem: That's the proposal for a wider range of software, isn't it? Let me just note that down.

Devika: That's right. I've just been talking to Lena and we were both saying that now could be the right time …

Naseem: Right, well, Lena's the finance director. Does she reckon we've got the budget for it?

Devika: Yes, that's the point. She says that since profits are definitely up this year, we should be looking to plough something back and reduce our tax exposure.

Naseem: OK, but the main reason for getting into a new project like this – and it would be a pretty big one – is that our existing clients have been asking for it. That would be the main selling point, er, in the proposal. Our clients want a whole range of compatible applications – compatible with the stuff we're selling them at the moment.

Devika: Exactly.

Naseem: OK, and what do you want to see in the proposal, Devika?

Devika: The reasons for adding to the product range, I guess. I mean, our existing products do well enough, but with the cut-throat market we're in, it wouldn't look too good if we spent a lot of cash developing a whole load of new products which just lost us money.

Naseem: Well, that doesn't sound too likely at the moment.

Devika: No. And could you also specify the types of product we are going to work on, you know, especially stock-control tools and applications for automatic online ordering, that sort of thing.

Naseem: OK. Those will do for a start anyway.

Devika: And you'll also have to cover resources in the proposal.

Naseem: Yes. Right.

Devika: I mean, this will mean quite a lot of people working on it and it will swallow a fair amount of cash before we start getting any return on our investment. Fortunately Lena will be keeping us to a tight budget, though.

Naseem: Quite. But it would be useful to know what the extra costs involved in this are likely to be.

Devika: OK, so you'd better include a section on them in your proposal, and then hopefully we should have everything pretty clear.

Naseem: Great. When's the next board meeting?

Devika: Wednesday of the week after next. Do you think you can get your proposal together by then?

Naseem: I'll try to get it ready by Friday of next week if possible so we can mull it over a bit before giving it to the board, though I can't promise that. Otherwise, definitely by the Wednesday.

Devika: That sounds fantastic. Thanks a lot, Naseem.

Naseem: My pleasure. I'll get cracking on this right away. I've been wanting it to happen for some time now.

Devika: Sure.

Naseem: Anything else, Devika?

Devika: Not just now, Naseem. Thanks.

Naseem: OK, bye, then.

Devika: Bye.

Naseem: Bye.

UNIT 8

15 Listening, page 40

Nils: Good, thank you all for coming. Shall we get started, then? As you know, the purpose of our meeting is to start thinking about expanding our operations to China. Before getting down to the finer details, please remember that our discussions in this meeting are confidential, OK? So, Catalina's going to get the ball rolling by giving us a brief run-down of the Chinese market. OK, Cati?

Catalina: Sure, Nils, thanks. Now, I'm just going to give you a number of key facts, which should help you to concentrate your minds on the opportunities and difficulties of breaking into China, OK?

Nils: Sure, go ahead.

Catalina: Right, well, I've got three main points to make: firstly, the Chinese market, unlike markets here in Europe or the US, is growing steadily and rapidly, so it represents a major business opportunity. Last year, the total market in terms of ice-cream sales was 23 billion yuan – that's about 2.3 billion euros – so pretty considerable. I've been reading recently that China is likely to overtake the USA as the leading market for consumer goods within the next 25 years, and when you take into account that the market growth rate is a steady 10% a year, you can see that there's an opportunity there, if we can get in. Now, my second point: at the moment, there are five major players selling on the Chinese market, along with a lot of smaller local companies. These big ones have a market share between them of rather more than half – 57% to be exact – and that's split up between our usual competitors: Nestlé, Wall's – that is, Unilever – and Meadow Gold, with 30% of the market, and a couple of local companies: Yili and Mengniu – I'm not sure I've got the right pronunciation there – but anyway they've got about 27% of the market. And now my third and final point: to give you a bit more background, in China, on average people buy far less ice-cream than in Europe – the annual purchase is about 1 litre a head which is still a lot less than the 23 litres per head of the Europeans, so you can see that, as Chinese incomes rise, ice-cream consumption is a pretty hot prospect.

Nils: Thanks, Cati. That was interesting. Now, any of you got any questions?

Paul: Yes, Cati, can you tell me how Chinese companies are reacting to this competition from abroad and also how these competitors are going about increasing their market share?

Catalina: Sure, Paul. I've got something on the biggest national manufacturer – that's Yili. Apparently, they recently announced plans to build more production facilities in different parts of the country. The reasoning behind this is logical. China is a huge country – the distances between major centres such as Shanghai, Beijing and Hong Kong are vast – so they'll then be able to save a lot on transportation costs. Also, if you have a factory in each region along with a regional product development team, you can adapt your ice-creams to regional markets more easily and thereby satisfy local tastes. That, I think, answers the first part of your question as far as I can; as to the second, while companies have been advertising pretty heavily, their main tactic for gaining more market has been to fight a fierce price war. Most products sell at about 1 to 2 yuan which is between 10 and 20 cents. So you can imagine that, even with cheap production costs, no companies as yet have been announcing big profits there.

Nils: Any more questions? Yes, Tanya?

Tanya: Our products, as you know, are a bit more upmarket than the companies you've mentioned so far. I wonder what sort of price you think we could sell them at. What I want to know is how we would position them.

UNIT 9

16 Listening, page 48

I = interviewer; NI = Neil Ivey

I: What in your experience is the best way to advertise?

NI: That's a very difficult question to answer because there are different answers for different types of product. And in some cases, the most cost-effective can be the most expensive, so television still remains probably the most expensive medium, but is possibly the best way still of … of … of getting to people, and given that our biggest ambition is to sell as much product as we can, then we want to reach as many people as we can most effectively.

I: And is advertising always the most successful way of promoting a product?

NI: Not entirely. I think there are a number of people who believe that a decision about, a final decision about a brand is made actually at the point of purchase, so anything that can be done within the store to attract a person, whether it be some sort of promotional activity within the store or something that actually sits on the shelf and attracts your attention or just simply the price.

I: And who decides where something should be advertised?

NI: We in the media company make that decision. We put together a proposal based on the size of the budget, which is, um, a major factor, because television is obviously the most expensive medium we can use, but also the … sort of time of day or the sort of, er, mood that the person is in will affect the … the place that we'll advertise. So, for example, if we were advertising a cosmetic brand, we might think that women reading a … a glossy monthly magazine might find that a more appropriate place to see an advertisement for a cosmetic brand or a fragrance, for example, whereas Fairy Liquid might well be suited much more to the television and have less of … of an appeal to people reading a newspaper or a magazine.

I: And who decides when to go on air on television?

NI: The media company would … would decide on that, and we would have a budget which we would, which would mean that we would have to buy a certain number of, er, slots within prime time, which is generally from about 5.30 in the evening until about 10.30 in the evening, but then again, to get a … a broad range of potential consumers, we would advertise throughout the day. And, for example, the morning time is cheaper than evening time.

UNIT 10

17 Listening, page 50

Presenter: Good evening. I'm Serena Godby, and tonight on *Your Computer,* we're talking about how you can use the Internet to buy things and what sort of things the Internet can really help you to purchase. Now that questions of security and Internet fraud are no longer such an issue, e-commerce and e-shopping are becoming an increasingly attractive option to both businesses and consumers. I have five people with me in the studio: the writer and broadcaster Bruce Myers, up-and-coming young actress Tanya Balham, computer programmer Paddy Smith, Petra Ferriero, the fashion critic, and of course our regular expert on this programme, Salim Mahmud. Now, if I could just kick off by asking each of you about something you bought recently and why you used the Internet to buy it. What about you, Bruce?

Bruce: Well, you know, I use the Internet quite a lot for my work – I research articles and the like, stuff on the economy, background facts and what have you. Anyway, I'd been thinking for some time that it was time for me to get away from it all and take a break. Normally I just call in at my local travel agent's while I'm in the High Street, and they book the tickets and send them round. Anyway, almost subconsciously the other day, while I was reading the online edition of the *Financial Times*, I clicked on this banner ad, just to see how much things might cost, you know. I certainly wasn't thinking of booking anything up there and then. Still, it came as a bit of a shock, I must say, to see how much cheaper things are online and how much money I could have been saving.

Tanya: Yes, they say you can pick up some great bargains on the Internet, but I still think that unless you shop around plenty, you can get taken for a pretty big ride.

Presenter: Tell us about it, Tanya.

Tanya: Well, before I buy something I like to see it, touch it, get the feel of it, so I'm most likely to use the Yellow Pages online to find the local showroom and one or two others – which street they're in, that sort of thing. It's not bad, because nowadays you can filter out pop-up boxes and such like. Then I go down there and check if they have any special offers, see what's going, perhaps kick the tyres and take a test drive if they'll let me. I mean, I don't think we'll ever want to make a purchase like that online, do you?

Presenter: Well, not as yet, but you never know. It could come, I suppose. Paddy, you're next.

Paddy: Er, well, I've just changed jobs, and that's been a pretty big thing for me. It means I've had to move and I've been using the web for checking out estate agents and what they've got on their books, see what's going in the area and look at a few photos before getting on the phone.

Presenter: Petra. How have you used the Internet for shopping?

Petra: Not for shopping, actually. Last time I was in London I bought a new PC, but they didn't have the one I wanted in stock – only a showroom model – so I arranged to have it sent on, which they did. I used my old one to check where it had got to and when it was arriving.

Tanya: I think that's wonderful, actually, to be able to do that.

Petra: So do I, because at least I knew it was coming – even if it didn't get here any quicker!

Presenter: Finally you, Salim.

Salim: Hm, I've been thinking about doing one of those online degrees, you know, so initially I went to Google and typed in the words, and then actually I clicked on various sponsored links which were pretty good, because, you know, they took me direct to more or less what I was looking for and I was able to look at the different options and what they were offering all in less than an hour. I mean, ten years ago it would have taken me weeks!

Presenter: Great. So let's go on from there and just consider together what options there are for …

18 Listening, page 53

I = interviewer; NI = Neil Ivey

I: How can advertisers use the Internet, do you think?

NI: The Internet is a … is a difficult one for advertisers at the moment because it's so new. I don't think a lot of people know quite how to use it. People tend to use the Internet for things that they're interested in … The places where the Internet can be very successful are in … in areas where there is high interest in the product involved, so for example, the motor-car industry, where you do a lot of research before you buy a car. Nowadays, most people do their research on the Internet, and therefore to advertise on the Internet is an obvious way to get people when they're again in the right frame of mind to … to be advertised to. And, that can be just simply brand advertising which tells people a little bit more about the car or redirects them to … to the website which will give them more information, or it can be direct response advertising, which will encourage them to send off for a brochure or to send … to … to ask for a test-drive which then gets them into the dealership in order to get the dealer himself then to persuade the … the customer that he might want to buy that particular model.

I: Can the Internet be used to advertise normal household products as well?

NI: There are ways that people try and get round that issue by the website or the advertisement on the Internet actually trying to give a solution to something, and … and what I'm thinking of here is that Persil, for example, the manufacturer of detergents, has a … has a part of its website which talks about tips and hints of how to get rid of stains out of clothes, so you might go and say, you might … you might go into a search engine and … say I want to get rid of a stain on my … on my shirt, a wine stain, and the search engine would then direct you to the Persil site which would then possibly encourage you to buy Persil to get rid of that stain if it was the right solution.

I: So how would advertising on the Internet increase sales or attract new customers?

NI: Um, I suppose in … in the same way that advertising in any medium will work – it's … it's not a static medium, so it's probably mistaken to use static images on the Internet. It's … it's very much nearer, very much nearer … more akin to television in that respect, so that you can do a lot more with it. There's a lot of what are called 'viral ads' being put out now by fairly, um, normal major international companies, who are making ads to look like they're spoof ads, but they're actually made by big advertising agencies at vast expense, because they might be a spoof on a … on an existing ad or they might do something that you wouldn't necessarily expect an advertiser to do, and then they're sent around to a few people, who will then pass them on to a hundred of their people in their mailing list, who will then pass them on and on and on, and that's … that's an interesting way where advertising is developing, because at the end of the 30 seconds or whatever, you suddenly realise it is actually a brand message.

I: If a business wanted to set up an e-commerce operation or sell its products over the Internet, what would be the best way to go about it?

NI: I think it depends very much on what brand they're … they're trying to sell and, um, the danger is that there are now so many different websites that it would be a very difficult thing, I think, to set up a … an e-commerce site from scratch that … that could be successful because just about every market that you would want is catered for. The main reason that people go to the Internet, I think, is because they can shop around for price, and if you're offering something that offers people better value for money, then there's an opportunity then to attract people's attention. Otherwise I think small companies trying to set up e-commerce nowadays would find it very difficult to achieve, because most of the major manufacturers in the world are now savvy to … Internet and setting up their own websites which have a lot more, um, money spent on them.

UNIT 11

19 Listening, page 55

So, our company's been in existence for more than 15 years now, and during that time, we have, of course, I s'pose just like everyone else, experienced big changes. Probably more than most industries. Our products have evolved, and our production processes have changed out of all recognition. Our customers have also become more savvy and more demanding. And the whole global marketplace has been transformed, so, we've had to adapt our sales activities to meet the challenges. I mean, ten years ago, most of our sales were done by sales staff making personal visits to prospects and explaining our products, how they worked and their selling points. Now all that area of activity has been declining because our customers know more now, and our products, of course, are much more intuitive. So there's not so much explanation needed. Sales by visiting reps have plummeted from about 40% to less than 20.

And another big change that you can see on the chart, although not quite so big, is that people just don't buy our software in shops so much these days. Over-the-counter sales volumes are about 10% lower than they were ten years ago.

On the other hand, though everyone hates being rung up about products, we find it surprisingly effective and comparatively cheap. Less time-consuming, no travel expenses. You know, what we do is actually call up prospects – that is, likely companies, potential customers – and make an intelligent sales pitch. Over the past ten years, these sales have soared from just a … a tenth of our total to around a quarter of our products, which is pretty good.

Our … our other big success story, I s'pose, is fairly predictable because, of course, ten years ago, few companies – well, or perhaps almost none – were online and the whole concept of e-commerce was in its infancy. I'm proud to admit, though, that we were among the pioneers, and this has really now rocketed to become our most important sales activity. As a result, we can sell much higher volumes nowadays with just about the same staffing levels as a decade ago. That in turn means better margins, and these are really driving our profitability.

The only other sales activity we do has been receding, and we're hard put to really know the reason: that's this one here, which has shrunk from 15 to just 3 per cent. People just don't fill in coupons or write in for things any more. I mean, we still advertise in the trade press and in specialist magazines, more than anything to maintain brand awareness, but I s'pose people like to go online and find things through Google, or some other search engine where they can download things instantly. Of course, people feel a bit more confident about using credit cards online as well …

UNIT 12

20 Listening, page 58

Richard: Richard Slade speaking.
Rosa: Hello, Mr Slade. You don't know me. My name's Rosa Levy, and I work for CSS Security.
Richard: OK. I've only got a few minutes …
Rosa: Yes, I'm sure you're very busy, so I'll be brief. We specialise in providing security not just for buildings and properties, but also for employees so that they can do their jobs in the safest possible conditions and work with confidence.
Richard: So why do you think we need your services?
Rosa: I don't know at the moment, Mr Slade, but with your permission, I'd like to ask you a few very quick questions to see if there's anything we can do which your company could benefit from. Do you mind? It won't take long.
Richard: OK, go ahead, but make it quick.
Rosa: Thank you very much. First, can you tell me: have any of your staff ever been attacked by members of the public or by clients of your company?
Richard: Well, that's rather a sensitive question, so I'll only answer very generally. From time to time, we've had members of staff who've been shouted at, or on one or two occasions physically threatened.
Rosa: And where have those incidents happened: in the office or when, for example, they're showing a client a property?
Richard: From time to time, on the telephone, though our staff are trained to deal with that. On odd occasions, here on our premises and several times, as you say, when visiting properties.
Rosa: And these members of staff, would I be right in thinking, when they visit properties are generally working on their own?
Richard: Generally speaking, yes.
Rosa: Can you tell me what protection you offer them when they're working alone outside the office?
Richard: Well, we have an arrangement with a large mobile-phone company. If one of our staff members presses a number on their phone, a call comes straight through to us. We then ring the person concerned – you see, if they're in a dangerous situation they can press the number without anyone realising. If necessary, after that we call the police.
Rosa: I see. And one last question – do you find this works satisfactorily? Is there anything you would like to see improved?
Richard: Frankly, it's not too satisfactory because sometimes there's nobody in the office. And there was one occasion quite recently when the worker in question felt threatened – she wasn't actually physically attacked – but she didn't feel it was safe to answer her mobile and we were unable to locate her exactly.
Rosa: So, you'd like to be able to offer your workers round-the-clock protection and be able to locate them automatically if an incident occurs?
Richard: That would be ideal.
Rosa: Well, Mr Slade, that's exactly the sort of service we'd be able to offer you, and probably at a price that you would find very competitive with your present service. Would you be interested in hearing about what we have to offer?
Richard: Yes, I think so. Quite probably.
Rosa: Well, that's great. Perhaps we could set up a meeting and I could show you exactly what we can do.
Richard: OK.
Rosa: Would sometime this week suit you?
Richard: Let me have a look in my diary. I could do Friday afternoon at about 4 p.m.
Rosa: Friday at four. That's fine by me. I'll come to your offices, shall I?
Richard: Yes, I'll meet you at the reception desk.
Rosa: OK, fine. I'll look forward to meeting you then. And thank you very much for your time, Mr Slade.
Richard: You're welcome. Goodbye.
Rosa: Goodbye.

21 Listening, page 61

Richard: So, come in and take a seat.
Rosa: Thanks, and thanks for finding the time to see me.
Richard: Not at all. Sorry it's a bit late on a Friday afternoon.
Rosa: No, that's fine. I'm used to working all hours.
Richard: Right. Now, tell me about your company's staff protection service. What does it consist of?
Rosa: OK. Now, as I understood from our phone conversation, you already have a service with a mobile-phone operator. They alert you when a member of your staff presses a button to signal that they've got a problem.
Richard: That's right, but the service has its limitations, as I mentioned to you on the phone.
Rosa: Right, so what we do is provide a more complete service. When a member of staff feels threatened or in danger, they press a button and alert us. Our service operates 24 hours a day, seven days a week, which means first that your staff know that they'll always get a response, second that the response will always be immediate, and third that the

people dealing with the call – that's us – are specially trained to deal with these types of situations.

Richard: OK so far, but what do you do when you get an emergency call?

Rosa: Well, it's not exactly an emergency call. The employee doesn't have to call us. All he or she has to do is press a button and that alerts us. We then call the employee and if they answer, we ask them the nature of the problem and take it from there.

Richard: Take it from there?

Rosa: Well, clearly, in some situations the worker may just want to let someone know that the client is acting strangely, but they don't feel in any immediate danger. In this case, they have a code word, and we can give them advice, you know, tell them how they should proceed and perhaps just generally to calm them down so that they don't feel quite so threatened. You know, it really helps in these situations if they know there's someone there if they need them. We can also alert your office of the potential problem, and if the situation warrants it, we can call the police.

Richard: How will the police know where to go?

Rosa: Because your staff will be supplied with equipment which is basically a slightly adapted mobile phone, but which also contains a satellite tracking system, so we know where they are to within a few metres. Of course, we make sure that the employees know this and sign an acceptance form when they get the equipment – you don't want to be accused of spying on them when they're not working!

Richard: No, of course not – that's a good point. But I'll tell you why I'm interested. In the last year or so, we've had a couple of incidents involving staff. Of course, they're given some training in how to handle difficult customers or tenants, but about three months ago, a member of staff was visiting one of the properties we manage, and he was actually physically attacked by the tenant of the property. You may have read about it in the local press. He had no opportunity to make a phone call, let alone have a phone conversation. Fortunately, he wasn't badly hurt, but he was badly shaken and was off work for a month after that. It's that sort of situation that we want to avoid.

Rosa: Precisely, and in that case he'd just have pressed the button and not responded to our phone call. Often just the fact that the phone rings is enough to make a potential attacker desist. We'd then have alerted your office, or if there was no one in the office, we'd call a contact number you'd have supplied us with, and at the same time we'd have phoned the police.

Richard: That sounds fine, but the other incident we had was when one of our workers called in saying she was being threatened, and we responded by calling the police. The police, however, took nearly 45 minutes to come to her rescue. Again, fortunately, nothing very serious happened to her, but it could have been very serious.

Rosa: We actually try to keep track of the police. I mean, we direct them to the location, we phone every five or ten minutes to find out what the situation is and if they've resolved it. Our aim is to provide the completest possible protection without actually giving your staff bodyguards. But if the police have been informed, it's the police who have to deal with the situation. You and we have done everything we can.

Richard: And the cost of this? What's the bottom line?

Rosa: That's the interesting part. It really isn't going to hurt. The costs you'll have are for leasing the equipment – a more sophisticated mobile phone. The charge you'll have to pay for that is really not very high, especially when you consider it in the context of the confidence and security it will give your staff. All you have to pay apart from that is a fixed monthly charge, about the same as you'd pay if your burglar alarm was connected to us and nothing else. There are no extra costs and no hidden charges.

Richard: Not even when one of our staff presses the emergency button?

Rosa: Certainly not. The last thing we want is people to be calculating the cost of calling for help. Look, I have a list of our charges here.

Richard: And can you tell me the names of other clients you have, other companies who use this service?

UNIT 13

22 Listening, page 64

Presenter: Good evening and welcome to *Business Growth*, the weekly programme about business and finance. My name is Max Edwards, and tonight we're going to look at that recurring nightmare, the sales forecast, where sales and finance directors bang their heads together, supposedly gaze into a crystal ball and then pull some figures out of the air. Or perhaps it's not quite like that! We asked five company directors to tell us how they do it and how accurate their forecasts have been in the past. First, Olivia Howe of SPG Holidays. How do you do it?

Olivia: Well, I'm basically an economist, so sales forecasts are really not my speciality. But I am asked about how general circumstances might affect our sales figures and I usually give a projection for bank rates and how they'll affect demand. Last year, though, the company actually underestimated its sales forecast quite considerably when the holidays we sell suddenly rather unexpectedly caught on, and everyone, it seemed, was wanting to go on one. I mean, we used to think of our holidays as a niche product and suddenly they seemed to be mainstream.

Presenter: So, you were running to catch up with demand?

Olivia: Exactly.

Presenter: Jaime Almendro, you're a director of the up-and-coming Spanish clothing retailers, Próximo, which is appearing in every shopping mall in Europe. How do you predict sales?

Jaime: Oh, in any number of ways, but my particular contribution comes from my involvement with marketing and market research. I and my team track our rivals' activities and likely sales, and, on the basis that whatever they can do, we can do better, we work out what they're selling and add on a percentage. Like Olivia, we also fell short of our forecast last year when a Spanish Formula One driver won the championship and at the same time we talked him into wearing our clothes. That really was a knock-out, and we hurriedly had to source extra suppliers.

Presenter: Fabulous. Gary Summerwell, managing director of the bicycle importers, 'Free Wheel', how do you do your sales forecast?

Gary: Hard to tell, really. I mean, I've been to business school and learnt all the conventional techniques, like making computer extrapolations based on past sales and such like, but honestly I think, in the end, I just go on a hunch and, as you so nicely put it, pull a figure out of the air. You know, what I imagine will be the sales for next year, because however much calculating you do, you're never going to get it quite right. It's always, in my opinion, better to be optimistic and plan for more sales than fewer. Sometimes you have a hiccup, though, like the time a year or two ago when someone comparing bikes in a magazine said ours were overpriced for what they were. Completely untrue, of course, but sales took a bit of a nose-dive for several months. We survived, though. I think good quality and good service always survive if you stick in there and believe in what you're doing.

Presenter: Thanks, Gary. Sylvie Lemaître, your company, 'La Chaise', is a leading player in the French furniture market. How do you go about making sales predictions?

Sylvie: It's a complex process as you know, Max, and I really don't agree with Gary about computer extrapolations. I do think they have a place. But my role is more to look at how our promotional activities can affect sales figures and what we can do as a company to increase our sales. So, I look at the money we're thinking of spending and what bearing this will have on how much we sell. I really believe that what you spend in that area should have a quantifiable effect on what you sell. You've got to know that your investment is paying off. Of course, there are always the things you can't predict, like the fire that destroyed our factory in Cognac last winter and meant we couldn't complete all our orders on time.

Presenter: Bad luck, in other words.

Sylvie: Very.

Presenter: Thank you, Sylvie. Finally, Nesreen Nasr. You're director of one of the Middle East's most important translation and interpretation consultancies. How important are sales forecasts for a company like yours?

Nesreen: Very important, though I should say that, though we make annual forecasts, we do adjust them on a monthly basis, as I expect all the rest of you do. They're important because we have to get our staffing levels right, we have to be training the right number of new personnel, and we have, like everyone else, to keep a tight control on our cashflow. So we do sales forecasts and cashflow forecasts, and my part is to get our agents in the field to tell us what their likely needs are going to be. I then collate this information and pass it on. Even so, over the past few years, demand has been growing faster than we can train new personnel and retain them – a lot of staff after a time tend to go freelance – and this has meant that rather too frequently recently we've had to turn down lucrative contracts that we'd counted on in our forecasts.

Presenter: Very frustrating.

Nesreen: Very, and in a labour-intensive industry like ours, not one with an easy solution.

UNIT 14

23 Listening, page 69

I = interviewer; PF = Philip Franks

I: How do you think the theatre business is different from other businesses?

PF: Um, well, probably in no way at all. But the theatre business isn't just a business. The business side of it, i.e. something which has to produce a product that people want and which people are prepared to pay for, is exactly the same as any other business. It must be planned, it must be budgeted, it must be marketed and it must be successful in order to survive. However, the theatre's also an art form, and you can't, um, apply strict business standards to art. You just can't. The theatre has to have, in some way shape or form, the right to fail and the right to be unpopular.

I: And when a new production is going to be put on, where does the initial impulse come from?

PF: A commercial producer, er, for whom money is absolutely paramount, because they're not supported by the state in any way, um, will find a star, somebody maybe with a high film and/or television profile, and try and build a production round him or her.

I: How would you go about, um, setting, putting on a commercial play?

PF: Well, if … if I was, if … if I had a play in my head that I wanted to direct, and it had a cast of more than, say, ten, um, I'd be pretty foolish to take it to a commercial management, because they would just say, I'm sorry we can't afford it, unless you have Brad Pitt in it, in which case we'll fill every theatre in the country. Um, we simply can't afford it. You have to be practical about these things. You have to know your audience, you have to know your producer. And most commercial, most theatre managers spend most of their time trying to second-guess what an audience will like. And more often than not, the things that are huge runaway successes both artistically and commercially, you couldn't have predicted in a million years.

I: How would you go about making financial forecasts and budgeting for a new production?

PF: How would I go about making financial forecasts? Um, I suppose if you knew that you had a certain bankable star, um, then your forecasts would be higher than if you were just taking the risk on a new play. If … you were performing a brand-new play with a good but not necessarily bankable cast, you would limit the number of performances. I think it would seem wise to do maybe 20 or 24 performances of … of a new play, not try and run it forever. Um, and be very careful about the size of cast, because an awful lot of the … the budget of a production goes in, um, actors' wages.

I: Yes, when you've got a budget, say you've got a production that you're going to mount and you're doing the budget, how does it break down?

PF: It breaks down into, um, creative team's fees, i.e. director, designer, lighting designer, sound designer, choreographer maybe – this is at sort of full stretch – actors' fees, a set budget for … for building, making and maintaining the set, a costume budget for either hire or making of the costumes, um, a properties budget, i.e. the things that are on the set, the objects that you will either have to, again, either hire or buy, um, and certain, some of those will be called 'running props'. That might be things that are consumed, er, cigarettes that are smoked, food that's eaten, plates that are broken. That has to be budgeted for as well. Um, and then, er, it's the running costs of the building, and that differs from, if it's again, if it's, if it's a subsidised repertory house or if it's not, if it's commercial. For instance, many subsidised reps have their own workshops where things are built, so you don't have to budget that over and above. Commercial projects which don't have a fixed building home, you would have to budget for having your set built out and then transported in to wherever you go.

I: And … a budget then has to be reduced, are there certain things that you would always go to first to cut?

PF: Um, I think you would look at, you would look very, very, very carefully at how many people you could afford, because to change that at a late stage is fraught with peril, er, not … not only from a sensitive and emotional side, but from a legal side – if somebody is … is sacked without deserving it simply because you can't afford to hire them, then they would be well within their rights – and I'm sure Equity would, Equity, the actors' union, would help them – to sue you and management for every penny they had. So you get the people right and you stick to it. Scenic elements are the next most expensive thing. You might find that a set has a piece of very expensive technical equipment for instance, a video screen or something like that which you might decide, we just can't afford it, or a revolving stage, we just can't afford the revolve. Or, for instance, many plays are set in rooms with three walls, obviously not four because you wouldn't be able to see.

I: So how would you finance a production? A commercial production, we're talking about.

PF: A commercial production, er, I would go to a producer. Assuming that I'm the director, I would go to a producer and say, 'I've got a marvellous idea. Let's do *A Flea in her Ear* by Feydeau ... I've got actors X and Y lined up who are interested in being in it. Can you do it for me?' If the producer says, yes I think we might be able to do this, it is then his or her job to raise the money ... They ... they would either put up money of their own, or, if they're the big ones and they own theatres, then that makes it a little bit simpler because you'd go into one of their theatres. ... Or a smaller, more independent producer ... would go to some rich backers, known as 'angels', and they would say to them, we have this production coming out, do you want to buy a share in it? Um, they might be sent, they might, for instance, sit down and say, 'OK, we'll ... we'll send a hundred packages out to people who we think might be interested in investing in our production and they can invest in it at a level of their choice'. They can buy units, if you like, in the ... in the production. And if ... if you just fancy a flutter, you can buy a couple of units. If this is what you do and you want to take a big financial gamble in order, possibly, to reap a big financial reward, then you'll buy correspondingly a lot more units.

I: How long do you think a play has to run before it can break even in the West End?

PF: I think, um, a play that's been carefully budgeted and is not a hugely expensive one to front can probably break even in about 12 weeks.

I: Can you think of the proportion of London productions that make money versus the ones that don't make money?

PF: Um, no, I don't ... no I don't know the answer to that. I would have thought that the ones that don't make money are ... massively outweigh the ones that do. However, if you get one that does, it can be a cash cow for years and years.

I: Mm, and also, presumably, if the production company don't make money, they don't get to produce much ... much more because they haven't got the money to put it on.

PF: No, although producers are huge risk-takers.

24 Listening, page 71

Jenny: First tonight, we talk to Paul Keene from the National Gallery in London about corporate sponsorship of arts events. Paul, is sponsorship growing or is it going out of fashion?

Paul: Huh! Definitely not going out of fashion, Jenny. Corporate sponsorship of the arts is up about 50% on ten years ago.

Jenny: So it obviously takes quite a whack out of their budget. Why do they do it?

Paul: Well, there are lots of advantages to it. It can be great publicity if you get the right event or activity. You can get to people who would normally be impervious to your advertising, you can leave a pretty permanent reminder of your company's existence in a high-class public place, for example a theatre bar might be named after you or have the company logo in it, and you can associate yourself with some really high-class art or music or theatre which does no end of good for your company image. Actually, for big organisations, I'd say that last point is the one which really gets them on board.

Jenny: We hear about companies sponsoring arts events which actually appeal to quite a narrow audience, such as opera or ballet. Why do they do that?

Paul: Mm, that's interesting, but you must remember it's not the quantity of the audience but the quality which counts. These elitist events tend to attract people with money – not necessarily company directors, though I suppose there are a few of them, but certainly people who are likely to put money into the stock exchange. I mean, you may not sell more product, but you bring your company name to people who invest, and up goes your share price, hopefully. Neat, isn't it?

Jenny: It sounds clever if it works like that. We've always heard about corporate sponsorship in the United States. Is it something which is catching on more in Europe?

Paul: In the last ten years or so, certainly. Governments used to subsidise the arts much more than they do nowadays, so arts institutions have to get out there and find backers. Though they've really been helped in a lot of countries by bigger tax breaks. You know, what costs the company in real terms just about £200,000 can mean income of up to a million for the organisation receiving it.

Jenny: What sort of activities do companies most like to sponsor?

Paul: I'd say that exhibitions in world-class galleries like the Tate are just about the most popular. It depends on what they're exhibiting though. Music concerts are still pretty popular, although not so much nowadays, because they're fairly one-off. Er, exhibitions, on the other hand, um, go on for months and have people strolling around and taking their time and can be very beneficial for corporate image. Wouldn't you like your company to be associated with Matisse or Picasso? Then you read in the papers about Barclays Bank sponsoring the National Theatre, so there are no clear trends.

Jenny: What gives an arts organisation an advantage in attracting money?

Paul: They need to be big and well known. Nowadays, they have full time fund-raisers – perhaps as many as 20 or 30 – working for them, and I think that's the crucial point. They're able to put a professionalism into it that smaller organisations find hard to compete with. Although it also helps to be located in somewhere like London, Paris or Berlin. Places out in the provinces are at a disadvantage unless they're really well known, like, um, the Salzburg Festival or that sort of thing.

Jenny: Now, what about smaller businesses? How can they benefit from sponsoring the arts?

Paul: In a number of ways, actually, and they can do it on quite a modest scale and still reap the benefits. Particularly, their employees feel that they're working to put something back into the local community and that the profits are not just going to the shareholders. It makes them feel more motivated and more closely tied to the company. A lesser point is that people in the local community may also view them differently, and companies may hope that they'll get more favourable treatment from their local politicians. But politicians are a changeable lot, and I wouldn't count on it.

Jenny: Now, say an organisation – a theatre or an orchestra – was going to approach a company for funds, how should they go about it?

Paul: Um, good question. One thing which is definitely not too effective is to flood people with glossy brochures and videos and the like. Company decision-makers see hundreds of them. No, the personal approach is better – one of your executives should go along and give a presentation accompanied by a two-page executive summary explaining goals, needs, budgets and activities. Something snappy and ... and businesslike.

Jenny: OK, and one final question: when a company is looking for something to sponsor, what criteria should they use?

Paul: In my opinion, you shouldn't look too much at visitor numbers. It may be OK, but it can rebound on you – you know, those exhibitions which attract thousands of people, long queues, many of whom are tourists from overseas and are never going to be your customers anyway. The main objective is that the event is compatible with the way you want people to see your company. What the newspapers say doesn't matter because they're not going to mention your sponsorship. Basically, the event has got to look right for you. Nothing else.

Jenny: Thank you, Paul Keene. And now, troubles in the fixed-line phone industry. Is it an obsolete technology, or can it adapt to changing times?

UNIT 15

2 Listening, page 74

Astrid: Hello. Could I speak to Rajiv Narayan, please?
Rajiv: Speaking.
Astrid: Hello, Rajiv. It's Astrid Kloof here.
Rajiv: Hello, Astrid. Er, what can I do for you?
Astrid: It's about this invoice which you still haven't paid, and I was wondering when you were intending to pay it.
Rajiv: Oh that. Yes, I'm terribly sorry. We're hoping to pay it as soon as we possibly can.
Astrid: And when do you think that might be, Rajiv? It's beginning to cause us serious problems.
Rajiv: Well, the problem is that two major customers haven't paid us for what they owe us, and so we're also having cashflow difficulties.
Astrid: I see. So that's causing a sort of chain reaction, and we're at the end of it.
Rajiv: Yes, it's very embarrassing for us. We *are* hoping to pay you.
Astrid: Yes, but when?
Rajiv: Hopefully by the end of the month. Just as soon as we have some cash available. Our customers have promised to pay us by then.
Astrid: You know, Rajiv, the trouble is, it's beginning to cause us problems, too.
Rajiv: Oh dear.
Astrid: Yes, we've had to ask our bank to allow us to extend our overdraft, which is working out pretty expensive.
Rajiv: I'm sorry to hear that. In our case, to tell you the truth, we just can't ask the bank for any more money. We're right up to our credit limit now.
Astrid: I see – I'm sorry to hear it.
Rajiv: Look, Astrid, I'll keep you informed, and just as soon as the money comes in, I'll let you have what we owe you. Is … is that all right?
Astrid: OK, Rajiv. I suppose it'll have to be. What I'd really like is a firm commitment to pay this month.
Rajiv: I think I can give you that, Astrid.
Astrid: I'd like that commitment in writing, Rajiv. Can you do that for me?
Rajiv: Sure. I don't see why not. I'll put a registered letter in the post to you today. You should get it tomorrow.
Astrid: OK, Rajiv. Today's the 20th. I look forward to receiving your cheque within the next 11 days.
Rajiv: Fine, Astrid, and thanks for calling.
Astrid: You're welcome. Goodbye.
Rajiv: Goodbye.

3 Listening, page 75

I = interviewer; WBH = William Brook-Hart

I: Does Gifford's have problems with late payers or non-payers? And if so, how do you deal with them?
WBH: Well, er, that has been a theme of recent years, and the need to, um, improve our cashflow is something which we've targeted during the last few years. We have a team of very friendly, um, people who contact our late payers amongst our clients and, um, politely remind them of the need to, er, pay promptly. Um, so it's very much done on a friendly, er, basis of encouraging to start with, um, but clearly if we have a client who, um, who's a very late payer and they had no good reason for … for delaying payment, then … then other measures have to be taken.
I: So this is outsourced from Gifford's, it's not a department within …
WBH: No, it's within Gifford, yep, so they're very much part of our team.
I: Part of the finance team.
WBH: Part of the finance team who'll … who'll look to recover late payment. And because we're looking to, um, have future jobs with clients, of course, um, it's preferably done on a very friendly, amicable basis.
I: But does it happen often that, um, that people are, that companies don't pay or that, um, I mean, they can be a slow payer? I suppose you get to know them.
WBH: It's … very rare that a company won't actually ever pay. There are some who are slow payers, but of course some of them may reckon that they've got very legitimate reasons for paying slowly. They may not be satisfied with the work we've done and they'll hold back payment until they're satisfied that we've done everything that we have to do.

UNIT 16

4 Listening, page 76

Tutor: So, let's initiate today's session by talking about negotiating problems and things we can do to get round them or get over them. Negotiating is a big part of all your jobs, er, so let's have a quick buzz session where each of you briefly describes a negotiating problem you've had in the past, and then we'll go on to look at how we can deal with these things. How does that sound to you? All right? So, um, who'd like to start? Vasili?
Vasili: Er, sure. Um, this wasn't in my present job, I'll start by saying. Er, I was working in procurement for a processed-food manufacturer at the time, you know a … a large multinational, and, er, working on a deal for a pretty large consignment of flour, and by that I mean several hundred tonnes. Of course, I wanted them to knock something off the price, I mean, taking into account the fact that we were buying in bulk. I was expecting to haggle a bit. You know, I'd ask for six and settle for three, reach a compromise, but when I put it to them, their sales people, I mean, they said that they didn't have the authority and would have to ask someone higher up. I mean, that's pretty frustrating when you think you're talking to the right people and then it … it turns out you're not.
Tutor: Um, so, pretty irritating. Er, who's next? Melinda?
Melinda: Yes. This was, er, before I was promoted, when I was still a fairly inexperienced office manager and we were talking about installing a new computer network in the office. I … I should say that we were running a pretty big but temporary operation to meet an order that had come in, so we were in larger temporary offices and, since it was just for a few months, we didn't want to buy the stuff, just hire it. Being relatively junior and fairly new in the job, I didn't have much leverage – you know, bargaining power. Well, when I met their reps, they only wanted to sell us the stuff and didn't seem to take in the fact that we wouldn't be needing it in six months' time. And they refused to take me seriously because I was so young.

Tutor: Um, ageism in reverse. And you, Glenn?

Glenn: I work in air-conditioning, and we were working on this deal with one of those big hotel chains where they'd buy the stuff and we'd install it. Then they insisted that the maintenance should be thrown in free, even when we'd already given them quite a hefty discount. I mean you can't do that; one thing is the price and another thing is the cost of labour and parts over years and years. Even when I told them what my bottom line was, they just refused to budge. I mean, their buildings manager said take it or leave it and that was it; we'd reached a deadlock. So, no deal.

Tutor: Very disappointing. Carla?

Carla: We import clothes from the Far East and really we have to have them in the stores by the beginning of October to make the winter season. These were a range of coats that we'd had designed and ordered and we were negotiating all the terms. The real sticking point was that if they were late delivering, we said they'd have to pay, or rather, they'd only get 50% of the final price. I think the real problem was that they didn't even know when they'd be able to get the things out and they were afraid of taking on something they couldn't do.

Tutor: Mm, frustrating. Finally you, Naomi.

Naomi: Well, these people had outlets all over the country, so we were hoping they'd agree to stock and sell our products. You know, they didn't have to do much more than that, except perhaps organise the publicity, which shouldn't have been a problem for them. Everything was going fine, you know, I was talking about the constraints on us caused by our suppliers' prices – it was just a bargaining point, really, because that's one of the enjoyable parts of my job, you know, the horse-trading – when suddenly my opposite number interrupted me by saying that it was too soon to be talking about this and that the market was not right yet. I was very put out because we'd already been discussing it for several months. I mean he could have come out with this information sooner.

Tutor: Um, well, OK, thanks all of you. That was very good. Um, now, let's take all of these one at a time and analyse them and see exactly what's happening and what we can do about it …

5 Listening, page 78

CS = Company Secretary; RD = Regional Director

RD: So, um, let's go over what they're asking for again.

CS: Fine, I'll just get it up on the screen and then we can go through it point by point and see what we think. Um …

RD: That's it.

CS: OK, here it is. First, apart from the monthly rent, which we discussed before, they're asking for another half year as an upfront deposit. What do you think of that, Ramón?

RD: It's a bit steep. Supposing we offered them two months and settled for three. Do you think they'd accept that?

CS: Mm, it's possible, I suppose. We could try – after all, I don't think there are too many companies who'd be willing to shell out six months' rent as a lump sum.

RD: No, still, let's go through the rest and then we can put together a counter offer.

CS: Right. The next point, which shouldn't give us too many problems, I imagine, is that we'll have to keep to the same commercial activity unless we obtain the owner's approval in writing.

RD: Mm, no problem there. I suppose if we were to start doing something different, they could use it as an excuse to try to up the rent. I mean, we're an insurance company, and as long as we continue to be an insurance company, we won't have anything to worry about. We could perhaps use it as a bargaining point, though – you know, pretend that we might change and then haggle over it to get an advantage somewhere else.

CS: Um, possibly. Er, there's one thing here which I'm not too keen on – they want the right to raise the rent every year according to the inflation rate, and I think we'd be better going for a two-year deal on that.

RD: Mm, OK, but provided rents didn't rise by more than that, I'd be quite happy with that clause myself. I can't see it as a big issue, frankly.

CS: True, so perhaps we could let that one pass, though again we might use it as a bargaining point.

RD: Um, quite.

CS: Er, another point in this document is that we, the leaseholders, must foot the bill for any alterations or repairs we might decide to make. This is quite serious, as we have to be sure the building is in good condition before signing anything. We'll need a thorough survey, and we can only agree to this provided we're given a fairly long lease. I mean, we don't want to go to the expense of a lot of building work and then be evicted soon afterwards.

RD: Um, correct. So we should look for some guarantees there.

CS: Sure, and I think they'll be quite amenable on that one, because there aren't that many companies looking to lease round here at the moment. Er, the only thing about it that I don't like is that they want to reserve the right to change the conditions of the lease – i.e. making them renewable – after five years.

RD: Um, personally, I think we should go for ten.

CS: Mm, me too. In fact, I'd only take the lease on condition that we had a ten-year agreement.

RD: Good. Well, we have the basis for a counter-offer then. I think we should be able to negotiate something very much to our advantage. And the landlord should be happy, because we're prepared to offer him a pretty generous rent.

CS: True. And he's thrown in something which is quite attractive – it's not here on the document, but his secretary phoned to say that there was also the possibility of us renting staff parking space in the basement as part of the deal.

RD: Well, that's pretty attractive. If we were to get that, it would make life much easier for everyone. Did he mention a price or how many places were available?

CS: Mm, he told me there was room for up to 30 cars, which might mean we had some room for customers as well.

UNIT 17

6 Listening, page 84

Sue: Good evening and welcome to *Business Night*. Now, stress has been a favourite topic amongst workers and employers for a good number of years, and according to recent figures published by the Health and Safety Executive, it's still on the increase. The government is worried and has issued new guidelines to employers on how to deal with it. Tonight, we have in the studio Mariella Kinsky, an occupational psychologist who's just written a book about stress. Mariella, who is most likely to be affected by stress?

Mariella: Not an easy question to answer, because stress is such a subjective thing, and one person's stress is another person's excitement. Rather flippantly, I might suggest that housewives suffer the most from a fatal combination of boredom, isolation and low status, but there are no figures on this, because of course housewives don't come into data on work-related stress. The people who statistically come top of the league are routine office workers, which is surprising when you consider that, in many ways, their working lives are more comfortable than their predecessors' lives ever were. In general, their bosses seem to thrive on it, which perhaps explains in part how they became bosses in the first place. It also shows that it has its positive and negative sides. Positive stress is seen as a challenge which gives you a … a zest for living and doing more. Negative stress comes, I think, often from a perception one has of lack of control over one's life.

Sue: Mm, interesting. What is stress exactly? Can you give me a definition?

Mariella: Not easily, and that's the major problem doctors have when faced with a patient who says he's too stressed to go to work. I mean, how do you diagnose something you can't measure or examine? In that sense, it's a bit like pain; I mean, if you say you've got it, you've got it.

Sue: So, what do they do about it?

Mariella: Well, you can't just tell someone they're not really stressed and that they should pull themselves together and get on with things. Doctors do have a number of things in their armoury, though. They give people time off, they prescribe pills, in extreme cases they send them to a therapist …

Sue: Like you.

Mariella: Like me.

Sue: And are these things effective?

Mariella: In some cases. Not many.

Sue: So, how is stress affecting productivity, Mariella? Is it a major industrial problem or just something we all like to complain about?

Mariella: It's certainly something we like to complain about nowadays. In the old days, people had other ways of letting off their stress, I think. They weren't so supervised, so they could get their own back on their employers, you know, by not working too hard, perhaps even by stealing or damaging things at work, though I like to think that those were extreme cases, and this was part of the sort of 'them and us' battle which was fought out in the workplace. That's not so easy to do nowadays – I mean, it's socially frowned upon, and people can get found out more easily, especially as most of them spend their days sitting in front of a computer, not operating a machine at the back of a workshop. On the other hand, people change their jobs more frequently than was possible in the past, though it's hard to say what part stress plays in this, or whether it's due to other factors. After all, starting anew in a new place must be at least as stressful as staying put. What we can measure and what shows a sharp increase is sick leave due to workplace pressure.

Sue: Mm … and what's causing it? Is it boredom, or surveillance, or overwork, or what?

Mariella: Again, there's plenty of debate about this amongst occupational psychologists. We certainly don't spend so much time at work as we did in the past. All the figures will bear me out on that one. While we're at work, the pace has certainly hotted up: they give us perks like laptops and mobiles, and as a result we're always on call and we end up working very much more intensively than we did in the past. I think it has to be that. I mean, you mention that Big Brother bugbear – they can monitor your computer activity, they can record your phone calls and so on – all technically feasible, but it only happens in large companies with the resources to do this. Most companies really don't have the time or the personnel, while reports of workplace stress are pretty much across the board. So the cause has to be what I mentioned before.

Sue: Do you think the way our work is organised has changed, and that that's a stressor?

Mariella: Well, that's an interesting point. There's no doubt that our parents and grandparents in general lived harder lives, they worked more for less, but their work gave them a social cohesion which isn't so evident now. They got companionship from work, they were protected by their trade unions and professional associations in ways which disappeared 20-or-so years ago, and when they stopped work, they stopped thinking about it and really devoted themselves to their family and freetime activities, and I think that last point is the one which has really made the difference.

Sue: Mm … we often hear the consumer society cited as a reason for stress. What part does it play in the equation?

Mariella: Clearly, we're better off than our parents and grandparents, and this means that we're liberated from a lot of the routine drudgery which they had to put up with in their non-working time. This means we have more time to worry, and not only that, I think we even expect and want to worry about our work. Strange isn't it, considering that in most ways we're safer and more prosperous than was ever the case in the past?

Sue: Mm … you say we're expected to worry. What exactly do you mean by that?

Mariella: Yes, our work has become very central to our identity, who we are as people, and work-related stress has become an acceptable, even a respectable thing to complain about. You can do it, and the fact that it's stressful is almost a sign of how difficult the job is and how hard you have to work, and therefore people will look up to you for doing something despite the difficulties.

Sue: So, finally, what can employers do to cut down on stress in the workplace?

Mariella: I don't think you're going to like my answer to this one, but, frankly, I think there's almost nothing to be done. It's a fashion and a reflection of our social climate. You know, you can, individually, get advice from professionals. In my experience, it's hardly ever cost-effective, or effective in any sense. Giving people social support by organising them in teams might, you would think, bring a favourable outcome, but it often results in more pressure on individuals prone to stress. What the Health and Safety Executive, a … government body, seem to think can improve things is getting people to take part in the change process within their workplaces. The idea is that they have a feeling of more control over their lives. I personally see very little evidence for this being effective; people were less stressed in the past when they had even less control.

UNIT 18

7 Listening, page 88

… and in actual fact, there are more than a million people in this country participating in some sort of job sharing scheme, so it's not all that unusual, really. What are its advantages and disadvantages? Well, for employees, if they have other things they want to do in life, for example, sing in a professional choir or do a university course as a mature student, career continuity is one of the main things in its favour. You don't have to totally give up one thing in order to do something else and, while you're satisfying your other longings, you can carry on working and earning a living. People who need to juggle their jobs and their family responsibilities get an element of flexibility which lets them carry on working when they might otherwise not be able to. Similarly, people who have had to give up working for one reason or other, can, through job sharing, rejoin the workforce in a way which they find practicable, er, especially if they can't work full-time.

There are a number of drawbacks for employees. First, for people who are a bit ambitious, job sharing lessens your chances of climbing the corporate ladder. The way round this is to put in your CV alongside that of your job-sharing colleague and go for promotion on a joint basis – and, er, this can work very well if both people in the partnership are performing well. Another drawback is that you're likely to come in for less training just because the cost of sending two people on a course is twice the cost of sending just one. Finally on this one, you'll probably never be paid overtime, as each of you is counted as a part-time worker, and you never get up to the maximum working hours.

There are quite a lot of advantages for employers to job sharing. Er, to start with, part-time workers generally work harder than full-time workers because they don't have to pace themselves through an eight-hour day or a five-day week. As a consequence, job sharers tend to be more productive, and this can reflect very favourably on the overall profitability of a department. Also, job-sharing schemes can make the difference between employees going off somewhere else and staying, so staff turnover on many occasions is lower in companies operating these schemes. Another thing: because job sharers have that extra flexibility to look after sick children or parents, they're less likely to take sickness absences than their full-time colleagues.

Finally, to … to wind up, I'd better just point out the difficulties for employers when they want to implement a scheme like this, and it's not necessarily easy to do, even with the best will in the world. Because job sharers sometimes don't see each other, it can mean that job functions suffer – er, a task started by one person may not be continued by the other, so it takes longer to complete. Also, because working hours are different, bosses may not see the employees on the scheme regularly, and this can lead to communication problems. Finally, there's the training problem mentioned earlier and the costs involved in training two people instead of one. There is a way round this, which is to get the more experienced partner to train up the less experienced one.

However, I think that where employers and employees are willing to make the effort, job sharing can be a very positive experience for everyone involved and well worth giving a try. Thank you.

8 Listening, page 89

Presenter: In today's edition of *The Lowdown*, we talk about work and how it's changing. To start with, we invited five people from around the world to our studios to talk about their present jobs and their future ambitions. Here are some of the things they said.

Lechsinska: Well, my name's Lechsinska, and I'm an industrial electrician working in a large food-processing plant in Gdansk in Poland. Basically, I like my job, apart from the smell, but you can't have everything. I get on pretty well with my colleagues and I think they're pretty good to have placed their confidence in me, being a woman doing what's traditionally a man's job. On the other hand, I'm hardly getting what's the going rate for my job in this part of the world, and unless I get a more competitive wage, I think I'll soon be moving on, because I think, with my skills, I could make a better living being self-employed. I mean, I can't see myself working for them forever, even though I like the social side of things there.

Ganesh: I'm Ganesh and I work for the Indian subsidiary of a Swiss multinational as a pay clerk. Er, the job doesn't sound too exciting and it isn't. I've been in it for a few years now, and while computerisation has meant big changes in the way we work, I feel I'm stuck in a rut and stagnating. It's a sort of feeling of 'once a pay clerk, always a pay clerk'. I'm in my early thirties and with not too many commitments – I mean, I can easily make ends meet so – I'm thinking of doing one of those distance-learning courses where I can convert to being a proper accountant rather than what I'm doing now.

Francesca: My name's Francesca Morelli. My parents are Italian, though I was born and brought up in South London. Recently I've moved to Prague, where I work as a loss adjuster for a big insurance company. I'm on the go all the time and don't get much chance to wind down, not even at weekends, because they give me a mobile phone and I'm expected to be on call. Working hours are reasonable, in fact, but the job is pretty high pressure, and I sometimes worry that in the long run, it will affect my health. Well, basically I enjoy it, but I think I probably need a break from it for a year or so to take stock – just temporarily, I mean.

Darron: My name's Darron Corral, and I do temping for an agency just filling in for people off sick, or on maternity leave, or when there's a rush on. The place I'm working at the moment is pretty dire, actually – I mean, no one seems to speak to anyone, and when they do, it's only to complain – but, in general, I like temping because it suits my lifestyle. I can work when I want to work and I can concentrate on my career when I'm not. Er, in case you don't recognise me yet, I'm an aspiring actor waiting for my big break, and this job makes ends meet between the bit-parts I'm getting offered at the moment. My dream is to get taken on by the Royal Shakespeare Company and work for them till I retire in 40 years' time, 'cause this temping will become a bit of a strain if I carry it on for too long.

Irenke: So, I'm Irenke, and I'm from Hungary. At present, I'm working as a trainee stockbroker with a big firm in Budapest. We don't stop and there's lots of excitement because I'm buying and selling millions of euros' worth of shares every day. I think my boss supervises my work too much, which annoys me. I know he's worried I'll make a mistake, but I haven't so far. Still, I suppose it's his responsibility if I do. The money's good because we get a cut of the profits, and when I've made enough, I'll probably launch my own firm, but perhaps not a stockbroker's.

UNIT 19

9 Listening, page 92

Presenter: Tonight on *Business Night*, we look at productivity. With the advent of information technology, robots and the Internet, the drive towards increased productivity has become increasingly intense. I have in the studio three production managers, each from different industries: Lee Kah Seng of Radiolux, a manufacturer of household appliances, Ferenc Kovács from Kovács Shoes, and Mike Drewer from the producer of frozen convenience foods, Unifreeze. First, I'd like to ask Lee: should production managers always be looking for higher productivity?

Lee: It's one of the factors, but really they should be going for efficiency, reliability, quality, satisfying customer requirements and a whole range of requirements which are central to competing effectively, not just churning out products at the lowest possible price. In my company, in one factory, productivity actually went down quite sharply a year or so ago. Alarm bells started sounding at Head Office, but when they came for an explanation, there was a perfectly simple answer: the gadgets we were making were more reliable and more complex, with more added features, so they took longer to produce. But they met customer needs better and, while we produced less, we stopped producing things and stockpiling them because we couldn't shift them quickly enough. Our activities as a provider of unwanted goods with excess production capacity were cut short, and everyone was happier! So no, productivity is one of the factors to watch, but it's not the be-all-and-end-all of a production manager's life.

Presenter: In today's highly complex world, how reliable are traditional ways of measuring productivity?

Lee: Quite unreliable. You know, you're measuring output per worker, but in an industry like ours where we're constantly innovating, large numbers of man hours are swallowed up in developing and modifying the product, designing, preparing and testing the production process for the new product, modifying the assembly line, and so on. It's a very complicated business, which in some cases can take months or years, and in other cases be comparatively quick. You have also to take into account the parts you'll need to buy in, get these designed and budgeted for and ordered. So, with so many people involved in the process, productivity measures are bound to suffer.

Presenter: So what would you rate as the best measure?

Lee: Well, we've got to look at profitability and what we can bring to a product to make it worth buying at a price which is going to earn us revenue, I suppose. Though, this may involve a loss of productivity and an increase in the time it takes per shop-floor worker to produce each product. Traditional production managers used to be very much product-led in their attitude to how the company should be run, but we've moved on from there and become more centred on bringing the product to the end-user when and where they want it. And measures of how successfully and consistently you can do that are what I would rate most highly. That's, after all, what's going to keep you in business and add value to your company.

Presenter: Ferenc, what's your view on this?

Ferenc: I'm also pretty sceptical about productivity measures. Trouble is they tend to measure what's happened rather than what's happening, and it takes up a whole load of your time and leads to nothing useful, even though you have to be highly trained to understand them. You could probably make the same or better decisions without them. On the other hand, I'm a big fan of automation. It's taken over a lot of the more unpleasant manufacturing jobs and made us less reliant on the vagaries of the labour market. It has its downside, of course, like anything else – you know, technical glitches, need to hire more expensive technical operators, that sort of thing, which all mean that very often you're not saving on production costs at all; you're just streamlining the process.

Presenter: Mike Drewer?

Drewer: Can I just come in here to say that I think there's a serious hazard involved in industry's collective fascination, as it seems to me, with productivity. Productivity increases are usually at the expense of jobs, as companies replace workers with obedient technological marvels. What happens, though, to all those depressed redundant workers? Out of a job and no money to spend. Unlikely to find another job because companies prefer machines or outsourcing, so they stop spending because they've got nothing to spend and, hey presto, we've lost our customer base!

Presenter: But isn't that being a little alarmist?

Drewer: I don't think so. But to move onto another point: a lot of our stuff is now not made by us at all. We give that job to modern specialist producers and then buy it in according to demand. It allows us to switch products, innovate relatively cheaply, since we don't have to retool and concentrate on marketing the product, an activity where productivity measures are largely irrelevant.

Presenter: Ferenc Kovács. Do you think productivity has a ceiling, or will it continue to grow?

Ferenc: It'll grow, and in Europe it's got to grow. I don't know if there's some great new thing on the horizon like the Internet has been in the last ten years, and outsourcing will undoubtedly erode our manufacturing base, but I'm quite sure that sooner or later employment regulations in Europe will have to change to make it easier to hire and fire workers, reduce their holiday time (as has happened in the United States), otherwise we just won't be able to compete, and productivity, you know, is really about making the product in the cheapest and most efficient way and increasing profit margins while giving customers the best value for money possible.

Presenter: Gentlemen, thank you. And now to France, where the French prime minister appeared on television last week to announce a shake-up in their telecommunications industry …

UNIT 20

10 Listening, page 95

Peter: Hi, Wendy, have you got a few minutes?

Wendy: Er, sure, Pete. You got my email, then?

Peter: Yeah, and I'd just like to clarify a few things before my meeting with management next week. What exactly is it you want? It wasn't terribly clear from your email.

Wendy: Sorry, I wrote it in a bit of a rush. Um, my point is that we're all working round the clock here to make this company a success, and management don't give any sort of acknowledgement of our hard work. I mean, for what we do, I think we should all be moved up a point on the pay scale. I mean, if it weren't for us, this company would fold overnight, wouldn't it?

Peter: I agree with you and, er, I'll put it to them, but I don't think they'll jump at that one. Thanks anyway, Wendy.

***

Peter: Er, Demitri, I was looking at your comment before the meeting we've got with management next week. Could you talk me through it, please?

Demitri: Sure, Pete. You know the rumours about plans to open offices in other parts of the country? Well, I know they're only rumours, but, before they become reality, I just want to say that I don't want to be relocated to one of those against my will. I mean, I've got my home and family life here. Now, had the bosses spoken to us about this possibility, I'd have told them what I thought, but no doubt it never occurred to them, because they never ask us, and we're left to get hot under the collar and channel our complaints through you. It's them who should be asking us our opinions, not you!

Peter: Er, thanks, Demitri. So, er, next week I must go into the meeting and demand a complete change in management style! They'll love that! But you're right, of course.

***

Peter: Hi, Naline!

Naline: Hi, Pete. Here for one of your chats by the water dispenser?

Peter: Well, it seems a convenient moment. I've, um, got this meeting with management next week. What was your email all about?

Naline: Something which a lot of us think is a pretty big issue round here. We've got all this newly installed electrical and electronic equipment in the building, and no one seems to have much idea what it's for, but my question is what would we do in the event of a fire? And by the way, I think there's quite a good chance of one, the way this place is wired up. They could at least show us what to do, give some time to basic safety procedures and how to get out of this fire trap, don't you think?

Peter: Erm, you're right there. I was going to bring that up anyway, but, er, thanks all the same. I'll let you know what they say.

***

Peter: Hi, Claudio, er, is this a good moment?

Claudio: Good as any. What brings you to this remote workstation on the 7th floor … Pete, isn't it?

Peter: That's right. Your staff rep.

Claudio: Now I know why you're here. It's that email I sent you a week or so ago, isn't it?

Peter: That's right, because we've got the meeting with management next week, so, um, could you fill me in a bit?

Claudio: Yes, I'll tell you. What I like to do is get my desk clear, know what I mean? And as a result they keep putting more on my plate. It's not as if I'm averse to a bit of hard work, but I do feel that I get picked on just because I'm a fast worker. I mean, I'd be happy to do all this provided other people were being asked to do the same amount. But the managers give the hard workers like myself extra stuff to do and they never say a word. I suppose they think that if they were to say something, then they'd have to put their money where their mouth is and give us a bonus. But as long as I'm not passed over when the next round of promotion comes along next year, I'll be happy. You got that clear?

Peter: Thanks, Claudio. Pretty clear, er, it's not me you should be angry with, you know.

***

Peter: Toya! You got a mo'?

Toya: Hi, Pete. Long time no see. You been on holiday, then?

Peter: Er, not exactly. I've been completely caught up in a new project. Now, I … I want to consult you about the meeting with the bosses next week, following your email.

Toya: Oh, right. Well, yes, it … it's not such a big deal really, Pete. I just get a bit fed up with having the bosses breathing down my neck all day, and that goes for all of us round here. We wouldn't mind it if they just let us get on with things instead of continually checking what we're doing. I mean, I've been here a few years now and given the circumstances, I think that they should know that my work is consistently up to scratch, don't you?

Peter: Toya, you're not the first person I've consulted who is looking for a change in management style. Still, I'll find a way of suggesting some changes, I s'pose.

11 Grammar workshop, page 96

1 Honestly! They could have given us more notice instead of springing this on us almost at the last moment! Really, those managers seem to live in their own little world and have very little idea of communication. I mean, in my case, had I known, I wouldn't have bought a new house here just six months ago!

2 For me personally, it would be a big upheaval. I mean, er, I've got my kids in local schools and so on. On the other hand, I guess several people in my department would be interested in relocating … if the company were to offer the right package. It would have to be pretty generous, though.

3 This is the sixth job I've had in five years and I've really had it up to here with these short-term contracts. I'd jump at the chance to move, providing I was offered some sort of permanent contract, but I guess it's just as likely that they'll just lay me off instead.

4 Well, you know Travelsafe's quite a small, limited place for someone who's interested in building a career, and I'd regard this as a great opportunity to go to a big city with more scope if it weren't for the fact that I have all my friends and family in this area.

5 Actually, I'm originally from Liverpool, as you know, so for me the thing isn't as awful as some people seem to be trying to make out. I'll happily move back to Liverpool, as long as I'm given a section supervisor's job as an incentive. You see, I want to get on and I'm not prepared to move just for the sake of it.

6 My line manager told me that they had their eye on me to move to Glasgow and that I'd get a pretty decent promotion if I agreed to go. I'm not sure I like the way things are being handled, with people being taken on one side like this, but anyway, apart from promotion, I've told him I'll only move to Glasgow on condition that they give me a generous resettlement package as well, because I'm not prepared to end up out of pocket as a result of all this. I'd have to sell my house as well, you see.

7 I'm quite a lowly employee in the hierarchy of Travelsafe Insurance and frankly I'm not the principal breadwinner in my household. That's my wife, who's running her own business here in the town. I mean, if it weren't for my wife's job, I'd consider moving as a possibility, but as it is, I can't expect her to close down her company and follow me. That would be totally unreasonable.

8 The trouble is, most of it's still just rumours, you know. For instance, one rumour that's been going the rounds is that they're going to close departments here completely and open them again in places like Plymouth. I don't honestly know how much truth there is in the rumour, but I must say that in the event of my entire department being relocated, I'll move with them to stay with the team. That's if they all agree to go, of course. Which is unlikely, I guess.

12 Listening, page 97

Frank: So, Peter, I called you in to just let you know in advance what our plans are for reformulating the company.

Peter: OK, Frank, go ahead. I'll just take notes and listen at this stage.

Frank: Fine. First, I'd like to start by saying that this reformulation is an expansion of the company and an expansion of our operations. Our total projected number of staff is set to rise from 450 to 600, although a certain amount of decentralisation will take place as we open offices in different cities, and so there will be a certain amount of cutting back here at our head office in Norwich, where we plan to make cuts of 20% – that is, 90 out of our 450 staff. However, that said, I'd like to stress that nobody'll be out of a job unwillingly. We'd like a maximum of 60 employees to go to our new centres in Glasgow, Liverpool and Plymouth, and we'll give them financial incentives to do so. To start with, anyone who transfers will get a 5% salary increase straightaway, independently of whatever post they transfer to. Also, we know that there are a lot of costs involved in moving to another part of the country – you know, buying and selling houses and so on, so we're prepared to foot the bill by giving a one-off payment of £12,000 to anyone who goes to make sure that they're not out of pocket. Finally, to cover the time involved in uprooting themselves, all these people will get two extra weeks' paid leave when they transfer. We are, as you see, keen to get experienced and trustworthy staff from our head office into our new operations.

The other aspect of our reformulation is for those who don't want to or can't move, and here we're offering totally voluntary redundancies for people who want the opportunity for a career change or a career break. What I mean is to arrive at the correct number of posts, we'll pay people to leave to the tune of one month's gross salary on top of their legal entitlement. In other words, if they were to be made redundant for other reasons, they'd get whatever the law states, but we'll give them a month extra on top of that. And to help them find a new job if they wish to, we'll provide an outplacement service entirely free of charge so that they can do so.
I do want to emphasise most strongly that we want to make these changes with a maximum of goodwill and a minimum of friction. Now, Peter, what's your reaction? Are there any questions you'd like to ask?

UNIT 21

13 Listening, page 102

Presenter: This week is fair-trade week, and tonight I have in the studio Professor Bernard Hill from the University of the South Bank, an expert in fair trade. Professor Hill, how does fair trade benefit third-world producers?

Hill: Er, producers are paid more for their produce, often cutting out the middle men who may take an enormous cut, and selling directly to ethically run businesses in richer countries. This is what, for example, has happened in the Maraba region of Rwanda, where, as a consequence, farmers can devote part of their land to growing a variety of crops to feed their families and another part of their land to a cash crop against which they can raise loans and develop their business, er, buy equipment and send their children to school. Er, it can and, in the case of Maraba, has, transformed the region.

Presenter: Fair trade has been taking off in this country. Growth in sales according to many reports has been in the region of 40 or 50 per cent over several years now. How have the big supermarkets reacted to it?

Hill: Supermarkets have a reputation for driving down prices from their providers, er, and they do this with a view to maximising profits and making the products they sell cheaper in turn. On the other hand, they all have to look good to their customers. Customer loyalty is something no supermarket can count on once they start getting a bad reputation, and in view of this, their mission statements and other literature usually pay lip-service to ethical trading and ethical treatment of their suppliers. Still, the main reason given me by someone speaking on behalf of one of our best-known chains, was that it's what people want, just the same as a few years ago they started looking for organic food, and that, rather than publicity-seeking, is why they carry these products on their shelves.

Presenter: And how do you account for the success of the fair-trade movement in this country? Programmes such as this one, perhaps?

Hill: Oh, these undoubtedly help, but they're comparatively few and far between, and frankly, I think the media have been a little slow on picking up on this story. Similarly, the fair-trade movement has been loath to spend money on spreading the word and, er, more interested in spending the money they have on developing their fair-trade activities. Really, this is one of those things which people have just told each other about. The idea has got round, and it's been helped by having fair-trade shops in the high streets and shopping centres.

Presenter: So is fair trade something which will continue to grow and eventually become a touchstone of the world trading system?

Hill: I'd like to think so. But there are many hurdles in its way. Eventually, trade tariffs and subsidies to rich world farmers will disappear, I think – I mean, they've got to, though that'll take time. What may prove a greater difficulty is that fair trade, almost by definition, means paying more than would be the case if the market was just allowed to find its own level, and it'll only bear these artificial levels, I mean consumers will only accept this in the long run, if they feel they're getting value for money in terms of quality. So, long term, it's a complicated question.
On the other hand, also in the long term, it's in the interests of all of us that this movement is successful. The current differences between rich and poor countries can't be maintained indefinitely. It's not reasonable to continue to pour aid into poorer regions forever. This movement helps people to stand on their own two feet and become self-supporting. Quite apart from that, many people in rich countries like the idea of paying a fair price. It makes them feel good – they feel they're co-operating and not exploiting. People become interested in the places their coffee and other products come from and they become interested to know about the lives of these producers. It's all part of a developing educational process.

Presenter: Bernard Hill, thank you.

Hill: It's been a pleasure.

UNIT 22

14 Listening, page 105

I = interviewer; R = Richard Coates

I: Can you tell me about how your company breaks into new markets?

R: Mm, going into new markets, our company tends to acquire businesses. Er, if you look, for example, to the electronic market, a very big market, or the construction industry across Europe, it's an area in which we really don't have a customer base, a supply base, so what we use primarily is acquisition to acquire people and a company with experience in that sector.

I: Mm, OK. Do you ever choose to have distributors instead or form joint ventures with other organisations?

R: We are a distributor … what we … we wouldn't generally take on a joint venture, as it'd be difficult to see what a joint-venture partner would add to us. If we were taking over a distributor, that would be our area of expertise. We are primarily, as I say distributors … however, we don't do manufacturing. The products we distribute, we primarily source from a supplier or the original manufacturer.

I: Mm … how does Wolseley identify the markets it would like to expand into?

R: When you look at any market, you're looking at size and growth potential. So when we look across countries or we look to a new product range we can get into, we're looking for something where there's a big market and which is also a growing market so we can, in entering into that market, we can see lots of potential for further growth of the business.

I: Uh-huh. So once you have decided on a country, how do you identify a company in that target market which is suitable?

R: What we look for, what we acquire is expertise in the management group, so what you'd be looking for is a business that we believe is well run. You can assess that by how good their outlets are, their size, their growth rate within that market, through contact with the management and through the finances of the business; is there healthy financial performance and is it growing?

I: So why would an overseas company want to be acquired by Wolseley?

R: The owners of an overseas company might want to sell because it allows them to realise cash. Management would potentially want to join Wolseley because being owned by a business that is in the same trade allows them to benefit from, for example, lower purchasing prices, from the experience and expertise that Wolseley has in other markets, to help them grow and develop in their own markets in a way that they potentially couldn't do on their own.

15 Listening, page 107

I = interviewer; R = Richard Coates

I: And how do you supervise the companies once you've acquired them?

R: When you acquire a business, you … the first thing you need to do is share with them your view of the business plan you formed in advance that, as likely as not, you'll have discussed to some extent with them. You then set out the requirements of that, and then the supervision is done through regular contact that can be quarterly, semi-annually, where you'd meet with them face to face and discuss the objectives and how they're performing against those objectives, and then you have routine management reporting that comes in every month, which reports on the financial performance and that allows the business to report on the day-to-day running of the operations.

I: And how do you go about incorporating these companies into the Wolseley culture?

R: Ah, the important thing is about contact with senior management. Our senior management at a European level need to have contact with them, that's how you get alignment at a management level. There are then events and processes that they'll get tied into … as I said, they'll tie into six-monthly reviews, they'll meet with group management, they will get tied into annual conferences that we hold, where management groups from across Europe come together, and slowly, over time, they come to see the way Wolseley works and the people within it.

I: So that's how you create an international culture then for your management, is it?

R: Yes, the international management culture comes really down from the senior management. There are also processes ongoing within the business to develop our international management and the culture. We're currently in the second year of a European graduate programme, where we take recently graduated individuals of high calibre and get them working within our business, trained and developed, to enable them to grow and work across our European network. We also recruit at senior and mid-management level to bring different expertise and different management potential. We're looking to then move certain people across Wolseley Europe at mid-management level.

I: Um, OK, and when you expand into a new market, what sort of activities does Wolseley undertake to build up its brand and make itself known to customers in the new market?

R: Mm, there's … the major form of expansion that you'd … um, we tend to take a business we've acquired and look to develop it through its own branch network. What we've tended to do is to retain the local brand. Wolseley believes in the power of the local brand, the individual business that we've acquired. So we'd retain that local brand that's operated by, um, in that market and then look to grow their branches. As we open new branches, we do leafleting and other sorts of marketing campaigns to increase awareness and develop a customer demand prior to opening.

I: So do you think that it's an option for any company to say no, we don't want to grow – become international we're happy as we are?

R: For other companies that may be the case, it won't be the case for Wolseley, though

I: So it is possible then?

R: You could … I could imagine a business that … um, would want to stay entirely local. If we're a service business, I know many retailers are actually … have entirely focused on national boundaries only and haven't sought to go international.

I: And they could survive like that?

R: I think, in the longer term, they'll find it more difficult. Generally, those that have gone further and developed further are bigger. Therefore they've achieved economies of scale. The reason why … um, one of the major factors in international development is to achieve greater economies of scale through, for example in our business, purchasing greater volume of product which would then achieve lower costs.

I: Uh-huh. What do you think it is that makes Wolseley products so successful?

R: Hmm! Wolseley is a service business, it's about the service that's provided to the professional contractor who visits our branches What makes the service so successful is the experience and the service provided by the people in those branches, the availability of product, the service that's provided to deliver any products that aren't available the next day, and also other services, for example providing credit. So we primarily focus on service as opposed to price.

UNIT 23

16 Listening, page 108

Hello, Marion. Sorry to miss you this morning but I had to rush, as you know, so I thought I'd better just give you these instructions before I go, as I'd like to get this moving as soon as possible. You remember we were working on a list of contacts last Friday? Could you please draft the same basic letter to all of them, and then perhaps we'll be able to work out an itinerary when I get back from Shanghai? Write to them by name where possible – I know for some we only have the name of the company – and use a formal style. You're better than me at that, so it's better if you do the letter and you can email your draft to me later today if you want, and I'll send you any suggestions when I get to my hotel. I've got a few notes of what you should include in the letter. Give them details of our new product – the mirror, I mean – and also put in some sales figures from two or three years ago till now, as those should impress them a bit. I don't think you have to go into too much detail there – just the basics, really. Then tell them why we want to expand into Asia – I mean, we've increased our production capacity – and you know, we're now looking for other markets. Something fairly vague like that, but it sounds impressive. Also, you could put in something about our future plans, you know, marketing other products that we have in the pipeline, that sort of thing. Then you could also tell them that we may need someone to distribute our products in their country or even perhaps a joint-venture partner. I know that's not true in all cases, because it will really depend on the country and the type of operation they're running, but it could get some people interested, so that at least we can talk to them. You'd better also say that I'm hoping to go on an Asian tour in the next month or so so we'll need expressions of interest from people pretty quickly and then we'll take things from there. I think that's all for now, Marion. Don't send the letters straightaway, because we might just think about asking someone, perhaps an agency, to provide a translation of the letter into some other European languages. Not sure which languages at the moment.

Perhaps you've got some ideas on that one or you could look for an agency on the Web. Oh, that's my flight being called, so I'd better run. See you at the beginning of next week. Bye.

17 Listening, page 110

1 The initial investment is going to be pretty heavy, because we'll be opening and equipping a whole chain of outlets, so that'll eat into profits in the first year or so. Still, we should be able to lure some pretty good local people, especially if we offer competitive salaries, and when we've got the whole operation going, we'll have taken one step further in satisfying the company's ambition of becoming a global presence. And once the operation really gets off the ground, there'll be plenty of profits for us there.

2 Well, you know, when there's an opening, you can't just pass it by – and, er, with the things we have in the pipeline just now, we just have to be in the North American market, I mean, with the spending power they have there. Um, of course, we'll have to present things a bit differently to satisfy their rather different tastes, and, um, we've got a design consultant working on the boxes right now. I'll show you one as soon as he sends me a sample.

3 The competition in our main markets is just getting fiercer and fiercer, so I reckon that unless we move into other areas and spread our risks, so to speak, we'll find ourselves in real danger. Even so, any new market we move into will also be pretty tough, so we'll have to run some very streamlined operations when we do so, otherwise we'll never undercut the local players.

4 People sometimes say that business is the same the world over, but frankly that's not my experience, and it takes managers in the companies we take over some time to cotton on to our working methods. I expect that'll be the case this time, too. Often one of the most immediate problems is language. On the other hand, the effort will be worth it, because the enlarged distribution chains will allow us to cut costs and sell our products considerably more cheaply than our local competitors.

5 Quite frankly, I reckon they're asking for it – they've really pushed us into it with the price war they've been waging – so it seems the most logical move is to take over one of their competitors as close to home for them as possible and try and rob market share from them there. And we've got an agency working on the publicity already, because when we're selling our products there, we'll have to take account of the local culture. Otherwise, all we'll succeed in doing is alienating a new market, and that would be a real flop.

UNIT 24

18 Listening, page 112

Good morning. My name's Fedor Brodsky and, for those of you who don't know me, I'm marketing director for our consumer products division. I'm going to talk to you, briefly, about how to protect your brand's reputation, a question which should interest all of you in this company. By way of introduction, I should say that good reputations – both for brands and for people – don't come by accident but from good marketing activities, including particularly building up consistently high-quality, excellent packaging, shrewd pricing and, of course, effective promotional activities over a period of time. Remember, though, that however good a brand reputation is, it can be ruined overnight by critical media coverage, and companies have to do all in their power to avoid that.
I think there are three main points in defending one's brand. First, we have to make sure that we always satisfy customer expectations. Despite pressures from shareholders, the customer comes first in any business, and with good ongoing market research, we should always be aware of what our customers want from us. Second, we should never make sacrifices in quality. In particular, although your finance department may want to implement cost-cutting exercises, brand quality should never be compromised. Once it gets into the media that, for example, you're putting cheaper ingredients into your pies, people will just stop buying them, even though you spend millions on advertising. My third point concerns protecting the general image of the company because damage to company image will damage the brand. This is the area of corporate ethics; we know so many famous examples of companies polluting the environment – oil companies immediately spring to mind – though damage of this kind is often unintentional or accidental, or – another instance – companies passing part of their operations to subcontractors who then exploit their workers or don't pay attention to safety procedures.
In conclusion, the company has to be marketing-led. In other words, the company puts the customer and the customer's needs at the centre of all their strategies. This is really one of the golden rules of corporate culture, that whatever you do in whatever area of corporate activity, you should first consider whether this could affect the health of the brand, which must always be your prime objective.
Now, if you have any questions, I'd be happy to answer them.

19 Listening, page 115

So, following on from Fedor Brodsky's talk earlier today, I'm also going to talk about risk, but in more general terms. My first point is about risk in general. Many people have the perception that the world is a riskier place nowadays to do business. I'm not so sure that's entirely true. We hear much more about disasters and the like from the media, and this leads to scares, which in turn can affect consumer confidence and share prices. Then again, we keep hearing about global warming and how this is creating even more natural disasters, but these tend to affect business only in exceptional cases. What's true, though, is that business is far more international than ever before, and this means that something that happens in one part of the world can have unforeseen consequences somewhere quite different. A hundred years ago, a disaster in Europe would almost certainly not have affected businesses in Japan or Argentina the way it might in today's world of global supply chains and global sourcing.
The second thing I'd like to say is that in some ways, people in business run fewer risks. They can take out insurance against many things, and insurance companies make a living from calculating what the probability of a risk is going to be. Business people set up limited-liability companies, where they are not responsible for all the company's debts if it fails financially. And government regulations, linked with technological breakthroughs, have made the world and the workplace safer places to live and work in.
There are a number of problems connected with handling risk. While investors' willingness to accept risks varies according to their level of confidence at any one time, this is something which has always been part of the economic cycle. The principal problem is that managers find it hard to assess the real degree of risk that they face in their activities, and some risks seem far greater than they actually are, and so they waste resources preventing something which is unlikely to happen, while they're taken by surprise by something quite unexpected. We see the same with politicians, too.
Nowadays, of course, computer projections can predict the probabilities of all sorts of untoward events occurring, and these are the basis of how the insurance industry works. While there'll always be things computers can't predict, from rail strikes to storms, if used with confidence, they can be a useful tool. Having said that, managers feel very often that they're paid to assess risks and take appropriate action, and they feel a certain loss of control if they put all their faith in the machine.
Finally, I'd like to say that business is about taking risk; you have to take risks to make money, and it's this element of risk and gambling which attracts many people to become entrepreneurs. Risk is part of life, and our job as business people is to accept it and handle it responsibly. Thank you.

EXAM SKILLS AND EXAM PRACTICE

2 Exam skills, Listening Part 1

In actual fact, all aspects of corporate life, especially in large corporations like Unipro, have become increasingly complex, and it's this need to manage complexity which is really sorting the sheep from the goats in the corporate marketplace, if you'll forgive the expression. Why is it that companies are becoming so much more complex? The answer to this really lies in the consumer boom which has been an ongoing process since the 1950s and which in recent years has led to tremendous enlargements of companies' brand portfolios – there's the famous example of a well-known ice-cream company which sells over 1,000 different flavours and varieties of ice-cream. Both the general public and corporate clients have come to expect this sort of choice, and to meet the demand, companies have had to become increasingly specialist in what they offer. This has certainly been the case in Unipro over the last few years.
On top of that, I should also draw attention to the ongoing process of market consolidation in our sector, where Unipro's culture, products and processes have gained additional complexity through mergers and acquisitions both of rivals and as we expand into new markets. Also, it has to be said that in today's marketplace, where your customers are always expecting something new or improved, if you are to maintain a competitive edge, you have to constantly innovate, and this in itself almost guarantees added complications.
We've heard recently of, er, some consumer-products companies actually reducing the number of products they sell in order to simplify their processes. The problem with doing this is that you lay yourself open to the risk of losing market share to your rivals – something that can be demoralising, while at the same time being detrimental to the bottom line. It has to be said also that, by bringing out new products rather than just reducing variety, companies have been able to move upmarket, and this is what we've been doing over the past three or four years.
The downside of complexity comes in three main areas, in my experience. Firstly, because we're no longer able to concentrate on just a few things which we do well, our products have undergone a slight but noticeable loss of edge in terms of cost-competitiveness, and this is something we're continually struggling to regain. Secondly, because we now produce 500 different products, whereas before we concentrated on just 50, our manufacturing processes have lost what little simplicity they might once have had. Of course, automation and computerisation compensate for this to some extent, but behind every machine ultimately there has to be a human hand, and this brings me to my third point; that as a result of all this complexity, management decisions are often reached more slowly, as managers have so many different tasks to concentrate on and aspects to consider.
Interestingly, at Unipro, we have no plans to reduce the number of products we sell. Er, quite the contrary. We plan to continue expanding aggressively, even though just a few of the many products we produce are actually responsible for the bulk of our operating profits. This is because we believe that we have the know-how and the energy to get ahead of our rivals and that the keys to managing complexity lie in just two things. On the one hand, we believe in a rigorous analysis of our markets and we believe that this will ensure that we bring the right products to the right people in the right place and at the right price. At the same time, we believe, in our organisation, that we have to make a sustained effort to be continually streamlining the development, marketing, production and customer relationship processes and systems in order to reduce costs and increase efficiency. Er, we believe that by doing this, we set a benchmark in complexity management for the entire industry.

3 Exam practice, Listening Part 1

This is the Cambridge Business English Certificate Higher, Listening Test.
You will hear an introduction to each part of the test and you'll have time to look at the questions before you listen.
You'll hear each piece twice.
While you're listening, you should write your answers on the question paper.
You'll have time at the end of the test to copy your answers onto the separate answer sheet.
There will now be a pause. Please ask any questions now, because you must not speak during the test.
Now open your question paper and look at Part One.
Part 1. Questions 1–12.
You will hear a woman, Anna Grant, giving a talk about her recruitment company, PKS. As you listen, for questions 1 to 12, complete the notes using up to three words or a number.
You will hear the recording twice.
You now have 45 seconds to read through the notes.

Anna: Good afternoon. I've been asked to come and talk to you about the company I set up a few years ago – PKS. We did something that was very innovative at the time and that is: we started offering an integrated recruitment service to companies. In other words, companies outsource their recruitment to us. Like all great ideas, I didn't come up with this on my own. I set up the business with Alan Murton, who has now moved on to being a director of a new consultancy, though he is still a sleeping partner in my company, which I manage alone. And over the last seven years we've built up a huge business, with sales rising at roughly 15% per year and last year exceeding all expectations at 45%. Our client list is wide-ranging, including several large multinational clients. We help some of the biggest UK companies – if they need temporary or casual staff, they often use their HR departments, but we now recruit all permanent staff for these companies in over fifty markets.
We recruit senior management staff as well as caretakers, so it's important we have good sources. So how do we find the right staff to match the company? We are different from the normal recruitment company because we're in charge of the whole process until the company makes the final recruitment decision. Sometimes we're responsible for hiring thousands of people for companies, especially for our multinational clients. To do this we will decide on the best strategy for going about that hiring – we might use a direct search company or go through suppliers or place recruitment adverts in newspapers or in a job centre. One of the most fruitful sources we have for hiring is at job fairs because they tend to attract the kind of high achievers we are usually looking for. And it's not always a question of searching outside the company – we're also often given the role of evaluating internal candidates for promotions within companies. This is evidence of how much the companies trust the service we offer.
We are also committed to helping staff in their career aspirations. So we don't just help people on their way into a company but also with how they advance within that company and we also offer support on their way out. For example, when a company is downsizing, we can offer outplacement training. Our unique selling point is that we offer a complete package and, in order to do that, we need to be in a position where we can really get to know a company and its staff. So we demand that our clients agree to long-term contracts – though that's not as rigid a commitment as it sounds, as we can be flexible within those agreements.
And what might the future hold for us? Are competitors nipping at our heels? Well, at the moment we're hoping to expand even further and, to facilitate that, we're talking to a private equity group about them taking a majority stake in the

business. And I suppose if that is successful, my ultimate ambition would be to get to a point where, when many people would be thinking about whether they wanted to retire from work, I can consider whether or not to float the business. That would be a real reward for my hard work. As for the immediate expansion, the next stage of our development would be to utilise the clients we have who have very large customer bases and, through them, to add a further three sectors to our portfolio – though I'm not sure exactly which areas yet; maybe telecoms, retailing and financial services.

Now are there any questions?

Now you will hear the recording again.

That is the end of Part 1. You now have 20 seconds to check your answers.

4 Exam skills, Listening Part 2

1 This was a few years ago now. I don't suppose it's still happening because if it was, I imagine the company would be bankrupt by now, but the company I worked for was regularly delivering orders late. Our clients were definitely not happy and they were saying so. More and more, and in no uncertain terms. The helpline never seemed to stop ringing. Trouble was, we had a number of new recruits on the job and they hadn't been shown how to do things properly.

2 So he rang up the marketing director and said, 'That's it. I'm taking my custom elsewhere!' Frankly, it was a disaster which could have been avoided so easily if we'd bothered to check things carefully as they came off the production line. As it was, there were plenty of people standing around doing hardly anything, and they could have been usefully employed doing that.

3 The launch was pretty dispiriting. Almost no interest and almost no take-up in the first month. The promotional budget was quite low, but, um, I don't think it was that. In my view, the new product manager lacked the background for this type of product and activity.

4 Well, the board took the decision to substitute all our Macs for PCs, and we really weren't ready for it – this was a few years ago now, but it led to a lot of headaches. Anyway, we lost a lot of files – only temporarily, I'm glad to say, and nothing too sensitive – but it took the various directors quite some time to realise we all needed training up with the new equipment.

5 Exam practice, Listening Part 2

Part 2. Questions 13 to 22.

You will hear five different people talking about their company's recent expansion.

For each extract there are two tasks. Look at Task One. For each question, 13 to 17, choose the way the company chose to expand from the list A–H. Now look at Task Two. For each question 18 to 22, choose the challenge the company now faces from the list A–H.

You will hear the recording twice.

You have 30 seconds to read the two lists.

Now listen and do the two tasks.

1 We produce fitness products for gyms and private clients – we'd wanted to expand for a long time. We had a variety of options open to us. For example, our main competitors expanded by allowing other companies to make their products under a licensing agreement – a possibility for us in the future. We wanted to move slowly though, so we negotiated a partnership with a personal training firm, who gave us access to their list of contacts. It's really taken off beyond what we expected and we're struggling to find people with the right kind of background to manage our production teams. It's so frustrating as we've put a lot of money into the expansion but we're ending up with delays in our deliveries, which is bad for our reputation.

2 We sell sporting goods and we've got a very large customer base in several countries, so looking at how we could grow was difficult. We did it through a huge investment programme, which involved increasing the number of stores worldwide. Our brand is now so big that we plan to look at ways of franchising in the future, which will give us more expansion with limited risk. Something we'll have to sort out first though is how we're going to get the goods to so many different places in a cost-effective way. We've expanded so quickly that our current system isn't working very well and the costs are escalating. I think we need to take on someone to come in and restructure the whole system.

3 When we started looking at expansion we looked at how much money we might make out of franchising, which is the way a lot of companies have gone. In the end we felt it was more sensible to allow other companies to produce our goods under licence, so we had some control. It's very difficult though – there are so many administration issues that you have to get sorted in the contract and they're different for every country. We outsourced all that to a team of lawyers and we've got it all off the ground, but we've got several major schemes on the go at the same time and it's getting increasingly problematic to keep track of them all. We may need to take on more people.

4 Expansion is always a problem, especially in our business, which is electrical goods. We did it the easy way really – rather than invest in new products, which we perceived as a risk, we made a bid for one of our competitors and were successful, so we have access to all their warehousing and outlets. Plus we use their website for our retail operations. We've been monitoring everything closely and it's clear that getting the raw materials from abroad is causing delays. We can't depend on the steel manufacturers we currently use. So, although we've increased the efficiency of our own delivery system worldwide, we'll have to look elsewhere if we're to get materials into the factory in time for our production deadlines. It may push our costs up but it'll be worth it.

5 Our company sells packaged food in several very profitable regions in Europe. Last year we decided it was time to build on that and saw no reason why we shouldn't diversify – by offering frozen goods, for example. So we looked at what our main rival was doing and tried to increase our market share at their expense by undercutting them. Of course it's meant spending a lot more on machinery and re-training our production staff. But what we hadn't realised was how complicated it would be to make sure we satisfied all the standards set down by the various official bodies in each country – trading standards and so on – so in the end I'm not sure we will be able to undercut our competitors.

Now you will hear the recording again.

That is the end of Part 2.

6 Exam skills, Listening Part 3

Interviewer: I have in the studio this evening Jeremy Pollock, lecturer in psychology from the University of Leeds, who has made a study into the psychological factors which influence poor decision-making in business. Jeremy, are business people such poor decision-makers?

Jeremy: Um, not all of them, but a lot of them could improve, and one of the reasons is that, while they invest a lot of money in fancy computer equipment to help them make decisions, a lot of them don't like what their computers tell them and so they rely on their intuition instead.

Interviewer: And how does intuition lead to bad decisions?

Jeremy: In a number of ways. The first one is over-optimism. When people are optimistic, this reflects heightened morale, and as a result people often do better-quality work and produce better outcomes. Obviously a good thing, and footballers are a great example of this. That's not a problem. The problem is over-optimism, and in business it may lead managers to put too much effort into something which is not going to produce such good results as they expect. They waste resources, and the business in general would benefit from a more modest approach. More to the point, though, is that managers start thinking that everything they are doing will go well, and they tend to forget that they have rivals out there who might be even better than them. That's when things really start to go wrong.

Interviewer: As a matter of anecdote, which nationality do you think is the most over-optimistic?

Jeremy: I guess the Americans. They think their houses are always going to appreciate in value, they never expect to lose money on shares and, most tellingly, in a recent survey it was discovered that 40 % of Americans thought that eventually they would end up in the top 1 % of earners. I mean, how unrealistic can you get?

Interviewer: What other psychological influences are there on decision-making?

Jeremy: The next one I'd like to mention is what's called the 'anchor effect'.

Interviewer: What's that?

Jeremy: Well, in negotiation, this is where the first price mentioned, the opening position, becomes the point of reference around which all discussions seem to revolve. Negotiations become distorted because negotiators should be looking at real values so that they reach realistic agreement, rather than one which is based on an outrageous opening bid.

Interviewer: Can you give an example?

Jeremy: Sure. You're interested in buying a house whose market value is really £200,000, but the sellers are asking a million. The chances are your discussions (if you have any) will centre round the million figure, not the 200,000 figure. It's clear if you reach a deal that you're going to lose out.

Interviewer: Many people find it hard to make decisions when there is a wealth of information, don't they?

Jeremy: Maybe, but you know for … for business managers, actually making decisions is a central part of what their job consists of, so that making decisions as such is not generally the problem, and as long as you can differentiate useful from useless information, having lots of information is a bonus. The problem really arises when managers spend too much time analysing the information for each decision. I mean, some of the decisions are quite trivial: where to place the photocopier, when to have the Christmas party. This distracts them from analysing information for big decisions like that looming merger, for example.

Interviewer: I know managers who, once they've made a decision, find it very difficult to admit that the decision was wrong. Is this something which came into your study?

Jeremy: Mm … very much so. This is the stubbornness factor. Pharmaceutical companies who find it hard to admit that the product they decided to develop has no future, so they continue to pour money into researching and developing a no-hoper. Er, another more typical example is the manager who recruits a new member of staff who turns out to be a dud – just no good at the job. What do they do? Well, it's hard to believe on a theoretical basis, although we all see it every day: they stick with them. They don't give them the boot and admit their mistake, and they don't send them off to some other part of the company as an advertisement for their bad judgement. They just continue to live with them. Amazing, isn't it?

Interviewer: Yes, but it does sound very familiar. Are there any other psychological factors that affect decision-making?

Jeremy: Mm, just one more, called 'home bias'. This is where people tend to put money into things in their region or in their country, rather than looking further afield – I'm talking about stock market investments and also business investments. Reasonable, you may say, after all you probably understand those things closer to home better. But you can also get your fingers burnt, and, especially if you're a serious investor, investing in a variety of markets and properties is a much safer and more reasonable decision.

Interviewer: Jeremy Pollock, thank you.

Jeremy: My pleasure.

7 Exam practice, Listening Part 3

Part 3. Questions 23 to 30.

You will hear an interview with a consultant, Jason Copeland, on the competitiveness of small retail stores.

For each question, 23 to 30, mark one letter A, B or C, for the correct answer.

You will hear the recording twice.

You now have 45 seconds to read through the questions.

Now listen and mark A, B or C.

Interviewer: Jason, you have substantial experience in retail and you're concerned at the takeover by the big retail chains, aren't you?

Jason: Yes. I do consultancy for smaller stores because I believe they can compete with the big hitters.

Interviewer: Well, what would you say a retail store's success depends on?

Jason: Many stores focus on getting a range of products that will appeal to their target customers and, of course, price is an important part of this equation. Naturally you need to find out what customers want – your store is defined by what you stock and what you charge. None of this matters if your customers don't know you exist. For example, the wrong promotional campaign can mean your message is not heard and the result is too few people through the door.

Interviewer: And how do you think it's possible for smaller stores to compete with large chains?

Jason: They need to make a realistic choice about what to compete on. The advantage for small stores is the fact that they are individual. This means they can offer something special and they need to maximise that feature. Small stores do have a different character and that atmosphere can appeal to some people. And the same goes for the type of service small stores can give their customers – it's very personalised, which people like – but you need to attract them to the store first.

Interviewer: So which type of customer do you think these stores should focus on – er, the big spenders?

Jason: Actually it's much more important to concentrate on customers who may not spend much, but who are regular. You may not make a fortune off them, unlike say, your typical, average-spending customers, but if they're regular, it means they're satisfied with the store and will probably tell everyone they know about it. You should nurture them as your most valuable customers as they could be your future.

Interviewer: Do you think that online shopping will put the small retailer out of business?

Jason: It's true it's important for all stores to have an online presence. This may just be an informational website as not all stores want to invest in the security systems which are needed for online ordering. This doesn't matter as there will always be customers who want to inspect the quality of products and this will preserve the brick and mortar retailers. Also hold-ups in delivery are often seen as a disadvantage with online shopping – but I feel this is negated by the fact that the online shopping experience is instant.

Interviewer: When small stores expand they often relocate – but then they can end up going under, can't they?

Jason: Yes, relocating a store is inevitably expensive. However, if you've thought it through, it can be the best thing for your bottom line. Obviously you want to expand your customer base and attract new customers in the new location. Having said that, this will not be enough to keep you afloat, unless you advertise the move well, so that you concentrate on keeping old customers.

Interviewer: And do you think the old saying that the customer is always right is true?

Jason: No, the customer is not always right. But of course you can't tell them that. Sometimes they make an honest mistake about something or want something for nothing. But even if they're not right, it's our job to make them believe that they are valued and essential to the store. After all, it's their purchasing decision that makes a store a success or failure.

Interviewer: The retail industry has very high staff turnover, doesn't it? Do you think retailers should invest more in trying to keep staff?

Jason: Yes, given how important customer service is, stores should make every effort to keep staff who are good at their job. But I think sometimes stores think anybody can do sales – it's not seen as a very highly trained job and so staff needs are seen as very low on the agenda. Also salaries tend to be very low and prospects for rising up the ranks are few – it's by addressing these latter issues that good staff can be retained.

Interviewer: So there is money to be made in the small retail store?

Jason: Oh, indeed. The profit margin may be small but good sales can generate a reasonably healthy income for someone operating on their own. Surviving is easier, I think, if you decide to focus on one or two particular areas and become well-known for that. The real money, though, lies in gambling on an investment in growth when it may seem most chancy. You may be surprised at what takes off.

Interviewer: OK, thank you for your help on this …

Now you will hear the recording again.

That is the end of Part 3. You now have ten minutes to transfer your answers to your Answer Sheet.

You have one more minute.

That is the end of the test.

8 Exam skills, Speaking Part 2

My talk is about procedures for internal recruitment. This is an essential area of human resources, not just because it has implications for the efficiency of the company, but also because of the effect it can have on inter-staff relations. So the main point I'd like to make is about transparency. What I mean is that the process must be fair and seen by all staff involved to be fair. How can this be achieved? I think first that there must be a clear procedure for internal recruitment which has been agreed between management and staff representatives. This procedure must, for example, include internal advertising of all posts and allowing all suitably qualified staff to apply. It also includes a regular system of staff appraisal, which is also open and transparent. Staff know how they have been appraised and know what comments are on their personal files. They also have a right to appeal if they feel that any aspect of their appraisal has been unfair. A third aspect of this transparency is the composition of recruitment boards, and I say 'boards' because really internal recruitment is too sensitive to be the responsibility of one person. Anyway, these boards should really be made up of the director or manager of the department which has the vacant post, someone from the Human Resources department, and also, though this for many managers may sound rather controversial, an elected staff representative as well. Finally, and in conclusion, I'd like to say that I think Human Resources should circulate the reasons for choosing the person they finally choose, as this makes the process as transparent as possible, and makes it clear to staff what criteria were used.